Crime Scene Analysis
Practical Procedures and Techniques

WILSON T. SULLIVAN III

PEARSON

Prentice
Hall

Upper Saddle River, New Jersey 07458

Library of Congress Cataloging-in-Publication Data

Sullivan, Wilson T.
   Crime scene analysis : practical procedures and techniques / Wilson T. Sullivan III.
     p. cm.
   Includes bibliographical references and index.
   ISBN 0-13-119131-4
  1. Crime scene searches.   2. Criminal investigation   I. Title.
   HV8073.S76 2007
   363.25′2–dc22

2006025071

Editor-in-Chief: Vernon R. Anthony
Executive Editor: Tim Peyton
Associate Editor: Sarah Holle
Editorial Assistant: Jillian Allison
Managing Editor: Mary Carnis
Production Editor: Peggy Hood
Production Liaison: Janice Stangel
Manufacturing Manager: Ilene Sanford
Manufacturing Buyer: Cathleen Petersen
Marketing Manager: Adam Kloza
Cover Design Coordinator: Christoper Weigand
Cover Designer: Amy Rosen
Cover Image: Courtesy of Getty Images

This book was set in New Century School Book by *Techbooks*. It was printed and bound
by Hamilton Printing Company. The cover was printed by Phoenix Color.

Pearson Education LTD
Pearson Education Singapore, Pte. Ltd
Pearson Education Canada, Ltd
Pearson Education—Japan

Pearson Education Australia PTY, Limited
Pearson Education North Asia Ltd
Pearson Educación de Mexico, S.A. de C.V.
Pearson Education Malaysia, Pte. Ltd

10 9 8 7 6 5 4 3 2 1
ISBN: 0-13-119131-4

Contents

CHAPTER

6

CRIME SCENE DRAWINGS   72

Preface

There are many books available today covering forensic science and crime scene investigation. The availability of these books has expanded along with the interest in forensics programs on television, such as "CSI." There are some very good books that cover the introductory aspects of forensic science. So why would anyone want to read this book? What makes this book so different from all the others on the market today?

What really makes this text different is that it is a textbook and a reference book containing actual procedures and techniques. It addresses the *how to, when to, and in what order* to use the various procedures discussed. In other words, this book can be used in the field as a guide covering procedures in a step-by-step format. This is an especially valuable tool when you are faced with a procedure that you use only occasionally and might not remember exactly how to complete, or you are new and have never actually used it in the field. Other books tell you what can be done, but not how or when to do it.

This book was written by someone who has worked in the forensics field in one way or another since 1966. Every technique discussed in this text is one that is current and something you must know. It is written from the experience of not just the author, but also many associates. The author and these associates teach forensics at the college level, and are all still active in their fields as investigators, analysts, and consultants.

The structure of the text is such that it can be used as a teaching tool not only for college classes, but to train new crime scene investigators as well. Classes can be structured to follow the book for the various classes of evidence, and laboratory and field exercises can be conducted simultaneously so that the student actually performs the tasks as they read about them. The text can be used on the laboratory table as a reference for the new practitioner.

In addition, tips are provided throughout the book, not only to make the task as understandable and as simple as possible, but also to allow the reader to find these important bits of information rapidly. It is written in simple lay terms as much as possible to allow it to be of value both to detectives and other investigators who do not have the benefit of a formal forensic science background and to the beginning student, who is not yet familiar with the procedures. Too often, procedures are not used because the investigators are not aware that they even exist, or they have no idea of how or when to use them. They do not know or understand the critical interaction of these procedures. For example, luminol, a presumptive blood test, is usually used only after all sampling is done. Although luminol might not damage blood samples destined for DNA profiling, it is held back until samples of blood are recovered because there are other detrimental reactions of this and other chemicals with biological fluids.

Some of the many forensic organizations that the reader might be interested in joining are included and are a valuable tool used to seek further knowledge. These are of particular interest to the new investigator and to students because many of these organizations have student sections that are very well organized. Some, such as the American Academy of Forensic Sciences (AAFS) have very active student divisions and have programs at their annual training conferences. The training conferences are great for learning new techniques, but also for meeting those experts who might have an influence at some point in your career.

Some of the smaller agencies and colleges may not be aware of where to obtain many of the specialty supplies and instruments. To address that problem, many of these suppliers and their addresses, telephone and fax numbers, and e-mail addresses are included for your convenience. These supply houses are a wonderful source for detailed instructions concerning their kits, along with instructions and Manufacturers Safety Data Sheets (MSDS). Some of these kits are discussed in this text because they are often a viable answer for those agencies that either do not have staff trained to make their reagents or choose not to for whatever reason. Although these kits may add some cost to your operations, they may actually be cheaper because there is no need for a lot of laboratory glassware, chemicals, and apparatus. Another benefit is the lack of "left overs" or wastes to dispose of.

We also discuss methods that can be used if you cannot get the kit or supplies, for various reasons. We suggest sources that are not usually considered and substitutes for various pieces of equipment that you might not possess. These, of course, are meant to be used in an urgent situation.

This text contains safety points in each chapter to address those concerns that might result in not only injury, but also loss of evidence as a result of improper technique.

Mentioned earlier was the availability of MSDS from the supply houses. We suggest here that these documents not only be available as required by law in the laboratories, but that they also are available in the field. Should an employee need to go to the hospital because of an exposure, the emergency room staff will be able to address medical emergencies more rapidly if the MSDS is accompanying the injured person.

The intent of this book is not to make you an expert. Only the court can do that. The intended purpose of this book is to teach you as much as is feasible about the basics of crime scene procedures so you have the foundation to proceed at a competent level. From that point, you can strive to really master your profession.

Acknowledgments

This book could not have been written without the help of numerous people, and I attempt to acknowledge them here with the sincere hope that I miss no one. This must begin at a logical point—the beginning. Detective Sergeant Francis (Buster) Williams (ret.), Honolulu Police Department, took me under his wing when I was promoted to Detective Evidence Specialist. He taught me the basics and more. He encouraged me to experiment and try many new techniques, and he helped me at each step. Mr. Gilbert Chang (ret.), Crime Laboratory Director, Honolulu Police Department, who taught me crime lab procedures that I did not have to know, but wanted to know. Firearm/Tool Mark Examiner Sergeant Charles Davis (ret.), Honolulu Police Department and Forensic Ballistics Technology, who helped with photography and the firearms portion of this book. Dr. Anthony (Tony) Russo, Professor, University of Hawaii (ret.), who reviewed portions of the draft and gave me advice and encouragement. Dr. Robert (Bob) Mann, Deputy Director of Scientific Operations for the Central Identification Laboratory, Hawaii, who was always available to talk to and discuss anthropology and life. Mr. Max Leaver, Marketing Director for Forensics at Armor Forensics, who kindly allowed me to use their Sequential Processing Chart Reprint for this book. I promise never to mention the "fax" again.

A special thanks to Dr. Kanthi DeAlwis, Chief Medical Examiner of the City & County of Honolulu, who supported this effort because she believes we must educate the next generation of forensic scientists so they will not have to repeat what we have had to endure. Dr. M. Lee Goff, Dean of Math and Natural Sciences, Chair of the Forensic Science Department, Chaminade University of Honolulu, for his encouragement, direction, and guidance in allowing me to constantly pick his brain on entomology. He kept me sane—then again, maybe not. He allowed me time to work on this project and was always available to provide advice and work with me. Dr. Henry Lee, who needs no introduction. I learned something each time we met. He and Dr. Goff also reinforced my belief that we must keep a sense of humor and not take ourselves too seriously while maintaining a strict sense of professionalism and service.

My son-in-law, Sean, helped me with photography cases and my daughter, Masako Omine, helped with the drawings. Stephanie Ah Sam, Bryan Johnson, and Sharyse Hagino, who worked with me on some fingerprint cases and helped with photography, forms, and reading my manuscript for about the tenth time to date. We went through many gallons of coffee together and spent countless hours cramped in a small office or in the laboratory. And certainly this would not have happened without my wife, Kimiko, and the rest of my family, Chris, Maria, Elijah, Zachary, and Puna, who put up with me during the writing of this book.

Wilson Sullivan III
Honolulu, Hawaii Date

About the Author

Wilson T. Sullivan is a graduate of the University of Hawaii system with degrees in Police Science, Psychology, and Public Administration. He began his career in law enforcement as a military policeman in 1964. He joined the Honolulu Police Department in 1966, where he started in the Identification Section, fingerprinting persons and searching the fingerprint files. He was later promoted to detective, where he was a crime scene investigator and also did latent fingerprint examinations. After promotion to lieutenant, he headed the fingerprint unit, photo laboratory, and crime scene unit. On being promoted to captain, he headed the Scientific Investigation Section, which had been proposed as a new unit. After promotion to major, he headed the Research and Development Division of the department. On retiring, he worked for the Department of the Medical Examiner in Honolulu as a death investigator as well as starting and running a private company, Forensic Services. Today, Mr. Sullivan is an assistant professor of forensic science at Chaminade University of Honolulu, where he teaches forensic photography, crime scene investigation, and physical forensic science, as well as teamwork in seminars and internships. He continues to operate Forensic Services, where he uses advanced students when possible. He also teaches seminars in crime scene investigation and other related matters.

Introduction

Key Terms

Alternative light source (ALS)
Locard Exchange Principle
Trace evidence
Crime Scene Investigator (CSI)
Physical evidence
Class characteristics
Individualization
Individual characteristic

Crime Scene Investigators (CSIs) are persons who respond to scenes (because they are not always crimes) to document the scene and any evidence or lack thereof. There are some scenes where little or no evidence is found. However, we should keep in mind the old saying that "The absence of evidence is not evidence of absence." There are cases where evidence exists, but we may not recognize it as evidence because of a lack of experience, or do not have the technology to locate it. If proper procedures are used, we should have that evidence at our disposal when our science catches up. For example, we missed untold amounts of trace evidence and latent prints prior to the introduction of the **alternate light source (ALS)**. The ALS is really any light other than natural. It usually refers to a **laser**, xenon lamp, and **ultraviolet (UV)** both *long-wave (UVL)* and *short-wave (UVS)*. Also included are the *blue light* and *infrared (IR) light*, which we discuss later in detail.

Our search of scenes is based on the *theory of transfer*, or **Locard Exchange Principle**, which states that as we move about, we leave something and we take away something. That which we leave consists of our hairs, fibers, and other forms of **trace evidence**, which could include fingerprints and so on. When we refer to *trace evidence,* we are referring to usually small, often minute evidence that may or may not be readily visible to the naked eye. We take away other items that may be the same, hairs and fibers from the victim or scene such as dog hair, carpet fibers, and so on. Your imagination is your only limit to what might be found.

1

What then is evidence? *Evidence* is anything that might assist a court of law in the determination that a crime did or did not occur and of innocence or guilt. We are mostly concerned with physical evidence. *Physical evidence,* simply put, is that matter, large, small, and microscopic, that aids in the understanding of what occurred, where it occurred, how it occurred, when, and, it is hoped, why. We must learn to recognize potential evidence. We may not know something is evidence until we find it and understand its relationship with the event being investigated. Here is where we may find major difficulty. If the investigator is inexperienced, how will he or she recognize potential evidence? This is where education must accompany real and well-rounded investigative experience. Education alone does not make you a competent investigator. The more real-life experience one has, the better one is at recognizing of potential evidence. This is an ongoing, neverending task.

TIP: Visual dictionaries and glossary-type books of the physical objects are extremely valuable for learning about all of the objects around us from cars to the stars. These also provide you with proper terminology, which in turn makes you look more professional. What is even better is that these books are often on the discount tables of bookstores. They are well worth their cost.

Today, we refer to the crime scene investigator as a *Crime Scene Technician, Crime Scene Analyst,* or *Senior Crime Scene Analyst,* titles used for certification by the International Association for Identification, which is the scientific organization most representing the crime scene investigator and is the certifying body. To simplify reading of this book, we use the term **Crime Scene Investigator (CSI)** because it seems to be universally recognized today as a result of the publicity and coverage of crime scene investigation by mass media.

The CSI deals with **physical evidence**. That evidence that is tangible. We can see it, even though we may need assistance from lights, microscopes, and/or chemicals. We can recover and analyze it. As one should realize by now, we do not just document the evidence, we also recover the evidence and examine and interpret its meaning thereby enabling us to reconstruct the scene. Put simply, we look at a multiple step process, as follows:

1. *Recognition.* To document and recover potential evidence, we must first recognize those specific items as potential evidence.
2. *Identification.* We must identify the object. This is rather simple and can be accomplished in most instances. We are placing the object in a *class,* referred to as **class characteristics**. For example if we recover a piece of glass, it be can placed in one of several categories. This piece of glass is tempered glass, it is brown colored (usually used to store photosensitive liquids), it appears to be from a bottle of about 1 gallon capacity, and so on.
3. *Individualization.* This is our ultimate goal and unfortunately the most difficult to attain. We must identify this piece of evidence to the exclusion of all others in the world. We do this by looking at **individual characteristics**. A good example would be a plastic beverage bottle found at a scene and the cap

having been found in the suspect's car. When the top is removed it breaks a series of tabs on the perforated cap. The cap is removed and the ring portion remains on the bottleneck. These tabs can be examined to determine if the top found matches the ring on the bottle, therefore establishing individualization or identification to the exclusion of all others. Another example would be plastic bags that have been torn from a roll of bags. The perforation can be matched from one bag to another, and possibly even the variation in color if it is mottled.

4. *Reconstruction.* We use all of the evidence in its totality to reconstruct what occurred. This interpretation should be replicable under ideal conditions to prove the hypothesis. This is the ultimate for the crime scene analyst.

A well-trained and experienced CSI fits the title *crime scene analyst* because they, in fact, are able to have the scene "tell" what occurred. We discuss this in detail in Chapter Three. Detectives are well advised to consider what the CSI says and should seek their opinion. However, CSI staff, and all investigators for that matter, should be careful not to "think out loud" at crime scenes, because one never knows who might be listening. The next newspaper you pick up might be quoting you. Make your conclusions after careful study and thought, and then convey them in a secure environment.

TIP: One recommendation is to pick a spot where you can observe the scene prior to receiving a briefing or asking any questions, just look at the scene and allow your mind to take in all that you see and don't see and then you will have a foundation without bias. This is sometimes referred to as a **scene survey**. The reason we suggest you do this prior to being briefed is that in this way you will be unbiased as to what you observe. If you are briefed first, you may subconsciously look for evidence to support the opinion of the briefer, usually the scene detective.

There is an old saying regarding crime scene investigation. It states that there are three ways to investigate a scene. Only one is correct. You can look for evidence to prove a theory... incorrect. You can look for evidence to disprove a theory... incorrect. You can examine the evidence and let it dictate what occurred... correct.

REVIEW QUESTIONS

1. Briefly describe *transfer*, often referred to as the *Locard Exchange Principle.*
2. What is an alternate light source?
3. What is a *scene survey?*
4. What are the four goals we strive for with regard to evidence?
5. One of the four goals concerning evidence is the most elusive. Which one is it?
6. What do we mean by the term *trace evidence?*
7. When referring to trace evidence, what two categories of evidence are usually associated with it?

Planning, Training and Equipping

Key Terms

Minimum qualifications (MQ)
Certification
Manual of Operations (MOO)
Manual of Procedures (MOP)

No crime scene investigation can occur without having a staff. We discuss staffing options in this section, looking at both sworn officers and detectives and civilians as well as a combination of the two. The selection of staff requires **minimum qualifications (MQ)** for the position, which is usually thought of in terms of training and experience. We must understand that this is not just in the beginning, but is an ongoing process that ends only on termination of employment.

An applicant who has an undergraduate or even masters-level degree is not qualified to handle cases until they are trained in their specific duties and deemed qualified at the minimum acceptable standard. **Certification** is the goal, and maintenance means review and recertification every few years.

Once staffing is addressed, the task of position descriptions and actual duties and responsibilities must be addressed. This is spelled out in the **Manual of Operations (MOO)** or **Manual of Procedures (MOP)**. These are guidelines and not written in stone. There must be built-in avenues of flexibility. The MOP must also state the chain of command based on each employee answering to a specific supervisor.

The personnel considerations being met, it is time to move to equipment. If there are certain tasks and procedures expected of the staff, then it is obvious that the unit must have the proper operational equipment required to accomplish those tasks. We look at the minimum level of equipment needed and take it somewhat further to provide for a full-service crime scene unit. We address storage and transportation of that equipment, and later in the book we look at the actual operation of some of the equipment.

Preparation and Initial Steps

Key Terms

Manual of Procedures (MOP)
Standard Operating Procedure (SOP)
Sworn staff
Civilian staff

INTRODUCTION/OBJECTIVES

Preparation is critical because it covers many topics, some of which are addressed in this book. If your agency already has a staff of crime scene investigators (CSIs), your work here is half completed. If not, then you must decide which route to take. It is hoped that this part of the text covers some of these concerns. They include such staffing considerations as sworn or civilian staff and their training and deployment. What are their duties?

Prior to responding to any scene, the unit must be prepared. This is not something to take for granted, but something that must be planned far in advance. When you get the call, it is rather late to be thinking about these things. In this section, we examine the process as a whole, with the hope that it will result in a successful investigation.

Prior to performing any task, proper preparation is required. That means you must have a plan of action and the ability to complete each step in that plan of action. We address those steps here, beginning with research and training. We then move into the development of the plan, which is usually found in the form of a **Manual of Procedures (MOP)** or a **Standard Operating Procedure (SOP)**.

If you work for any government organization, prior to being hired you will most likely be required to provide a documented history of education at least to the level of BS in a natural or biological science or, ideally, a Bachelor of Forensic Science (BFS). Of course, a master's degree is even better, and rapidly coming to be expected. The former provides you with the foundation needed to learn forensic science, whereas the latter provides not just the foundation, but the actual experience in the duties put forth in your job description via advanced instrumentation and experience resulting from internships. This is the ideal situation, but there are many agencies that cannot bring on board a true forensic scientist for a variety of reasons, and this book is geared toward those agencies specifically. We show you how to take your existing staff and have them conduct credible investigations that are reasonably complete, all without that science degree. We should stress, however, that the intention here is not to bypass hiring a forensic specialist. You are always better served by staffing a qualified forensic scientist. Existing staff is to be considered only when qualified personnel are not a possibility. Many of the procedures covered in this book are hazardous, and could also destroy potential evidence when not applied properly.

SWORN VERSUS CIVILIAN STAFF

The question of sworn versus civilian staff is inevitable. There are two sides to every argument, and both must be understood. There may not be one perfect answer, but some of the arguments looking at both sides include the following:

- **Sworn staff**, or those who are actual law enforcement officers, have a "police perspective." They understand the needs of the investigator and the investigation as a whole. **Civilian staff** understand their specific duties, but seem to have little understanding of how everything and everybody relate to each other.
- Officers are easy to replace. If one leaves today, a replacement can be transferred in tomorrow. If the staff is civilian and someone leaves, the agency must advertise for replacements and go through the process of examinations, interviews, and everything else associated with new staff. There is a potentially serious problem here, however. It is unfortunate that some agencies use positions such as these as a "dumping" ground for misfits or persons who do not "fit in" with administration. This can have a disastrous effect on the desirability, credibility, and efficient operation of the unit. A unit such as this must be manned by staff who wants to be there and are willing to put out that great amount of effort necessary for successful investigations.
- If an officer is not right for the job, he or she can be transferred to another unit. If the member is a civilian, the question is, where do you transfer them? You must have a job within your agency or another in the same political subdivision in which to transfer them that has a similar job description. This may be extremely problematic when considering the need to work around deceased, decomposed, and dismembered persons. Having a science

degree does not in any way relate to a person's psychological ability to work with these stressors day after day. It sometimes ends in disaster when an employee commits suicide or becomes disabled as a result of these factors.

- Officers can protect themselves and therefore eliminate the need to have a police officer remain at the scene with the crime scene unit for protection and/or security. There is a definite need for civilian staff to have protection, as suspects do return to scenes and there are other persons who may also be a threat to staff.
- Dependant on pay scales, one may be cheaper than the other to employ.
- It may be difficult to find officers with proper education. With civilian positions, the job descriptions dictate educational and experience levels required for a specific position.
- Most officers are interested in advancement that would eventually put them out of the unit as they move higher in the agency. There are at least fewer opportunities for advancement. Civilian staff is employed with a clear understanding that there are very few upper-management positions. This might, however, result in civilian staff constantly shopping for better positions in other agencies.
- Specialty pay may be required and become expensive for officers, but as with any other job, such as bomb squad, SWAT, or hostage negotiators, these officers should receive incentive pay to keep on a par with their fellow officers in specialty work.
- As mentioned earlier, dependant on pay scale, officers may be quite a bit more expensive than civilians. We should stress that civilian staff should be paid for their educational level and certifications along with any additional training, among other factors. Civilian staffing should not be an attempt to get off with paying less.
- There is also the possibility of having a combination of staff, both civilian and sworn. Civilian staff might be used in the laboratory and sworn staff in the field. This has its pros and cons as well.

After a decision is made as to staffing types, position descriptions must be considered. Each duty must be broken down into components that can be addressed in a logical order. Each position description must have very specifically defined duties. In these organizations, often the position descriptions end with the statement "and all related duties." This allows for those unexpected duties that always pop up.

▲ SUMMARY

Preparation is a process that begins long before anyone is dispatched to a crime scene. Staffing, training, and equipment must be addressed prior to any actual work. These are not simple tasks, but require advanced planning on the part of the agency based on a solid foundation of what they intend to accomplish and how they intend to accomplish those goals. After these decisions have been made, the staff must be put in place, and they must also have a clear idea of what is expected of them, how they will accomplish those duties, and whom they will follow. These must be clearly stated and put in writing.

■■ REVIEW QUESTIONS

1. Why is the "police prospective" so very important to maintain?
2. Briefly discuss some arguments for civilians for the scientific investigation staff.
3. Why do we want to have our crime scene notes neat and orderly?
4. Discuss ways to solve the storage problems with regard to crime scene equipment.
5. What are some of the equipment kits we might carry in the crime scene vehicle?

Equipment and Supplies

Key Terms

Shelf life
Manufacturer's Safety Data Sheet (MSDS)
Plan of Operation
Delegation
Crime Scene Kits

INTRODUCTION/OBJECTIVES

Equipment and supplies are essential for the successful operation of a crime scene unit. Although this may seem to be a simple matter, it is far more complicated. We are concerned not only with having the proper equipment and supplies available, but they must also be in serviceable condition and in sufficient amounts.

STORAGE, PREPARATION, AND TRANSPORTATION

A major consideration with equipment is that of storage. Much of the equipment used for crime scene investigation is heat and/or light sensitive. This means that unless the crime scene vehicle is under covered parking and possibly with air conditioning running off a 115-VAC line, it may be necessary to offload much of the equipment after each case, or at least at the end of each day.

The equipment in kit form can simply be offloaded and placed on shelving provided in the vehicle and in the office or lab area. This method makes loading and unloading a relatively simple process. Equipment arranged as kits also has the advantage of keeping the storage and transport areas clean and neat, and helps avoid parts of kits becoming commingled. If the equipment is not in kit form, then portions must be unloaded. This makes it somewhat sloppy and also increases the chances of forgetting equipment and supplies when responding. Ideally, the vehicle should have proper parking and be equipped with both air conditioning and a refrigerator. The referigerator/freezer would eliminate the entire need to unload the vehicle.

When considering preparation, as mentioned earlier, a list prominently posted with the equipment reminding the operator of the need for reagents, batteries, and other items would be helpful. Another option is a checklist. However, these are often robotically completed, with no real attention being paid after the novelty wears off.

Transportation is another major concern. You must be aware that certain items such as gasoline must receive special attention with regard to fumes. It is also very important to have shelves that provide security for the contents with regard to falling off during starting, stopping, and cornering. Equipment falling from shelves can be dangerous to both the occupants of the vehicle as well as to the equipment itself. Of special interest are items like portable lasers that may be thrown out of alignment by simply hitting potholes in the roadway. These instruments should be either strapped down or, better yet, transported on some sort of suspension or shock-absorber system.

Protocols must be in place for replacement supplies in a timely manner. This requires staff to be aware of the **shelf life** of various chemicals and field kits. You should be aware that some of the reagents might have a shelf life of 3 months or even less. The shelf life or an expiration date is usually printed on the container. This information may also be found in the chemical's instructions or on the **Manufacturer's Safety Data Sheet (MSDS)**. Outdated supplies can mean the difference of obtaining good results and total failure, because some outdated chemicals not only fail to produce results, but can actually damage the evidence.

SUPPLIES

An army runs on its stomach, and a crime scene unit runs on its equipment and supplies. The investigation of a major crime scene can be a costly event. There are copious amounts of gloves needed in various sizes and of good quality. Also needed are bags and containers made of paper, plastic, and glass; permanent marking pens; graph paper; drafting equipment; cameras; film; and batteries of various sizes to power the equipment. Even industrial-quality trash bags are required. We provide a fairly complete list of each kind in this chapter.

Investigations require planning and constant modification when and where needed. Once the team arrives at a scene, planning is too late. Your **plan of operation** (working instructions) must be addressed prior to any response. Checklists, which can often be broken down into categories such as sexual assault, homicide, robbery, indoor and outdoor scene, and day and night time, are advisable. On notification of a case, the team gets the equipment ready and loaded into the response vehicle. Why not just keep the vehicle fully supplied? That might not be a bad idea if the agency has a very large mobile crime laboratory. Most, unfortunately, do not, and could not afford one in the first place. It would also require covered parking and onboard electricity to power a refrigerator/freezer, dehumidifier, and other equipment necessary to prevent deterioration of the supplies. The best we can do is to have nonperishable items stocked and the remaining grouped by specific need to facilitate rapid loading of the unit. The sooner you get there, the less chance there is for critical evidence to be damaged, altered, or destroyed. Drive carefully. You are needed at the scene, and should you become involved in a traffic collision you will be late, if you make it at all. Accidents waste time, and if the response vehicle is damaged severely, you might have no way to get the necessary items to the crime scene.

Film, batteries, and some chemicals and reagents require refrigeration. Others are light and heat sensitive, and certain equipment such as cameras and other optical devices need a controlled environment to prevent fungus from attacking the lenses. It is often a much simpler task to keep the equipment in the laboratory and load it as required. Film and batteries stored in a refrigerator must be returned to ambient temperature prior to use. This is accomplished during the drive to the scene; therefore, always remove them from the refrigerator prior to leaving for the scene.

A complete inventory must be kept on the amount of each item on stock and orders to replenish made on a timely basis to avoid shortages at critical times. These are tasks that can be **delegated** to team leaders, but remain the ultimate responsibility of the unit commander or director.

TIP: The midnight crew can clean and restock the vehicles and the day crew can order and stock the office and lab supplies. The evening team can also receive related assignments, although the evening team is often the busiest. The point here is that responsibility must be designated for these critical tasks.

TIP: Crime scene response vehicles should never leave the station without at least half a tank of gasoline. It is very easy to gas the vehicle on returning from all distant cases. Someone must also check oil, antifreeze, and other operational needs including tire pressure. Some departments have garage personnel take care of this, but be aware that many say it is the responsibility of the operator.

TIP: Make a list of the various batteries required for all of your equipment. Always keep extra batteries on stock. Do not store batteries in any equipment that is not used regularly, as they might ruin the instrument.

How much is too much? That is a very good question, and it is far better to be slightly oversupplied than short. For example, with reference to cameras, one camera can be used for those tasks requiring film and another a good digital camera can be used as the standard crime scene camera. A good digital camera can eliminate the need for concerns about black and white and color positive and negative film formats.

Fingerprint tape is another concern. It is not uncommon to have a defective roll or have the hot sun loosen the adhesive surface of the tape. Always keep extra tape with you.

CRIME SCENE KITS

Equipment must readily available to you when preparing to respond to a scene. It must also be complete as to all parts, reagents, and other related materials. One way to address this very important subject is to have your equipment stored as kits. Examples are fingerprint kits, photo kits, drawing kits, and so forth. There are some distinct advantages to this method, one being that all related parts are kept in the same container, which means fewer missing parts. The exception here might be batteries and some reagents that require refrigeration or mixing just prior to departure. In this instance, it might be a good idea to have a distinctive marking on the storage shelf or the equipment case itself, reminding you that batteries are required of a specific number and type. You do not want to find you are missing part of the kit at the scene.

Most agencies do not have a vehicle large enough to carry all of the equipment required for any situation, and therefore it is good to have a list of kits required for a specific type of investigation and a suggested list of additional equipment. When a case comes in, it is then possible to simply load the necessary equipment into the vehicle. Of course, things like generators and electric lines with lighting can be stored in the vehicle if the generator and gasoline are in a vented compartment designed for such storage.

Major supply houses carry and sell a variety of kits designed for forensic examinations. The problem is that these kits tend to be rather pricey and sometimes limited as to the number of tests that can be conducted. The obvious option is to make your own. The advantage to making your own is not only that they are less costly, but you can also design the kit to your own specific needs. Examples of some of these kits are included in this text. Briefly, we have found a few kits to be very useful almost on a daily basis, such as a photography kit for general crime scenes with equipment for macro photography and a fingerprint kit for latent print recovery. Also needed is a simple drawing kit with graph paper, an engineer's or architect's scale, a drawing pencil, an eraser, and a protractor.

Photography Kit

A photography kit can be a simple bag with a camera and film in it. However, more than likely you are going to have at least a good-size camera bag with a 35-mm single lens reflex (SLR) camera, one to three lenses, filters, electronic flash unit, photographic scales, and a tripod (Figure 2–1). This

FIGURE 2–1 A basic 35-mm camera kit with two bodies: 50 mm, 35 mm, macro and 35 135, macro lens combination, cable shutter release, flash extensions, slave units, and camera bag. Note that the film box ends that go in the slot on the back of the camera to indicate that there is film in camera.

would be a very basic kit. If, however, you are a full-service unit, then the following list might be of interest to you:

- At least one camera body
- Normal 50-mm lens
- 35-mm wide-angle lens
- Macro lens
- Latent print lens adapter
- Electronic flash unit(s) with master/slave capability
- Cable release or other form of shutter release
- Extended flash chord
- Tripod (heavy duty)
- Photo scales, which should include an ABFO#2 scale
- Filters such as Polaroid, red, blue, and ultraviolet including a 2-A; other filters depending on need
- Timer for time exposures in total darkness
- Small red light to make adjustments to equipment; a light emitting diode (LED) light is good for this task
- Supply of batteries for all equipment
- Lens hood
- Tape measure, at least 3 feet (but 10–12 feet better)
- Clipboard for photo logs
- Pencil for photo log (pens often do not write in the rain)
- Lens cloth, brush, and air
- Bubble level(s)

There is much more that can be found in a photographic unit that we address in Chapter 5.

Latent Print Kit

As with photography, we can have an officer's kit that may consist of a latent print brush, bottle of latent powder, and latent print tape with latent print cards. A more reasonable kit (Figure 2–2) for a crime scene investigator would consist of

- Latent print brush for each type of powder used. For the black powder, it is advisable to have at least two brushes, and a magnetic brush (wand).
- Various latent print powders that include black, bichromatic or silver black, magnetic black, gray, and white. Others might be advisable depending on the scope of your investigations.
- Latent print tape at least in one size, but better with some 3-in. tape as well. Frosted seems to be better than gloss clear.
- Good supply of white latent print cards or lifters. Some black cards are also a good idea.
- Latent print card transfer folders.
- Gloves to fit.
- Hand cleaner (towelettes are good).
- Flashlight.
- Short tape measure or ruler.
- Closable plastic bags to hold cards and other items to keep them clean.

FIGURE 2–2 Latent fingerprint kit, containing latent print tape, various powders, brush selection, and latent print cards.

- Empty container to mix "sticky-side" powder for prints on tape.
- Dishwashing detergent for sticky-side powder.
- Camel hair brush for sticky-side powder.

Fingerprint Kit

This kit is listed in addition to the latent print kit because it serves a different purpose and may not even be used in the field. It can be of real value under certain circumstances, such as printing persons for elimination prints or for processing deceased persons if your agency uses ink. A simple kit (Figure 2–3) would consist of

- Fingerprint ink
- Roller
- Glass slab to roll ink on
- Fingerprint cards (there are various kinds)
- Tabs for reprinting single fingers
- Fingerprint card holder
- Hand cleaner
- Paper towels
- Tape to hold down card holder and glass slab if not mounted on kit's case
- "Spoons" for deceased persons (if your agency uses ink for deceased persons)
- Gloves to fit

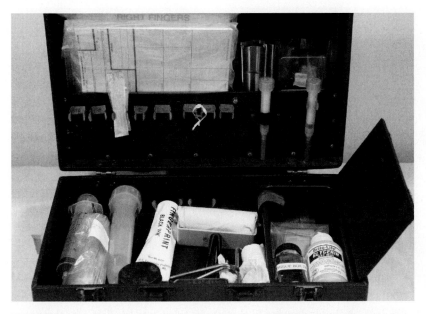

FIGURE 2–3 Postmortem fingerprint kit, containing ink, powder, cards, spoons, powder, tape, tissue builder, glycerin, syringe, scalpel, and roller.

Drawing Kit

There are kits designed for field use that are perfect for CSIs who have to make detailed scene drawings. With the addition of some other items, you will be well on your way to handle most scenes you come across. You will also be able to complete your drawing in the field, if necessary. Of course, another option is one of the crime scene computer programs now available. A good kit (Figure 2–4) consists of a rigid case containing

- A drawing board with small drawing machine (a drawing machine can be replaced by or used with the other listed equipment)
- T-square
- Triangles
- Drafting pencil
- Eraser
- Drawing paper
- Engineer's scale or architect's scale

In addition to this basic drafting set, the following additional items are either necessary or at least very helpful:

- One or two 100-foot metal measuring tapes. Do not use cloth because of stretch factor.
- One 25- to 30-foot steel tape
- Rolling measuring device (the author has found that these are fairly inaccurate)
- $\frac{1}{4}$-in. graph paper

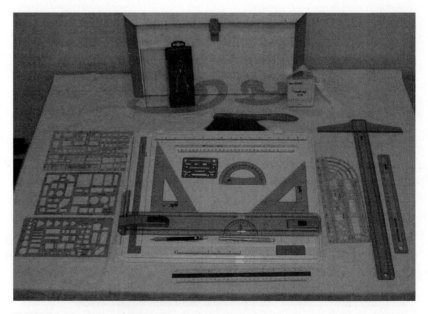

FIGURE 2–4   A simple drawing lit that can be taken into the field. The three templates on the left are architectural scales for house and office in 1/8- and $\frac{1}{4}$-in. scales. The template on the right is Northwestern University's Traffic Template.

- ¼-in. architect's templates for home, office, bathrooms, and a traffic scale from Northwestern University's Traffic Institute
- Drafting eraser, erasing template, and soft brush
- Drafting tabs to hold down drawing paper

Casting Kit

Casting can include many things, but we limit our discussion to two categories: the casting of foot and tire prints and the casting of tool marks. The purpose of each is the same. We want to recover as much detail with regard to the "signature" of the shoe, tire, or tool. To accomplish this, we must be capable of producing extremely fine detail in our **casts**. This can be accomplished with relative ease. We first examine the shoe and tire casts. The equipment needed includes

- Dental stone
- Spatula and/or chef's whisk or hand-cranked egg beater (if you can find one today)
- Wide putty knife that is used to break the fall of plaster when pouring mixture and also for smoothing the surface prior to marking
- Mixing bowl or similar container—plastic or nylon is best because it is easily cleaned (if it is the flexible type)
- Measuring cup
- Material for frames—cardboard will do, but aluminum is better

Evidence Collection Kit

- Zip-top bags of various sizes, from very small to larger 1-gallon size
- Plastic bags of various sizes
- Paper bags of various sizes
- Heavy-duty wrapping paper (such as meat wrapping paper)
- Standard and legal-size manila envelopes
- Plastic and glass tubes and vials (empty film containers are excellent)
- Blood vacutubes for recovery of flies and maggots
- Clean, new, unlined paint cans of quart and gallon size for fire evidence
- Permanent ink markers (these are wonderful for marking evidence without being destructive)
- Garbage bags (the heavy-duty industrial bags are the best choice; they are both very large and very strong)
- Gloves of various sizes

  TIP: These gloves can be bought in boxes of small, medium, and large, but you can also get them in specific sizes. If you are doing a lot of work in gloves and somewhat delicate work, do yourself a favor and get gloves in your size.

- Evidence tags and labels
- Evidence tape (tamper resistant)
- String, twine

- Scissors, box-cutter knife, and the like.
- Various tapes such as duct, masking, strapping, etc.
- Cotton-tip swabs and gauze pads, such as 4 × 4 in.
- Biohazard labels
- Warning labels for fingerprint contamination, indented writing, etc. (one label with check blocks is really sufficient)

There should be other packaging materials in your lab or workplace for mailing or using other delivery services. There are entirely too many to transport around with you. Much of the material mentioned here can simply be placed in a box in your vehicle.

▲ SUMMARY

We discussed the need to arrive at the scene safely and properly equipped to do the job. Check lists are an obvious choice to ensure nothing gets left behind in the confusion of getting ready to respond. It is a time when many things are going through our minds and concentration has not yet kicked into gear.

Delegation is a way to assign some responsibility for specific tasks, even though the unit supervisor is ultimately responsible. Delegation is a standard management tool and works well in this type of team concept. Although we looked at a few options, there are many more available to you, and you should explore these.

With regard to equipment and supplies, more is often better than less. If you should err, then err on the side of excess as a general rule.

■ REVIEW QUESTIONS

1. Discuss the need for planning with regard to crime scene investigation.
2. Why should film and batteries only be removed from the refrigerator just prior to leaving for the scene?
3. Discuss in a few sentences the process of "delegation" with regard to crime scene vehicles.
4. Why is delegation so important?
5. What are some options you can think of concerning our having the proper equipment at the scene when we need it?

◆ REFERENCES AND SUGGESTED READINGS

Handbook of Forensic Science, US Department of Justice, FBI. US Government Printing Office, Washington, DC.

STEVEN STAGGS, *Crime Scene and Evidence Photographer's Guide.* (Staggs Publishing Temecula, CA:1997).

DAVID R. REDSOCKER, *The Practical Methodology of Forensic Photography,* (Endicott, NY: CRC Press, 2001).

LARRY S. MILLER, *Police Photography*. (Cincinnati, OH: Anderson Publishing Co., 1998).

JAMES A. MCDONALD, *The Police Photographer's Guide.* (Arlington Heights, IL: Photo Text Books, 1992).

HENRY C. LEE, TIMOTHY PALMBACH, and MARILYN T. MILLER, *Henry Lee's Crime Scene Handbook.* (San Diego: Academic Press, 2001).

CHAPTER 3

Arrival at the Scene

Key Terms _____

Crime scene
Briefing
Walk through
Crime scene survey
Crime scene search
Line search
Grid search

INTRODUCTION/OBJECTIVES

The term **crime scene** implies that it is the location where a crime was committed. Of course, that is, in fact, true, but possibly not that simple. Many, if not most, crimes are committed at a single location, but it is not that unusual for various activities directly related to that crime to occur in other locations. To address this, the terms *primary crime scene* and *secondary crime scene* came to be. We are going to examine what you, as the crime scene investigator, must accomplish when you first arrive at the scene and just how to accomplish those tasks.

The primary crime scene is open to some discussion or debate. It is where the initial crime occurred, but could also be implied to mean where the major part of the crime occurred. For instance, a person is killed in one location, but the body is taken to another location and dumped. Is the location where the body was found the primary crime scene, or the location where the person was actually killed? The point is, there is a main crime scene and any other scenes are known as **secondary crime scenes**. A case in point involves a kidnapping/murder case that involved the following scenes:

- Scene of abduction
- Scene of killing
- Scene where body was dumped
- Location where suspect vehicle was first encountered
- Location where suspect vehicle was being repaired
- Police garage where vehicle was processed
- Location that suspect used as an alibi
- Morgue where body was processed
- Mortuary where body was again processed

One of these scenes was the primary scene and the rest were secondary scenes. Each one of the locations required a significant amount of investigation and processing. Furthermore, each of these scenes involved very critical evidence concerning the outcome of the case.

It is important that these scenes be handled properly and efficiently to keep the integrity of the investigation intact. There must be a clear progression or transition from one scene to the next. In this section, we address those initial steps that start you on the right road.

ARRIVAL AT THE SCENE

When you first pull up to the scene, you must determine the best place to park. Although this seems like such a simple task, there are some important factors that we tend to forget.

- Is our parking spot legal? Remember, we must set an example, and some agencies do not take care of traffic violations resulting from parking unless it is an emergency.
- Is our parking location causing a traffic hazard or undue traffic congestion? Although we have a job to do, the public is not very sympathetic when they are inconvenienced, and this seems to grow in direct proportion to the length of time we keep them in that state of mind.
- Does the parking place provide accessibility to our equipment, including electric generators? When you work out of a mobile crime laboratory, you may be surprised at just how many times you must go back and forth to the van during an investigation. This is even more of a nuisance when the equipment is large, heavy, and bulky.
- Does your location provide security for the vehicle and equipment? This is extremely important if evidence is going to be stored in the vehicle. Crime scene investigators have had equipment stolen from them while unattended at a crime scene. What about the evidence you might have in the vehicle? That is a possible target of theft as well.
- Is our vehicle in the "scene," where we might damage evidence?
- Is your parking spot free from "prying eyes"? Remember, the media take pictures of whatever they can get, and some of them might compromise your

case or, in some other way, come back to haunt you. Remember the O.J. Simpson case. We must keep the spirit of cooperation, but there must be a limit. There may be some evidence that only you and the person responsible for the crime is aware of, and it should remain that way to prevent the offenders knowing what evidence you have and to keep other persons who have the "need" to "confess" to crimes they did not commit from knowing exactly what to say.

- Have you set up garbage bags? You should set up a garbage bag for rubbish that is not hazardous and can simply be thrown away and another bag that is specifically for biohazardous materials. The latter must be either autoclaved or taken directly to an incinerator. Imagine what would happen if you were to throw the container in the garbage and some innocent person picked it up.

On arrival at the scene, your note taking is immediately resumed. What time did you arrive? Whom did you observe at the scene? Whom did you see? Whom did you meet with?

When you arrive at a crime scene, you should advise the detective in charge that you have arrived and you may receive some preliminary information such as complainant, classification of case, report number, exact scene address, and other basic recordkeeping data that are usually the header for each page of the report. The detectives are usually very busy at this time, something that is welcome because it provides the CSI with some time to allow the scene to "talk to you." By this, we mean initial observations to allow you to begin to understand what has or has not happened at this scene.

LETTING THE SCENE "TALK TO YOU"

On arrival at the scene, you should take a few minutes to look around and make some initial and often very important observations. This can be thought of as a *sight survey*. We want to do this prior to receiving a detailed **briefing** because it allows us the opportunity to observe the scene and let the evidence speak for itself. If one receives a detailed briefing, one might have an unintentional bias toward a specific scenario based on what was said about the scene. To take this a step further, it is also a good idea not to concern yourself with the identity of the suspect or victim, because even that may cause bias. There are cases when you might not even need to know the identities of the participants. However, should you need to process these persons, you obviously must obtain their identity at that time. To continue with the process of surveying the scene, the following examples are just a small sample of what you might observe:

- Indoor or outdoor scene. Is what you see consistent with that type of scene? Is there a possibility that this is not the only scene?
- Time of day. Is the scene in agreement with the time? If you arrive and observe breakfast on the table, could that be an indicator of about when the incident occurred? Is blood or other similar evidence dried, wet, or in a state of

change? Is the victim in pajamas and it is afternoon? Is there a reason? Do you see medications?

- Outdoor lighting, including type, such as incandescent lighting, mercury vapor, fluorescent, and so on, and distance from scene. The type of lights can alter color perception, and distance can determine ability for witnesses to see.

TIP: Most utility poles have a pole number and possibly company name/indicator.

- Indoor lighting. Is it daytime and the lights are on? If the scene is well lit by sunlight, then this may be suspicious. What kind of light? If there are growing lights, for example, there may a possibility that marijuana could be grown in that location. Of course, there may be other legitimate reasons for such lights.
- What is at the scene?
- What is there that should not be in the scene? A cigarette package and there are no ashtrays; beer bottle, but no other signs of alcohol? Is there blood? Cartridge cases? Is there a missing knife from the knife block? Is there camera equipment present in a bedroom or office that doesn't fit the situation?
- What is not there that should be? Impressions in the carpet may be indicative of something being missing. A kitchen knife in the bathroom. A missing carpet. Missing curtains or blinds when they are present in other rooms. Are there obvious signs that other persons occupy the scene and they are not present? Are there baby supplies and related furniture but no baby?
- What is out of place? A chair turned over. A desk with the chair missing. Gloves in the rubbish can or on the floor. An open drawer in the kitchen. A watch on the floor. Are there marks in the carpeting indicative of furniture having been moved?
- What are your gut feelings? This can be important. What may have the elements of a burglary could be to cover what actually occurred.
- What do you smell? Ether? This could indicate a clandestine drug lab.
- What do you hear? Sometimes sounds can be important, such as in the instance of background noise in telephone calls, tape recordings, and so on.
- What do you feel? If you are at the scene of a baby death and the room is extremely hot, this might be related to the cause of death.
- Is food being prepared or on the table? Are there signs that another person had eaten or drank at the scene?
- Are there newspapers piled up outside? What are the earliest and latest dates?
- Was the door locked from the inside?
- Are the windows locked?

The observations described here are just a small sample of actual observations from scenes. As you gain experience, more and more of this sort of communications with the scene will occur.

After having completed this little introduction to the scene, it is time for the briefing. The reason for the initial observations is simply to allow you to better understand the briefing and, more importantly, to help you maintain a neutral view of the scene and not be led in a particular direction or bias, even though that is not the intent of the briefer. This initial period can also help you to determine what you can do immediately to assist in the progress of the investigation and, in some instances, to suggest redirection of the investigation. If the evidence you have observed does not agree with that view being taken by the investigators, you should advise them of this fact. Remember diplomacy. Be tactful. We are all on the same team, and your suggestions should indicate just that, and certainly not indicate cockiness.

BRIEFING

Next, arrange to meet with the investigator in charge of the crime scene and discuss what must be accomplished. There are certainly tasks that need not be mentioned because they are standard to each scene, such as the photography, diagrams, latent print recovery, and other regular tasks. There may be some specialized technical photography, tire or shoe prints, and other less than routine procedures that may be desired. These should be discussed and their order of processing determined. Always remember that many crime scene procedures may have a negative effect on other procedures, and therefore their order of completion and other necessary precautions must be well thought out.

Some investigators may have already come to some conclusions in the case, but it cannot be overemphasized that you must remain unbiased in your investigation.

After the briefing, it is time to begin work. If you are alone, then you simply begin. If you are a member of a crime scene team, then you also must have a short briefing to finalize who accomplishes which tasks and how to process the scene as efficiently and timely as is possible. This is often not an easy task to accomplish.

TIP: Remove that equipment required for each task, and as you complete each task, put the equipment back where it belongs. This enables you to maintain custody of your equipment at all times, and should another person on the team require that equipment, it can be easily located. In addition, there is less chance of forgetting equipment when leaving the scene, and the task of packing up and leaving at least seems easier if you do not have to start from scratch cleaning up.

CRIME SCENE SURVEY

A **walk through**, or **crime scene survey**, is often used with the detective and supervisor for CSI staff. This is where each can communicate with the other and formulate a plan of action best suited for this specific investigation. This is sometimes a part of the briefing process, but not always. There are instances where the briefing may include all persons at the scene and may be rather general in nature. The survey is specific to certain staff and very limited with regard to participation because of contamination concerns.

CRIME SCENE SEARCH

The search of the crime scene for evidence varies depending on scene location, structure, topography, and other factors. The important point is that the **crime scene search** be consistent, complete, and competent. Again, when we are involved in searches, there are two views of working the scene. First is the *macro view* of the scene, where we consider the scene as a whole and what types of evidence and therefore procedures we will use. There is also the *micro view* of the scene, where we look at one particular aspect, such as trace evidence, latent prints, and so on.

SEARCH PATTERNS

There are various search patterns commonly discussed in books, each having both positive and negative points.

Line Search

When searching an area such as a large field or very rough terrain, a **line search** may be more practical. The distance between each searcher depends on how many persons you have at your disposal and the size of the evidence being sought. The important thing here is that the searchers are in a line and that they are close enough to cover the entire area completely (Figure 3–1). This search pattern allows a large area to be searched in a relatively short period of time. It is commonly used in large area searches when a large number of searchers are available and can be controlled.

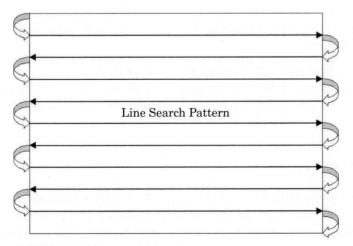

Line Search Pattern

FIGURE 3–1   Line search pattern.

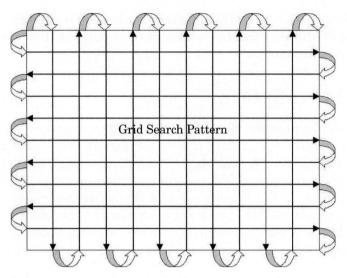

FIGURE 3–2   Grid search pattern.

Grid Search

The **grid search** can be used in two different ways. Most commonly it is thought of as a line search that when completed is subjected to another line search crossing from side-to-side of the previous search, thereby making a grid (Figure 3–2). This is useful outside, but is more time-consuming and may not be feasible if a very large area is to be searched.

A variation of the grid search is used in smaller areas such as rooms where the room is broken down into a grid pattern of small blocks of responsibility. This method is great for locating extremely small items of evidence and for using the tape-lift method and vacuum to search for trace evidence. A diagram of the room is made and a grid pattern is created using appropriate measurements. An example would be a linoleum floor with standard 12 × 12-in. tiles. If you were to kneel down, you could easily handle two blocks deep by three blocks wide as a grid section. In this manner, you could conduct a very detailed search of the room for trace evidence.

TIP: It is very difficult to work for long periods of time on your knees. A suggestion is to get one of the small kneeling pads used by gardeners, or to wear thick kneepads such as those worn by skateboarders and in-line skaters.

Spiral Pattern

While this pattern is discussed in most books, this method has limited use. It is very difficult to keep an even **spiral pattern** in real life, and even circular scenes can be searched using a grid search. More important is consistency. Whatever pattern you use, always conduct the search the same way. There is much less chance for mistakes if everything is done the same each time. For example, if you do choose to use the spiral, then move consistently in the same direction. Does it matter if you are moving clockwise or counterclockwise? Not really. Do what feels best for you as an individual.

◣ SUMMARY

We cover some preliminary but very important material concerning your arrival at the scene. Possibly the most important piece of information in this chapter and possibly the book is letting the scene "talk to you." It is this ability that helps you to become a true crime scene analyst. Also covered are suggestions covering such topics as the walk through, which is of course limited as to number of participants. We also looked at the sometimes difficult task of keeping track of your equipment.

We cover search patterns, which vary from scene to scene, but a single scene can use more than one. This is really something you must decide on based on experience.

◼ REVIEW QUESTIONS

1. Discuss briefly the difference between a line search and a grid search.
2. What do you think would be a good general search pattern and why?
3. Do you think the media has a place in the crime scene? Defend your choice.
4. What do we mean by letting the scene "talk to you"? Can you give examples not mentioned?
5. What is your perspective concerning the subject of the previous question?

◆ REFERENCES AND SUGGESTED READINGS

Crime Scene Search as a Process, US Department of Justice, FBI Laboratory Unit.

RICHARD SAFERSTEIN, *Criminalistics: An Introduction to Forensic Science* (Saddle River, NJ: Pearson Prentice Hall, 2004).

Forensic Science: An Introduction to Scientific and Investigative Techniques STUART H. JAMES and JON J. NORDBY, (Boca Raton: CRC Press, 2005).

HENRY C. LEE, TIMOTHY M. PALMBACH, and MARILYN T. MILLER, *Henry Lee's Crime Scene Handbook* (San Diego: Academic Press, 2001).

BARRY A. J. FISHER, *Techniques of Crime Scene Investigation* (Boca Raton, CRC Press, 2004).

The Crime Scene

In Part I, we address personnel and equipment concerns, now, we must proceed to the scene and actually begin the process of investigation. In this section, we look at arrival on scene and what we must accomplish before we actually get down to the work for which this book was written. The preliminary steps taken at a scene can be the difference between success and failure, but even more often it means a scene investigation that is run in an efficient manner and in a reasonable time.

Some of the topics we discuss are of a legal nature, whereas others deal with the safety of those persons at the scene and everyone who comes in contact with the material we recover and the procedures completed at the scene.

While investigating a crime scene, we must consider today what to do with the garbage accumulated as the result of our procedures. How do we dispose of the garbage? Should the rubbish be treated prior to its being burned? What are some other concerns about security and safety?

Notes and Forms

Key Terms _____

Field-work forms
Anatomic chart
Narrative report
Evidence report
Chain of custody

INTRODUCTION/OBJECTIVES

Now we turn to various methods and tools to record or document our crime scene. We usually think of notes as handwritten, and this is true, for the most part. There are some exceptions that are useful if done properly. They have very distinct advantages as well as some concerns. Let's look at the handwritten notes and each of the methods that can be used to enhance your note taking. We examine various field investigation forms to understand what they look like and how they are used.

NOTES

One of the most important tasks during any phase of an investigation is the compilation of notes. This is also one of the least thought-out tasks, which can result in incomplete, inaccurate, or insufficient notes. Poor note taking results in reports that are incomplete and a poor reflection on the writer and the agency for which he or she works. This refers to everything you do. Your work product will be seen by other investigators; attorneys on both sides; other agencies, including the courts; and sometimes even end up in the newspaper. Sloppy work follows you for years to come.

Notes are your memory. You may be called to testify many years after an investigation. Sometimes all that might remain are your notes. There is no **statute of limitations** on murder, and as a result you might be called to testify in a case 20 or more years after the initial investigation. This is sometimes after retirement and the only thing left might be your notes. There are instances where the original records are lost and you have nothing else on which to depend.

Notes should be in a bound book, never a loose-leaf notebook. If there is a possibility of removing or adding pages to the notebook, then your notes may be suspect if examined. Bound books ensure notes have not been tampered with and that nothing has been lost or added. A spiral steno pad is often used. Although it is possible to tamper with these pads, they are certainly better than loose-leaf binders and are generally acceptable as bound. A book that is bound with string and/or glue reveals any tampering immediately.

Plan a format for your notebook. Consistency is a virtue in forensic investigations. You want to *keep everything simple and consistent* so that you always know just where in your notebook specific bits of information are located. The key here is that you cannot take too many notes. They are the foundation for your product, and although you never include all the information in your notes in the final report, it may still turn out to be critical information down the road. Something that seems less important now may be a key factor years later when a "cold case" investigator reviews the case.

The types of information we want in the formatted portion of the notebook is suggested in Figure 4–1, with the understanding that you most likely will want to modify it to meet your specific needs or those of your agency.

Notes should be in ink, again, to avoid implications of altering or modifying the notes. Because of the permanent nature of ink, it is a good idea to mentally compose what you intend to write to avoid extremely sloppy notes. Black ink is suggested because it resists fading over the years, but you may be surprised just how much even it fades. Black ink provides a better photocopy than others and is accepted as the proper color for official documents, although that is beginning to change to blue, possibly because many persons have difficulty distinguishing the original from a photocopy because copy machines have improved so much.

Be careful when transcribing serial numbers and **vehicle identification numbers (VIN)** to your notebook. Cartridge head stamps should also be recorded with great care.

TIP: If you use your latent fingerprint brush to dust all engravings, head stamps, and serial numbers and then "lift" the engraving with fingerprint tape and place the tape in your notebook (Figure 4–2), you probably will never be questioned as to the possibility of recording information incorrectly. You have the actual impression of the information. When recording the cartridge information, if it is on a revolver, dust the cartridges while in the cylinder and place this entire lift in the book to show exact location of the evidence and then indicate the direction of rotation of the cylinder. Remember, direction of cylinder rotation varies from make to make.

Even though you are going to draw a diagram of the scene, make a rough sketch in your notes of anything important. Use the standard

(Suggested) Notebook Format

Report No: _____   Date: _____
Classification: _____   Time: _____

Time Sent: _____   Detective(s): _____
Time Arrived: _____   Sergeant(s): _____
Time Back: _____   Officer(s): _____

Scene:

Victim: _____
Address: _____
Phone: (___)___-_____

Work: _____
Address: _____
Phone: (___)___-_____

Witness: _____
Address: _____
Phone: (___)___-_____

Synopsis: _____
_____
_____
_____
_____
_____
_____
_____
_____
_____
_____
_____
_____
_____
_____
_____

FIGURE 4–1   Notebook format.

overhead line drawing as your pattern. This is a "bird's-eye view" of the scene. It is the easiest to draw and is described in detail in Chapter Five. It is not usually necessary to include measurements unless they are critical for your notes. That kind of detail is in the diagram or crime scene drawing. If you do put measurements in your notebook, be very sure that they are the same as those on your drawing. Attention to this sort of detail is critical.

Your notes are for you, and therefore write them with that in mind. If you find it advantageous to use abbreviations and symbols of various sorts, such as those found in the medical field, drafting, and so on, use them if they come naturally. Your notes are not the place to experiment with new techniques, however. You must be able to decipher them 25 years from now. Consistency is always the key consideration.

Tape Recorder

The voice recorder is not a replacement for notes, but as a compliment to notes on some occasions. Taking written notes is really necessary, but some detectives carry a tape recorder, and now more often the ***digital voice recorder***. Both serve the same purpose. The difference is that with the tape

FIGURE 4-2 (A) Dusting serial number and maker's marks on a Sig Sauer Pistol. (B) Placing tape on the marks. (C) Tapes in the investigator's notebook.

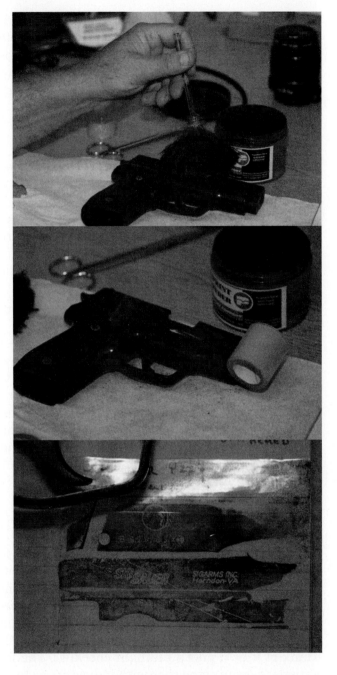

recorder you can remove the tape and break the security tab on the back corner to prevent the tape from being recorded over or accidentally being erased. The original tape can be placed in evidence and copies can be made to allow you the opportunity to work with your notes while being assured the original is in safe keeping. In the case of the digital recorder, a tape must be made of the recording prior to erasing the recording. It must be transferred to tape media. However, the new recorders can record information for

16–40 or more hours. The recorder can be downloaded to a computer, and computers with voice recognition can type the notes for you. It can be copied to a computer and a disc made for archival purposes.

When using a recorder, you can talk your way through your work while taking notes where appropriate. This frees you for other tasks requiring the use of your hands.

Personal Digital Assistant

Some investigators take a ***personal digital assistant (PDA)*** with them for notes, and while they have typing ability as well as speech recognition (some models), they also have a drawing pallet on which a sketch can be made. Some models allow photographs to be taken, although with limited quality, but then very good quality is not required for notes and it is certainly not meant to replace a camera. Another advantage of the PDA is that some can transpose your handwriting to print. We can expect more improvement as time passes.

FIELD-WORK FORMS

Another form of notes can be described as **field-work forms**. These forms are used as field notes and by some agencies as the product itself. Some of these may be designed by your agency and others you may design specifically for yourself. A suggestion is that as you receive various training or work with other agencies, pay attention to what they use and you can modify that to fit your needs. As you gain experience, you will develop the knowledge of what you do and do not need. Again, it is suggested you take your notes in ink to avoid being accused later of altering them.

CRIME SCENE WORKSHEET

The form included here is designed specifically for personal use. You may design one more appropriate for your use. It covers much of the information found in a notebook, but with more detail and in a format that is easy to use (see Appendix C). This form is more of a checklist to help you conduct all possible procedures appropriate to the case, and as a double check to see that nothing has been forgotten. The latter is the real asset to the form. Think of it as a pilot's preflight checklist. The form is structured to place various tasks in categories with indicators as to results, such as dusting for latent fingerprints and an indicator for positive or negative results.

MALE/FEMALE ANATOMIC CHART

This is a very useful chart to carry because it allows the investigator to indicate many important forms of information. Indicated on the chart would be all medical apparati attached or in-place on the body as well as injuries, scars, tattoos, birthmarks, and any other pertinent information. It is extremely useful for medical examiner's investigators and crime scene specialists who respond to both hospital and crime scene. If an individual has been shot or stabbed numerous times, it is much easier to write your detailed report using such a form. The chart provides both anterior and posterior view of the body and is very easy to understand (see Appendix C). These charts are available from various medical sources and universities. You can also develop your own, although it is so much simpler to use a commercially printed form. There is an excellent form for both male and female printed by the American Society of Clinical Pathologists (www.ascp.org).

PHOTOGRAPHIC LOG

The *photo log* (see Appendix C) is very useful for all types of photography and can be designed by you or acquired commercially. This log should include basic information regarding the type of camera, flash, film, film speed, and a description of the photograph taken. Some are more detailed than others. Again, it is good to be as complete as possible. If you do not need the information, so be it, but it is always better to have and not use than to need and not have. The form provides you with reference material for writing your **narrative report** at a later time. Even when taking a minimal amount of photos, it can be difficult to remember just what was photographed. Multiply this by 100 or more photographs and it becomes a very daunting task. There is a lot of repetition in forensic photography, such as photographing 20 or 30 spent cartridge cases at a crime scene. Which photograph represents which casing? A photo log provides that information.

MEDICATION WORKSHEET

The *medication worksheet* is commonly found with medical examiner's investigators, but is useful for all investigators. One case in which urine fluoresced turned out to be the result of a particular medication the victim was using. Had this medication not been noted, investigators might likely still be searching for the reason. In another case, the victim was coming out of rigor much sooner than expected, and it was determined that this was partially the result of medication and extremely violent activity resulting from mental illness.

The medication worksheet (see Appendix C) is in chart form and begins with the name, strength, and dose of medication, followed by the pharmacy, prescription number, address, and telephone number. This is followed by the name and telephone number of the physician and the date of the prescription. Next is the amount prescribed and the amount left in the container, and finally the person to whom the medication was prescribed. Not only does this form provide an inventory of medications found and their history, but it also can provide information regarding compliance or noncompliance to medical instructions, abuse of drugs, and "shopping" for medications like pain killers by going from one doctor to another to get the same prescriptions. This may explain a suspicious death resulting from overdose of medication. These forms are also a way to keep track of an unusual number of deaths related to a specific drug or even the overissuance of such a drug by a doctor. Did the medication belong to another person?

MODUS OPERANDI REPORT

The ***Modus Operandi (MO) report,*** or method of operation report (see Appendix C), can be thought of as the responsibility of the detective rather than the crime scene investigator, but experience has indicated it to be as important to the crime scene investigator as to the detective.

This report provides data that can indicate the possible relationship to other similar crimes, and could therefore result in multiple case closings on completion of this investigation. It provides detailed information as to the method of operation used at a particular crime scene. It can help determine age range of the suspect, mental/emotional status, specific behavioral characteristics of the suspect, potential for escalation, and sometimes patterns that might help in determining where the suspect will strike next. The MO report is also very effective when paired with geographic profiling.

EVIDENCE REPORT

The **evidence report** (see Appendix C) is one of the most important reports an investigator makes. This report documents the evidence in detail and all pertinent information related to that evidence. Just as important is the **chain of custody** portion usually found at the bottom of the report.

Extreme care should be taken when completing this report form. Although attention to detail is something we should always strive for, it is imperative here. Always take care when recording serial numbers, engravings, and any other descriptive information concerning each item of evidence.

TIP: When describing jewelry, be careful to describe it as "yellow metal," "silver-colored metal," "clear stones," "opaque white sphere," and so on. If you describe yellow metal as gold, even if it was not, it just became gold when the family makes their claim as to why the gold ring is missing and the brass ring took its place.

TIP: Try to use your item numbers from the evidence report on your drawing. That ensures you are not getting evidence confused when referring back and forth in court. Consistency has a direct correlation to a lack of mistakes. Strive to gain this trait.

TIP: When working with very valuable evidence, it is a good idea to include a photograph of that evidence, and when property is returned to the owner or their agent, photograph that person with the evidence and the report.

TIP: Marking your evidence should be consistent. It is not so much where you mark it, but that you always do it the same way, which ensures that you will not have to search for it on the witness stand. For example, you might always mark clothing and linens at the label. If there is no label, it is marked where a label would normally be found, such as the inside back of the collar; on bed sheets, mark on the label or on the left bottom of the sheet when looking from the foot of the bed toward the head.

With small evidence with insufficient space to mark the item, an evidence tag is attached or it is placed in a container with either a label or evidence tag attached, and this is noted in the evidence report.

▲ SUMMARY

In this chapter, we discuss how notes are so very critical to your writing accurate reports of all sorts. They are your memory many years down the road. We also discuss that there are various other methods to enhance your notes. The equipment required for these methods is well worth the money you might spend, but many agencies already issue this equipment; if not, you have nothing to lose by asking your agency to purchase them for you.

■ REVIEW QUESTIONS

1. Why do we suggest your notes be in ink and in a bound notebook?
2. Can you think of any other aids to your note taking?
3. Why do we suggest you remain consistent in everything you do?
4. Why is the evidence report of great importance?
5. What is the reason for using the same numbers from your evidence report in your diagram?
6. What are some of the uses for the medication report?

◆ REFERENCES AND SUGGESTED READINGS

VERNON J. GEBERTH, *Practical Homicide Investigation* (New York: Elsevier Science Publishing Co., Inc., 1983).

CHAPTER 5

Photography

Key Terms

Documentation process
Videography
Demonstrative evidence
Macro photography
Single lens reflex (SLR) camera
ABFO#2 scale
Painting with light
Luminescence photography
Fluorescence photography

INTRODUCTION/OBJECTIVES

The **documentation process** consists of three steps: The first step is photography, followed by the drawing or diagram. These two steps complement each other, along with the third step, the ***narrative report***. Photography is one of the most valuable methods of recording scenes, but can also be very misleading if not done properly. We end this chapter with a clear understanding of the advantages and weak points of photography.

VIDEO

Videography of the crime scene is becoming more common as time passes (Figure 5–1). There is nothing wrong with video as long as a person doing the videography is well versed in the process and the scene is well controlled. Video has a place in the documentation process, but if not done properly it tends to look very amateurish,

FIGURE 5–1   A decent digital movie camera with film and a memory stick. This camera has stabilization and night vision. A good tripod and a quality light round out this kit.

resembling something more like someone's vacation film than a crime scene. Following are some considerations. If you can overcome these, you may be successful in using this tool.

- The camera shakes when moving around. You can solve this to some extent by using a camera with Steady Shot or some similar stabilization tool or by using a tripod.
- Too much zooming in and out. Avoid zooming unless absolutely necessary, and then do this slowly and steadily.
- Too much extraneous noise and talking. Be careful of what you say around the camera. It may come back to haunt you at a later time. The microphone on some cameras is very sensitive and picks up extraneous noise and conversations. A wind shield or muffler prevents wind sounds, which are annoying.
- Panning too fast. Panning is similar to zooming and should be avoided when possible, but when used, it should be done in a slow and steady motion.
- Too much stammering and stuttering (*ah's* and *uh's*). The narration should be done by someone versed in this process, or possibly dubbed at a later time.
- Too much jumping back and forth between topics. The documentation must be done in a logical manner, telling the story in sequence.

Be very careful and remember that your tape, even though done "unofficially," just may end up in court. If this happens, you want to look professional and not have any surprising or damaging material recorded.

Video cameras are getting better each year, and are becoming easier and more "people-friendly" as well. Video has moved to the point that digital video is common and the cameras often have the capability of recording digital still shots as well. This is not necessarily good in that the quality of the digital still camera function in these cameras is not yet sufficient. Likewise, you can make still pictures from video on the computer.

Some inexpensive video cameras today can also take infrared images. This is an advantage in night photography, but also in some specialty fields such as bruise and bite-mark photography. Most new cameras have a built-in ***infrared filter*** that takes away the ability to do ***infrared photography***. Night-vision capability is also advantageous in photographing altered documents by visualizing differences in inks.

STILL PHOTOGRAPHY

"A picture is worth a thousand words." Perhaps, but if that picture is not accurate, or does not show what is needed, it is worthless or, worse yet, it might be misleading to the jurors. The report tells a story, and photographs, diagrams, and other forms of **demonstrative evidence** interact to compliment each other in ultimately making that story clear to 12 persons sitting on the jury who have never been to the scene and have no background in investigation or forensic science. Through the camera, the jury is actually taken to the scene. They can see what you saw. They see the scene through this type of evidence and ultimately understand what you are attempting to tell them. Because the photograph has this ability to influence people, we must be acutely aware that those photographs can be misleading and/or inflammatory, resulting in their being deemed inadmissible. This inaccuracy can be intentional or accidental, but the result is the same. A simple miscalculation on the lens ***aperture (f-stop)*** can result in two objects seeming to be closer or farther apart than they are in reality. The photographer should strive for a balance in ***depth of field*** to accomplish infinity, where all material in the photograph is in focus. This should not be confused with photographs that are altered as a part of the examination process, such as those showing a scene as initially observed and then after spraying luminol to visualize trace blood. In these instances, we take two photographs, one as we see it and the other after having been processed. Also when working with ***macro photography*** and ***photo microscopy***, the depth of field may be so shallow that everything cannot be in focus. This topic is covered in more detail later.

Photography has been one of the major methods of crime scene documentation since the days of the Mafia and other organized crime in the 1920s and 1930s. It was used in the Lindberg Kidnapping Case, and was extremely critical in the President Kennedy Assassination Case. It is even more important today because photography has become so very valuable at not only documenting the scene, but also documenting the examination process of evidence. Trace evidence uses photography, as does latent fingerprint examination and just about every other branch of forensic science. One of the interesting aspects of forensic photography is the examination of photographs to determine possible alteration of the image. We have succeeded in coming full circle, from the photographs becoming evidence of a crime being committed to the photograph becoming evidence of committing a crime.

Another use of *forensic photography* that is often used but rarely mentioned is the use of photographs from actual cases for training the next generation of investigators. This book is an example of that fact. Possibly no other method of teaching, other than actually taking the student to the crime scene, is as effective as looking at actual examples of forensic photography.

A question so often asked is how many photos should one take? It is always better to take more than required. You do not have to use them all, but if you did not take sufficient photos initially, you often will not be able to take more at a later time. The scene might not be available, and even if it were, any photos taken once the scene was released would be questionable. When in doubt, take the photograph. This is even more valid with the advent of *digital photography,* which can be downloaded to an archival disk and viewed without the expense of printing photos you will not ultimately use in your report. Do not delete any photos, however. Even if you are not going to use them, the opposition might want to see all of them to determine your honesty and lack of bias. By keeping all of the photographs, you should be able to avoid or at least lessen such attacks.

FILM CAMERAS

The most common camera used today is the 35-mm **single lens reflex (SLR) camera**. There is a trend toward the 35-mm format digital SLR camera, and this will continue, possibly to the point of eventually completely replacing the film camera. Film manufacturers have already begun the process of eliminating certain types of film. As a result, there will be fewer sources of having your film processed, which results in film becoming more expensive to use.

The significance of the SLR camera is that the photographer is looking through the lens, so what you see is what you get on the photograph. The SLR is contrasted by the *viewfinder,* found on most point-and-shoot cameras. A viewfinder does not actually show what appears on the photograph. It is an approximation of what is actually captured.

The 35-mm SLR camera should be capable of complete *manual operation* if used for forensic photography. These cameras also have the option to function totally or partially automatically. For most crime scene photography, *automatic operation* is fine, but there are those photographs requiring time exposures and manipulation of aperture and shutter speed. The cost has come down substantially, and most agencies can afford a basic digital 35-mm SLR package. Shop carefully and buy the camera that fits your agency's needs.

For larger departments with more staff and a heavier case load, there are large-format cameras such as the old *4 × 5 format cameras* of the Kodak Speed Graphic and Kodak Crown Graphic "press cameras" types we associate with the 1930s to 1950s. These cameras and others such as the *fingerprint camera* and the Polaroid CU-5 *fixed-focus cameras*

FIGURE 5–2 Large- and medium-format cameras. (*Left*) A Kodak Speed Graphic 4 × 5 camera. (*Middle*) A Kodak Crown Graphic 4 × 5 camera. (*Right*) A Polaroid 2¼ × 3¼ CU-5 1:1 camera.

(Figure 5–2) with their built in ***ring lights*** are still very useful when a large negative is desired, such as photographing fingerprints and shoe and tire prints. Although they are very good cameras, they are not recommended for agencies with small budgets and those not having dedicated crime scene staff, as they require more photographic skill and are not used enough to warrant their cost if case load is not substantial. They would definitely be classified as special equipment for those agencies that can justify the additional cost. There are various backs that can be affixed to these cameras to make them digital, but the cost is usually prohibitive. With the quality of digital cameras increasing rapidly, these will most likely not be in wide use much longer.

In short, the 35-mm SLR is the recommended way to go. It can fulfill your needs and means less equipment to learn to operate and less to break and lose. It can be purchased on a small budget, and as funds and case load justify more equipment, these units can be updated and expanded to fit specific needs without having to start over.

Choose a camera with certain abilities. These are usually found in most mid-level and higher 35-mm SLR cameras today. Some of these are

1. The camera can use a wide variety of films, or if digital replicate these film types. Most new film cameras have the ability to "read" the film cartridges' code and automatically set the ***film speed***, also known as ASA, DIN, and ISO. If the camera does not have automatic reading capabilities, check the film speed dial to determine the range of settings.

   TIP: Some cameras come equipped with a small frame on the back door to the camera body that holds the end tab from your film box. If yours does not have this, they may be purchased and are very inexpensive. They tell you that your camera is loaded and just what type of film you have in the camera (Figure 5–3).

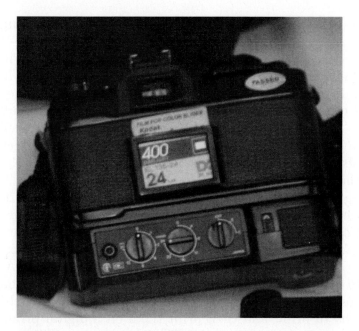

FIGURE 5-3   The back of a 35-mm SLR camera with a motor drive and a window for the film box end to designate the film in the camera.

2. Has a wide range of **shutter speeds** from bulb (time) to speeds up to about 1/4000 second.
3. The camera is capable of using a wide variety of lenses. Canon is well known for its extensive selection. Nikon also has a wide variety available. This is important; even though you might be starting with one lens, which is ideally a multipurpose lens. This allows you to expend later.
4. The camera can have a fully automatic function, but you definitely want full manual capability as well.
5. The camera must be sturdy. The Pentax K-1000 is an example of an aluminum-frame camera that was very sturdy and popular for forensic use. It is still widely used even though it is no longer manufactured. Most cameras today are plastic bodied. A very good film camera in use today is the Canon Elan 7/7E. The Canon EOS series of cameras have a wide variety of lenses, flash units, and just about everything else you would require for photography. For this reason, it is a good choice for scientific use, forensic or otherwise. These plastic cameras should never be left in a hot vehicle. For that matter, it is a prudent practice not to leave any camera equipment or supplies in the vehicle, whether plastic or metal. It is not good for the camera, film, or batteries. Heat is a photographer's enemy.

DIGITAL CAMERAS

If you are opting for the digital SLR camera, it should have the same capabilities as you would in the film format. Quality-wise, present philosophy contends your chip should allow for a minimum of 3.3 megapixels, but today, most quality cameras have 6.0 or more.

However, if detectives, officers, or supervisors are doing the photography and are not well versed in photography, the 35-mm point-and-shoot camera is sufficient for general photography, with the understanding there are severe limitations as to capability with little or no control over the operation of the camera. There are some very good ones that offer wide angle to telephoto as part of the noninterchangeable lens and others that offer clip-on adapters for close-up and *telephoto photography*. Their quality is fairly good, with chips of 6.0 megapixels and greater. These should be avoided unless they are the only option.

Digital cameras have become more affordable and can be found in formats from the point-and-shoot style to 35-mm SLR format, the latter being the camera of choice. This camera has a very short learning curve for those photographers who have used the 35-mm SLR film camera, and a good one can do almost everything the film camera can do. Another advantage to this camera is that you can see your results immediately without the cost of printing all of the photographs. You can choose what photographs to print, and then print them on a digital printer directly from the camera or via a computer. The latter is your best option, as you should download your entire files for archival purposes and then choose your preferences. Storage and transmittal of images can be accomplished via computer as well. Many agencies have already converted to digital and even more are using a combination of both digital and film formats. In the near future, we may see digital as the standard and film become the exception. A very good quality 35-mm SLR format camera such as the Canon Digital Rebel can be purchased for slightly more than its film counterpart.

When we think of point-and-shoot cameras, the digital format is much better than the film version in that most have both a viewfinder sighting device as well as a small LCD screen on the back of the camera, making it very similar to the SLR camera. One problem with these camera screens is that they are very difficult to see in bright sunlight, but that problem is not major and easily solved with shading of the screen, or you can simply use the viewfinder. An example of an excellent point-and-shoot camera is the Olympus Camedia series of digital point-and-shoot viewfinder cameras that have some adjustment capabilities and attachments for telephoto and close-up functions.

These cameras take very detailed photographs when used properly. They have taken passable fingerprint photographs and can take photos of such evidence as flies, even stopping them in flight.

PHOTOGRAPHIC TRANSPARENCIES

Photographic transparencies, commonly referred to as *color slides* in film photography, can be taken with the digital camera by using the PowerPoint program that is so rapidly replacing film.

LENSES

There are three basic lenses used in forensic photography, including the 50- or 55-mm *standard lens*, the 35-mm *wide-angle lens*, and the *macro lens* used for close-up photography. The *telephoto lens* was not included because although it is used, it is most often found in surveillance photography, which is not really a concern of this book. The variety of lenses available today is almost limitless. This makes them extremely versatile.

TIP: It is a good practice to keep an *ultraviolet (UV) filter*, or *haze filter*, on your lens if for no other reason than to protect the lens. The lens is an expensive item, and this filter can prevent scratches on the actual lens surface. It is far less costly to replace the filter than the entire lens.

Standard Lens

The standard lens, or the 50-mm lens, is the most often used and accomplishes the vast majority of crime scene documentation. It does a wonderful job of providing a reasonable and accurate depiction of the scene. If your agency could have only one lens, this would be your obvious choice, unless you opted for a *multifunction lens*, which is the recommended choice. The lens should be of excellent quality and construction. Remember, larger aperture openings equate to better lenses in general. Therefore, a 1.2 lens is much better than a 2.5. The 1.2 lens allows more light to enter the camera, thereby allowing photographs to be taken in low *ambient light* situations without a long time exposure, the use of an external flash, or other source of alternate light, such as flood lights.

All lenses have both positive and negative attributes. On the negative side is the inability of the standard lens to show wide areas, such as entire walls. It is possible to take several photographs and make a mosaic of sorts, but a much simpler answer is the wide-angle lens.

Wide-Angle Lens

The wide-angle lens (35 mm) provides the crime scene investigator with the ability to show much larger areas in a single photograph. For example, a single photograph might be capable of showing an entire wall of a room, where the 50-mm lens might require two or three photographs to accomplish this task. Although it is fairly common to see a 28-mm lens being used, it sometimes elicits questions of *distortion*, something similar to the "fish-eye" lens, which is simply a super wide-angle lens. The actual amount of distortion is certainly open to debate, but it is a good practice to avoid such questioning whenever possible. The rule is simply to use the wide-angle lens when needed, but do not overuse it and avoid extreme wide-angle lenses. An often heard bit of advice is to not use anything wider than 35 mm. Others argue that 28 mm is fine. Your courts may have the last word on this debate.

Close-up Lens (Macro)

The macro lens can be either a dedicated macro lens or a combination lens. This lens is ideal for photographs depicting such things as serial numbers, maker's marks, tool marks, hairs, fibers, and the like. In short, the macro lens allows you to record very detailed and intricate patterns on evidence. It is the next best thing to a microscope, and certainly a lot easier and versatile to work with at scenes. It provides the photographer with a very valuable tool, but does require a little getting used to, because the entire camera is moved backward and forward to achieve proper focus, where a conventional lens is focused by turning the focus ring on the barrel of the camera.

Multipurpose Lenses

The use of multipurpose lenses seems to be growing more common these days. Traditionally, a standard lens of 50 to 55 mm was used. Wide angle was 35 mm. It seems to be common today to see lenses that vary from 28 mm to 80 mm, or even 35 mm to 135 mm, with macro being included as a part of the lens. The forensic photographer should be very careful with these. Be prepared to defend their use in court. Again, this is a subject open to debate, and it seems courts are becoming more open to this newer technology, but determine how your courts look at this matter. It is much cheaper to get the answers to these questions before spending a lot of money on the equipment only to learn it will not be allowed in your jurisdiction. If there is no problem in court, these multipurpose lenses are economical as well as very convenient. It is certainly nice to have a single lens that can accomplish everything for you.

FILMS

Another often-posed question concerns the use of color versus black and white film. There is little advantage to black and white film today. Most likely, any reference you consult will advise you to go with color. Even cost as a factor has switched places, with color being the cheaper way to go. It is actually easier to have color film processed today than black and white, because most processors do not process black and white but send it to another company for processing. The use of color and black and white images is addressed further in areas of this book dealing with specialty work. In short, go with color when in doubt. In general, black and white may be something to consider when photographing particularly gruesome scenes as an additional method of documentation. The theory here is that if a color photograph is too inflammatory for the jury to see, you can use black and white in its place. If black and white photos are challenged, we may have to resort to a model or forensic art illustrations. The use of black and white film may still not be required, because it is possible to print a black and white photograph from a color negative, but not the reverse. With digital photography, this can all be addressed in the camera program and is really not a problem. Another use for black and white film is for fingerprint photography.

There is now available a Kodak Professional black and white film (T400CN) that uses the C-41 color process, meaning you can have it developed at any of the 1-hour photo processors if your agency does not have in-house processing. This eliminates the need to send the film to a specialty shop.

There are many films to consider in forensic photography, with the main consideration being speed of the film. The films' sensitivity to light is indicated by a designator referred to on the film canister as *ISO,* or by an earlier interchangeable indicator, *ASA.* Generally speaking, the more sensitive the film, the higher the designator number, such as 64, 100, 200, 400, 800, 1600, 3200, and so on. Therefore, the less available light, the higher the ISO number you would use. These higher ISO numbers are referred to as *fast films,* and contrasted by the lower numbers indicating slower films. There is a trade-off involved, however. The faster the film, the more grain, which in turn takes away from clarity and detail. This is why portrait photographers would use a slow film. In digital photography, the grain is referred to as **noise**. Forensic photographers usually shoot faster films such as 400 ISO as their standard, but it is a good idea to stock a fairly wide range of film such as 100, 200, 400, 800, and maybe 1600 ISO.

The next consideration again concerns two types of color films, **positive print film** (transparency or slide) and **negative print film**. This is something you should decide, with consideration being given to the purpose of the photographs. If the photography is strictly case/court use, then the obvious answer is print film using a film negative. Slide film is a good choice for presentations when giving talks or teaching. However, with the popularity of Microsoft PowerPoint presentation software, slides may be a thing of the past in the very near future. Many organizations have dropped slides for the most part in favor of Microsoft PowerPoint.

Infrared Film

When using **infrared film**, which is discussed in more detail a little later, do not keep it in stock, but buy it as you need it. It cannot be stored for long periods of time and must be kept in total darkness and refrigerated. It has a very short shelf life and is not used very often. It is valuable in document examination with reference to inks, faded writing, and burned paper. It is also useful in bite mark and bruise photography.

When purchasing film in 35 mm, it might be advisable to get a selection of 12, 24, and 36 exposures. This may not seem significant, but after a period of time you may experience a significant cost savings. Many cases require only two or three photographs, and there is no justification in wasting the excess film. One option is putting more than one case on a roll of film, but this may not be a wise decision. There are instances where the investigators may want the photographs on a rush basis, and then there is the possibility of getting cases mixed, even though you take precautions to avoid this possibly serious problem. Better safe than sorry. You may also be questioned in court why a portion of the role of film is missing. It might be insinuated that you are trying to hide something. Why put yourself through this?

Photo Log

The **photo log** (see Appendix C) is an important document that becomes part of your photographic report. Remember, the photo log contains the technical information, and the photo report contains the narrative report. There are various formats for the logs, and in the end you might design one that best fits your needs. There is a standard amount of information needed and additional information may be included as you see fit. Some of the basic information that should be on the log would be

- Report number and classification and date of case
- Date and time photographs were taken
- Locations where photographs were taken (This could be significant in the case of multiple scenes.)
- Camera description
- The lens used and all lens changes should be noted
- Lens and shutter speed should be noted
- The lighting present and any additional or alternate light sources used
- Film(s) indicating color print, slide, or black and white, as well as film speed (ASA, ISO, or DIN)
- Photographer's name and title
- Description of each individual photograph with reference to subject, location, and direction lens is pointed
- Additional information as dictated by agency requirements or those of the individual scene's unique needs

The photo log enables you to remember the subject and purpose for each photograph when you write your narrative report and provide testimony later on your assignment. When a photographer takes photographs numbering in the hundreds, there is no way to independently remember each and every one after you receive the proof sheet or completed photographs. Remember, there will be instances when you will take many photographs at each of several scenes pertaining to the same case. These may contain photographs of the same type of evidence, thereby multiplying the possibility of confusion and misidentification.

GENERAL CRIME SCENE

A simple rule to follow is to take the photographs in a logical manner; for instance, you might choose to work in clockwise direction. Be consistent, however. Consistency is the key to fewer mistakes and forgotten photos and better quality in general. When photographing an object, take a photograph of the object in relation to the general scene and then a close up of the object. Then take a third photo of the object with a measuring device in place for reference purposes. Today, the standard seems to be the **ABFO No. 2 scale**. In forensics we usually use the metric system, but many forensic scales today have both standard and metric. This is best because although scientists use metrics, many, if not most, laypersons in this country do not understand the metric system. Use a rigid ruler versus a cloth ruler. Cloth tapes have the potential for stretch and can open you up to accuracy difficulty in court. *Do not use pencils, pens, or fingers and so on as references or pointing devices.* These are extremely unprofessional. This also pertains to people. As a general rule, do not have people in your photographs unless there is a specific reason for doing so. You might want to have a witness stand in his/her vantage point looking in the direction being described. Another reason might be to photograph the crowd. While investigating a case such as homicide or fire, additional photographs including the persons watching may be the key to identification of a suspect who is in that crowd.

Much of the photography is similar, whether indoor or outdoor, but obviously there is some photography specific to night scenes. For example, you might want photographs taken with lamps or with available light to provide some understanding of what the unaided eye could see. However, you might want to "paint with light" in order that all detail might be seen in the photograph. You might want to photograph the locations of street lights and so forth. The goal is complete coverage in logical order. Throughout this book, we stress consistency. If you are consistent with everything you do, you tend to make less mistakes and to forget fewer tasks.

When you approach the crime scene, it is good practice to photograph the street fronting the scene, preferably with the street numbers of the scene in the photograph. Then photograph from the scene looking back toward the street and showing both directions. If the exterior of the building is important, then photograph from each of the corners to show two sides at a time. If not too important, the two photos will suffice, one showing the front and left side of the house and the second showing the rear and right side of the house.

If there is a car outside, then take a photograph of the front and left (driver's) side of the car and the second with the rear and right (passenger) side of the car. There is another advantage to photographing vehicles using this technique, and that is your flash strikes the license plate at an angle, which prevents the light from reflecting back into your lens, resulting in a ***"hot spot"*** or washing out of the numbers. Many if not all license plates today are constructed of reflective material.

INDOOR CRIME SCENE

Next we want to move to the interior of the building (Figure 5–4). A photograph of the entrance is first. If there is a room number or name, this should be included in this photograph. Then a photograph is taken from the entrance looking into the interior of the room. Again, being consistent, we work around the interior of the room. It is a good idea to move about each room in the same manner. You might choose clockwise or counterclockwise, depending on what you are comfortable with.

As you move around the room, take a photograph from each corner of the room. By taking a photograph from each of the corners looking toward the opposite corner, it is possible to get the entire room or a good portion thereof with the four photographs. If needed, a photograph can be taken from the center of each wall looking at the opposite wall to complete the coverage.

After these preliminary photographs are taken, the detailed photographs of the interior and evidence can be taken. These are usually dependent on the circumstances of the scene and case classification. Remember, however, items of evidence should be photographed in a manner making it clear as to their relationship in the scene. A close-up photograph is taken, and if the object is relatively small, take an additional photograph with an ABFO#2 photo scale.

TIP: A good rule of thumb is that for every item of small evidence you document, a photograph without a scale and another with a scale should be

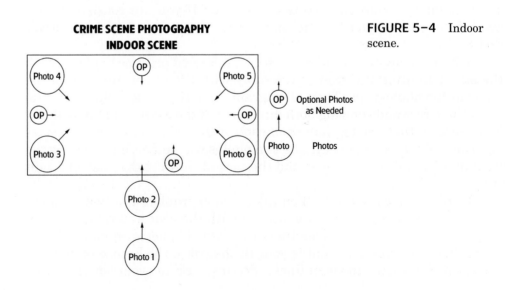

FIGURE 5–4 Indoor scene.

taken. This is also true of any evidence that scale or measurements are critical. Always take these photographs at 90°.

OUTDOOR SCENE

Outdoor scenes are very similar to indoor scenes, with the exception of the number of problems resulting from weather, sun, people wandering around, and other interferences. We begin with the approach to the scene, possibly with the first photograph showing a corner with street signs for the nearest cross street, or a street sign with the block numbers visible in the photograph.

At the scene proper, take the same photographs of the outer limits of the scene, not an easy task because there are no walls. Reference might be made to compass directions. If the scene is remote and not near a road, new technology can come to your assistance. A good method is a starting point referenced to geographic positioning system (GPS) coordinates. With the new Wide Area (WAAS) enabled GPS units, it is possible to get the position located within about 3 feet on the Earth's surface. Use some imagination in documenting outdoor scenes. If, for instance, you do not have access to a GPS, a car odometer reading can be used from the nearest cross road to the entrance to the scene, such as a forest. A location could be something on the order of: Forest area 7/10 mile east of Highway 90 West, on Log Road 432, and 500 yards north of the road. Still another option is to use a topographic map. These are discussed in the diagram portion of this book.

If there are multiple scenes or an escape route, such as a prison escape, then *aerial photographs* may be very useful to both the investigators and the jury. Often, if your agency has its own aircraft, especially a helicopter, you might have the unit meet with you and photograph the scene from the air from the beginning. This can help indicate weather conditions, traffic load, visibility, and possibly the actual vehicles and/or body while still at the scene. If the jury can see the scene as it actually was during the investigation, it would enhance their understanding of the scene.

FLASH PHOTOGRAPHY

Following are some things you might want to consider when looking at electronic flash units:

- The flash should be adjustable as to powder output.
- The flash should be capable of focus for wide angle, normal, and telephoto. The Vivitar Thryster electronic flash has a hood that extends to different lengths for these settings. Canon's reflector moves forward or to the rear internally to accomplish this task.
- Canon has several really good flash units that have filters for dispersion of light for close-up photos. Vivitar has a separate slide-in filter that accomplishes the same task.

- Flash unit should be capable of fully automatic and manual operation.
- Flash unit should be capable of operation both on and off the camera using an extension cable or IR sensor. On the camera it should be capable of "***hot-shoe***" operation.
- The flash should be capable of operating as a "***slave***" or a "***master***" unit. Canon flashes have built in IR transmitters and receivers for slave or master operation, and the head can be rotated side to side, furthering its capabilities even more. Other flashes like the Vivitar have a hot-shoe connection that allows a photo electric cell sensor to be mounted for slave use. These units are very inexpensive.
- The flash head should be capable of movement (tilt) from the horizontal to 45° up and vertical for bounce or reflective lighting.
- The flash unit should have a fairly rapid **recycle time**. Many excellent flash units can operate on an external accessory battery pack for both high-capacity flash work and fast recycle time.
- There should be some mechanism for the use of filters. The flash gives off the basic color of normal daylight conditions.

   TIP: Vivitar has a slot for the **diffusion filter**, and one can easily make additional filters of Plexiglas of varying colors and diffusion abilities that simply slide into the existing slot.

- Flash units using manual operation have a "calculator" dial on the flash. After setting the ASA of the film and f-stop, it indicates what power to set the flash on.
- Be aware that some dedicated flash units, those manufactured by a camera company for a specific camera or series of cameras, may or may not work with another camera. If you are using different brands of cameras you might want to get a generic flash that works with all of them. The Vivitar 285HV is an example of a good flash unit, with versatility being one of its best features.

Electronic Flash

The electronic flash we usually think of and the most common type used is the camera-mounted electronic strobe light used for lighting and fill purposes in general photography. There is another fairly common flash used for close-up and macro photography called a *ring flash*. This unit is sometimes a part of the camera, such as that found on the Polaroid CU-5 close-up camera. The other is a separate unit that is mounted on the barrel of the lens. It is used with fingerprint photography, forensic odontology, and lab applications such as photography of images on a cathode ray tube (CRT). Another variation of this flash unit is the ***macro twin flash unit***. It consists of two small flash units positioned on booms attached to the lens ring mount. The purpose of these lights is to put the flash at the end of the lens barrel to avoid a shadow or partial obstruction of the light when it is part of the camera main body or top mounted to the camera. Electronic flash requires the "sync" switch on the camera (if there is one) be set on X.

DC Flash (Bulb)

This flash uses flash bulbs and uses a sync switch set on M. If your camera has this switch, be careful to set it properly, or you will end up with photos that are half black.

The BC, or **DC flash** as it is also called, runs on batteries and in place of the now common strobe cell. It uses a flash bulb that is filled with a very long filament that meanders almost as if it were just stuffed into the bulb. This entire filament flashes instantly to provide the light. Although the flash bulb is not in common use today, there are instances when it is of use in technical photography for a source of infrared illumination as an example. The flash is also used for the 4 × 5 sheet film camera, but they can also be fitted with a **strobe flash**.

USING THE FLASH

The flash is a tool that is essential in the dark, but what many photographers do not seem to realize is that it is also an essential piece of equipment for daylight photography as well. When we talk about flash for the 35-mm camera, we are not talking about the small flash built into the camera. These are extremely basic and are all right for snapshot photography, but little else.

There are many flash units that are considered accessories for the camera. These external flash units are very versatile tools. For forensic photography, the flash should not be looked on as an accessory, but an essential and standard piece of equipment for the camera.

Some cameras have flash units designed for them, such as Canon cameras. There is a wide selection of flash units available that will cover your needs. These units can be used on and off the camera and as both slave and master units. Similarly, there are very good flash units available that can work with just about any camera. Both Canon and the Vivitar 285HV Zoom Thyristor flash are commonly used. This unit can work with a hot shoe, cable, and electric-eye slave attachment. Its power is adjustable and has a computer that lights and can compute ASA and f-stop to determine power both in fractions and in a color-code system. The flash is operated on four AA batteries and can also operate using an optional rechargeable battery pack for heavy use. The flash head adjusts for 90°, 75°, 60°, and 45° and a tube on the flash head adjusts for normal, wide, and telephoto shots. It also comes with a slot and diffusion filter. Other filters can easily be made for the unit. The author has made orange filters as well as other types of diffusion filters for this flash. The only downside to this flash is the plastic mounting foot has a tendency to break, but a metal one can be purchased. This is actually a small inconvenience when considering the overall dependability and versatility of this flash unit.

There are limitations to the flash concerning synchronization. The typical 35-mm SLR camera typically synchronizes at 1/60th of a second, and you are advised not to push it past 1/125th of a second. There are extremely fast flashes that can be used in total darkness with the shutter open on bulb or time. An example of such a time would be high-speed photography to stop a bullet in flight. These are not flash units the typical forensic laboratory will have, although some of the larger ones or those specializing in forensic photography might have such equipment. In these cases it is not the shutter speed that captures the bullet, but the extremely fast flash that could be at 1/300,000th of a second to 1/1,000,000th of a second.

TIP: Be sure to check and be familiar with the speed(s) your camera is synced for. You do not want to go faster than that speed. If your photographs seem to be half photos with the other half black, you have gone faster than your camera can handle. If you are using one of the older cameras with the X and M **sync speeds**, then you have it set on the wrong one. The X is for electronic flash, whereas the M is for the manual or flash-bulb type of flash unit.

TRIPOD, MONOPOD, AND COPY STAND

Photographers often get the best camera and lens but purchase the least expensive tripod possible. What many fail to realize is that the tripod is one of the most important accessory items you can buy and is critical to good photography. Photographs that are taken at shutter speeds slower than 1/60th of a second must be on a tripod to avoid blurring.

A good tripod should be sturdy enough to support your camera and flash while remaining firmly on the ground with absolutely no shake. It should be adjustable for a wide range of elevation movement, and have legs that move independently with their own length adjustments in addition to the previously mentioned main shaft height adjustments. The tripod should have rubber feet that also have pointed spikes to avoid slippage on any surface. In addition, it should have at least one leveling bubble to ensure it is at 90°.

A good tripod allows the head to be removed from the top and placed between the legs as well as allowance of the vertical boom to be removed and mounted horizontally. This allows the camera to extend over a surface such as a car hood with the tripod being on the ground.

TIP: You can hang your camera bag on a good tripod to add additional downward force to keep the tripod from tipping.

The tripod should be capable of handling any piece of camera equipment you have. In other words it must be very versatile. And this is just your main tripod. You may require additional tripods for slave flash units, laser mounting, and other uses. Fortunately, you require only one really good tripod, and the others may be of a considerably lower quality.

There are various very good units available at fairly reasonable costs. Those manufactured by Manfrotto (Bogen) are outstanding. You most likely will have to purchase the tripod and head as separate items. In addition, because of the value of this equipment it is a good idea to purchase a case to protect your investment.

FIGURE 5–5   (A) Keys under camera without fill flash.
(B) Keys using a fill flash.

Bogen also puts out a very good monopod that allows you to move about more rapidly and keep a camera steady if you are not doing long exposures. It can also double as a hiking staff if you have a case way off the beaten path.

GENERAL SUGGESTIONS

Following are some suggestions that while seemingly common sense, we often forget when we are trying to drain the proverbial swamp:

- Try to avoid photographing into the sun. You get sunspots on your photos and there is a lot of shadowing. Many objects also appear in silhouette.
- Use a flash for fill even when outside. It lights up shadowed areas. Evidence under a car might not show up, but with a flash eliminating the shadow under the car, the evidence should be visible (Figure 5–5).[1]
- When photographing into water, consider a ***polarizing lens filter***. You cut out the glare and are able to see the objects on the ocean or lake bottom.

[1]Steven Staggs, *Crime Scene and Evidence Photographer's Guide* (Temeculah, CA: Staggs Publishing, 1997). p.15.

- A lens shade or hood is a good idea when working in the sun.

  TIP: Do not use a ***lens hood*** when taking very close-up photographs with a flash as you get a partial image and a black half-moon or quarter-moon effect. This is because the flash was not able to light the entire subject. Remove the hood and your photos turn out just fine.

- Use support such as monopod or tripod when shooting photos at 1/60th second and slower. If you are shooting slower than 1/60th of a second, you might be better off with a tripod.

- When unsure of exposure settings, ***bracket*** your photos. This means you shoot what you think is the proper exposure and time and then shoot a few photos above and below that setting. Bracketing can mean the difference between getting a photograph or not. With the relatively low cost of photography today, it is in your best interest to bracket.

- Always use a neck strap when shooting. No one is exempt from dropping a camera. A dropped and broken camera can ruin both your day and that of those investigators who are depending on you.

- Always carry spare batteries. This includes those needed for your camera, ***exposure meter,*** motor drive, flash, ***electronic shutter release,*** and anything else that might require batteries. You cannot afford to have batteries go out in the middle of the night in the middle of nowhere with every store closed.

- Always carry a small, 36-in. retractable tape measure to measure lens distance and likewise a small penlight to look at the camera settings.

- Always carry a lens cloth. *Do not use eye glass cleaners.* They can ruin your lens. You can wash the lens cloth from time to time, and if you use a fabric softener you should have no trouble. A small lens brush with air bulb attached is also a good idea.

- Always carry a ***cable release*** or two. A short one and another about 2-ft long are sufficient. Cable releases seem to break now and then so you should carry an extra. It is critical for timed photography.

Night Photography

Night photography has some unique concerns. For the most part, however, it is conducted the same as daytime photography except with a flash or flood lights. The number of photographs, what to photograph, and so on are no different than that of daytime photography.

Reflection is a concern any time in photography, but it has more consequences in night photography because we must work with lighting systems during the hours of darkness. A key technique to avoid reflection problems is to avoid shooting directly into a reflective surface such as a mirror, glass window, or license plate when using as flash. You can avoid both the photographer's reflection in the photograph or the likely hot spot where the light is reflected directly back into the camera. Shoot at an angle or bounce the flash off the ceiling or a reflector designed for this sort of photography. In a pinch, a white card of at least 8- × 10-in. can be used. A matte finish would be even better. Remember to do the same thing when photographing vehicles because most license plates are reflective and cause the same hot-spot problem.

Although flash units are the cause of most reflection difficulties, photo floodlights can cause the same kind of problems. This happens less frequently because the lights tend to be off to the side. They are easy to shield and reflect (bounce light). Care must be taken when bouncing light off ceilings and walls. If they are not white, you may have color balance problems, and it is wiser to use a white reflector when encountering surfaces that are another color. If you are using lighting systems, always remember to have the lights face away from the lens. There are two guidebooks that are excellent and cover lighting for the crime scene and evidence very well. They are *Crime Scene and Evidence Photographer's Guide* by Steven Staggs, and *The Police Photographer's Guide* by James A. McDonald. McDonald's book has the added feature of plasticized pages so it can be taken to the field.

PAINTING WITH LIGHT

Another unique problem encountered during night photography outdoors or in large interiors such as auditoriums is how to light up a large enough area. **Painting with light** is one technique. It is a fairly simple process and can be done with one or more flash units.

The simplest and least expensive is to use one flash unit. When using this method, the camera is placed on a very good tripod and a cable or electronic cable (shutter) release is used. This must be done in almost total darkness. The procedure is as follows:

1. Locate the camera where you want to shoot from and focus on infinity.
2. The camera shutter is put on time or bulb so it can remain open during this procedure.
3. Place a cover over the lens, such as a black card.
4. Trip the shutter and lock it open.
5. A second person uses the flash unit while you control the camera.
6. Remove the cover from the lens and, at the same time, have the second person immediately manually fire the flash, after which you cover the lens again.
7. The flash is taken about 20 feet down the road. (It is a good idea to use half the distance you flash as rated at for full power.)[2] This procedure is repeated.
8. This continues until you have covered the desired area, maybe 150 feet or so.
9. The shutter is then tripped to close.

Care must be taken to avoid any unnecessary light from entering the scene using this process. Have traffic stopped and have officers remain out of the field of view. It would be a good idea to bracket these photos. In this case, you would shoot perhaps three photos like this with different f-stops.

---

[2]ROBERT CARRUTHERS and RICHARD MCEVOY, *Night-time Imaging* (Workshop W44, International Association for Identification, 2004).

FIGURE 5–6   Painting with light. This was done with three flash units using a master and two slaves. The flash on the right was not used in this picture.

The second method is not as difficult, but requires more equipment. With this method, a single person can conduct the entire operation. You need the same camera and tripod along with the camera having a flash unit mounted on the hot shoe. Three or more additional tripods with flash units affixed complete the setup.

1. The camera is set up as in the first method.
2. Additional flash units on tripods with either slave sensors affixed or with built-in slave units, such as those found on Canon flash units. The flash units are again set up at 15–20 feet apart (or no more than 50% of the maximum reported distance for that flash unit), with the sensors facing the camera and the flash head away from the camera (Figure 5–6). In the case of Canon, the flash on the camera is set on "master," and the remaining flash units are set on "slave."
3. Take a light reading from the camera's light meter and set aperture with shutter speed at 1/60th second.
4. Take the photograph. The camera-mounted flash simultaneously triggers the other flash units.

Floodlights

Another option is to use floodlights. Care must be taken here to determine the need for possible color-balancing filters. The floodlights in any field situation require a generator for power use unless you have access to the battery-powered lights. Use a good generator capable of powering all of the equipment you might be using in the field. As mentioned previously, there are battery-operated floodlights designed for photography. These are usually camera mounted and a battery pack is contained in a belt, the type used by news videocamera operators. There are photo floodlights that can be mounted on stanchions and powered by a motorcycle battery. The advantage to both of these is that they can be recharged in the field using a power outlet in either the vehicle or by the generator if regular household electricity is not available.

Another consideration here is rain and fog. Be aware that moisture on the bulbs of many of these units results in a blown bulb, some of which are fairly expensive. When photographing outdoors or in fire scenes it is important to use weatherproof electrical chords, and the flood units should likewise be weatherproof. Just as important is the fact that these units become very hot and can cause both burns to personnel as well as fire to the surroundings.

An additional advantage to using floodlights is the fact that they are exceptionally useful when used as **oblique lighting** on a surface to search for trace evidence. Hairs, fibers, contact lenses, and blood stand out with the use of a bright oblique light, which causes shadows, enhancing the three-dimensional effect.

Be aware of the type of artificial light used because the frequency of the light might require the use of a filter on the camera lens. As a matter of fact, you should always be aware any lighting used at scenes, both indoors and outdoors. Street lights can change the way certain colors appear. This accounts for witnesses stating they saw a vehicle of one color when in fact the vehicle was of another color. By being aware of these situations, you are able to explain why their information was inaccurate. Incandescent light requires you to use a blue filter when using daylight film, for example.

TECHNICAL PHOTOGRAPHY

Much of the photography done in forensic science is of a technical nature, and although it is not particularly difficult, it does require some specialized equipment and a fairly good understanding of photography. We examine photography using a combination of **alternate light sources (ALSs),** filters, various films, and unusual exposure settings. Perhaps the starting point here might be an understanding of filters.

FILTERS

There are many different types of filters on the market, many of which are for effects. We are not looking for filters to dazzle anyone but for the specific purpose in mind, and that should be communicated to the jury. The filters are usually glass, but there are some that are gelatin and require very careful handling. Filters tend to be of two classes. The **barrier filter** blocks a certain frequency of light. For example, the 2A filter blocks ultra-violet (UV) light. There is also the ***bypass filter*** that allows a certain frequency of light to pass through. For example, the 18A filter allows UV light to pass through while blocking out other light.

Filters are used with both black and white and color photography. It is interesting to note that although some of our photography might be done in black and white, we use colored filters to accomplish specific tasks. As a general rule, we can say that should we desire to eliminate a color from the subject, we simply place a filter of that color over the lens (Figure 5–7). For example when conducting fingerprint photography and the print is on a surface that is red and white, such as Coke cans or some beer labels, the red interferes with our view of the latent print. We place a ***#25 red filter*** over the lens and take the photograph. The red either completely disappears or at least disappears to the point that it does not pose an interference problem for the latent print examiner. Again, should we have a blue police uniform with blood stains on it, it is very difficult to see the blood. By using a ***#47 blue filter*** on the lens, we lighten the blue to the point that the blood becomes quite visible.

When using filters it is a good practice to take two photographs. The first photograph is without the filter so the jury can see what the object actually looked like. Then the photograph with the filter is taken to emphasize the blood stain. This technique is usually sufficient for court purposes when an attorney wants to challenge the photograph as being altered. We are able

FIGURE 5–7   (A) With red color still in photo. (B) Using a No. 25 red filter to remove the red. Latent fingerprints are easier to see. This was printed in back and white.

to see the original view, then the alteration and why it was used. The filter did not add or remove evidence; the filter merely emphasized the evidence.

Another consideration to remember when using filters is that it is best to bracket your photographs with the filter. The aperture is typically opened from one to two stops with the filter in place, but may on occasion be as many as four stops. An example of this would be T-Max 100 or 400 films. For night effect, it would take a four-stop increase in exposure.[3]

Depending on your source, there are many filters described and recommended, but this text covers only a few of those in common use. The others can be covered in an in-depth study of forensic photography.

Common Filters

- *Skylight or UV Filter.* This filter absorbs UV light. It is used more as a filter to protect the lens of the camera, with the theory being it is much cheaper to buy another filter than to replace a scratched lens. However, the 2A filter is also used on the camera lens when conducting photography to document the trace metal detection test (TMDT). Kodak sells this as the Wratten 2A, a gelatin filter in squares, and Tiffen sells it as a glass filter.
- *Polarizing Filter.* This filter is very useful when photographing in bright, glaring sun and even more useful when photographing objects in the water. It takes the glare off the water, thereby allowing you to see the object under the water.
- ***80A and 80B Color-Conversion Filters***. These filters are important to have when photographing something using color daylight film and tungsten light.
- *25 (Red) filter.* Quite useful for latent print photography. This filter can also be used with infrared photography.
- ***Hoya 0 (G) Filter***. Orange and very useful for ALS photography with both the argon laser and the blue light. This filter is on the camera lens, and you must do your search with glasses or goggles of the same color.
- *Hoya R72 and RM80 infrared filters.* For bite-mark photography.

There are other filters that might be of use, but purchasing them might be something to do on a need basis to save money.

TIP: When using an ALS, the color of goggles or glasses worn to visualize the evidence is also the same color filter needed on the camera lens. Orange and yellow are the most common.

We have discussed how to lighten or remove colors, but you should also be aware that you can darken colors with filters as well. For example, the yellow and orange filters can darken blue, and the red darkens both blue and green. The blue filter darkens both orange and yellow.[4]

---

[3]*Kodak Guide to 35mm Photography* (Silver Pixel Press, 2000). p. 234.
[4]STEVEN STAGGS, *Crime Scene and Evidence Photographer's Guide,* (Temeculah, CA: Staggs Publishing, 1999). p. 54.

LATENT FINGERPRINT PHOTOGRAPHY

Fingerprint photography can be accomplished using several methods. We begin with the simplest and move on from there. Remember, better-quality photographs are obtained using the proper equipment, but it can be accomplished with a simple camera under less than ideal circumstances when there are no other options.

Method One: A camera with a close up or macro lens can take individual latent print impressions if a few precautions are taken (Figure 5–8).

1. The camera should be placed on a tripod or other suitable support, such as a copy stand, when possible. The camera lens should be perpendicular to the latent print, and care must be taken to have the print in focus.
2. Because this is not a 1:1 photograph, it is necessary to place a scale in the photograph so a 1:1 image can later be made.
3. A flash is used and should be off the camera on an ***extension cable*** and at an angle of about 45°. If left on the camera, the flash results in only a partial exposure, with the lens tube blocking some of the light.

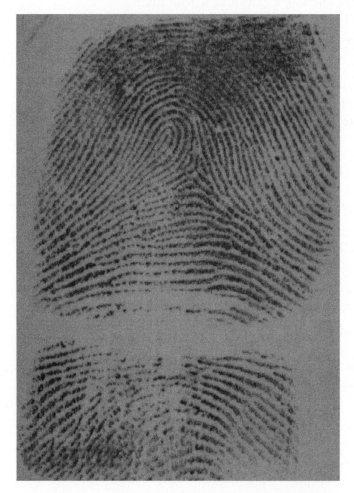

FIGURE 5–8 An inked print—in this case, a radial loop. Note the coverage and clarity of the print.

FIGURE 5–9 Latent print adapter.

4. Use the light meter on the camera for proper exposure.

5. A cable release is recommended.

6. Be sure to have a diagram or notes to explain the location and position of each latent print photographed.

7. Each latent print should include the photographer's evidence mark and photo or latent number.

Method Two: The camera with its normal 50- to 55-mm lens attached is fitted with a ***latent print adapter*** (Figure 5–9). The adapter is a clear acrylic tube with a magnifier in the base, and allows the photographer to take 1:1 photographs.

1. The adapter is fitted onto the lens via the filter attachment threads.

2. The camera is focused with the adapter sitting over the latent print. No other support (i.e., as tripod) is required with this method.

3. The flash is used as it is in Method One, off the camera and at a 45° angle, with the light penetrating the clear adapter tube.

4. The same marking considerations are taken as described in Method One.

A problem with both of these methods is that you can get, at most, three fingertips in each photograph. If an entire hand print is present, it must be recorded in portions.

Method Three: A ***latent print camera*** or close-up camera such as the Polaroid CU-5 is used. These cameras are medium to large format, with 2¼- × 3¼-in. or 4- × 5-in. negatives. These cameras can both use Polaroid positive film packs as well as film packs with print and negative and traditional film packs. The latent print camera uses regular 4 × 5 film packs, but the CU-5 required a modified Polaroid film pack to use regular negative film. The advantage of these cameras is that they can photograph almost an entire handprint. The CU-5 has a 1:1 adapter and the latent print camera is set for only 1:1 photography. Another advantage to these cameras is they have a ring flash as part of the camera, which is excellent for this sort of photography. The CU-5 is also capable of using an external flash.

1. Camera is focused at the factory, so it is necessary to place it only over the print.
2. Put the film pack in its compartment.
3. Turn on the flash unit.
4. Pull the trigger on the pistol-grip handle.
5. Remove the film for processing.

These cameras can be used for other small evidence as well, such as teeth and bite marks. If the organization has a lot of latent print cases, the purchase of the latent print camera is justified. It requires no special training.

TIRE AND SHOE PRINT PHOTOGRAPHY

Tire and shoe print photographs must be printed 1:1 for proper comparison purposes (Figure 5–10). For this reason, it is critical that a measuring device be placed in the photograph. The larger **L-shaped evidence rulers** resembling large ABFO rulers are ideal for this type of photography. The

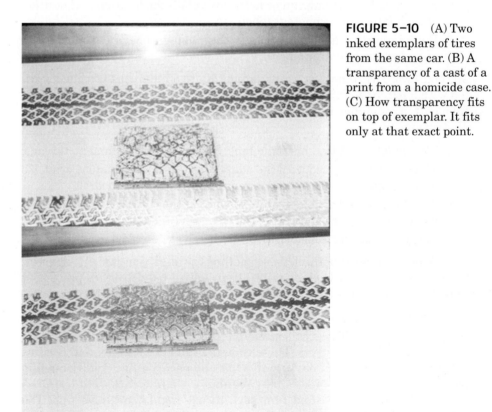

FIGURE 5–10 (A) Two inked exemplars of tires from the same car. (B) A transparency of a cast of a print from a homicide case. (C) How transparency fits on top of exemplar. It fits only at that exact point.

photographs must taken at 90° to the prints. Because tire patterns are different completely around the circumference of the tread pattern, it is necessary to photograph all print material found. These photographs must be taken prior to casting the prints.

1. The camera is placed on a tripod. It must be perpendicular to the print. If on a flat level surface, a bubble level can be used on the camera to confirm its being level. Some tripods come with a series of bubble levels for this purpose. If the surface is not level, you must be sure the film plane is perpendicular, which can be confirmed with the L-shaped scale described previously. It has focusing points that when all are in focus should indicate that the camera is in the proper position.

2. A remote shutter release or cable release is used for the exposure.

3. The camera is focused and settings appropriate for lighting conditions. Smaller lens opening (larger f-stop number) is better because you have more depth of field.

4. The flash is held at an oblique angle to the print to ensure detail is shown because of resulting shadow effect.

5. The photograph is taken, preferably with identification in the photograph.

A larger-format camera such as the 4×5 is better suited for this type of photography, but is not really necessary because of the better film quality today. If your agency does a lot of this sort of photography, the purchase of a larger-format camera might be justified.

TIP: We discuss the use of the ABFO#2 scale and the larger L-shaped evidence scale being used in ***technical photography***. These rulers have multiple circles with cross-hairs inside as focus points. It is useful to purchase stick-on white circles of the same size from an office supply store and use one of these stickers affixed to one of the circles with your evidence mark, photo number, and case number, printed on it. In this way, each of your photographs is identified for later use.

BLOODSTAIN PATTERN PHOTOGRAPHY

The key to photographing bloodstains for analysis is having the lens 90° to the stain and detailed enough to see and measure. It is a good idea to photograph the general scene and then take one wall overall and then work in on that wall. After the overall photograph has been taken, a close-up of the area of interest is next. Then place your measuring device for each bloodstain to be used in the analyses. The measuring ruler, sticker, or some similar device must be readable or it is of no value.

In cases where you do not have the expertise to conduct the analyses, the photographs you take are extremely important to the examiner. You must strive to produce excellent photos for them to be of use. But then, you should always strive for the best.

In cases where the analyses are conducted at the scene, the process should be documented. You should take photographs of the ***point of*** *convergence(s)*, and as the ***point of origin*** is determined, that should be photographed as well.

PHOTOGRAPHY OF LUMINOL

The area of interest is photographed with a camera on a tripod using standard camera settings like any other photograph. This photograph shows the scene as you see it. Next is the image of your luminol examination. The camera is still on the tripod, the lens aperture is set on f-22, and your strobe flash is set at 1/16th power. The shutter is set on bulb. The photograph is taken in total or near-total darkness, and the lens is kept wide open for about 3 minutes. Bracketing is recommended. In this manner, you will not have to deal with anything other than time and lens opening. You now have a photograph of the scene as it had looked and then what appears to be a duplicate photograph but with the **luminescence** visible on the same photograph. This method does not need to use an overlay of the luminescence, and is therefore less troublesome in court. It does, however, require an adjustable electronic flash.

PHOTOGRAPHY OF BULLET TRAJECTORY WITH LASER

We are sometimes asked to show the trajectory of a bullet in order to determine where the shooter was in reference to the victim. There are various methods of determining trajectory, and for the most part the photography of those methods is no different than any other crime scene photograph. The exception is the photography of trajectory using a ***laser*** (Figure 5–11). A

FIGURE 5–11   A shooting reconstruction using a red laser. The laser passes through the defect in the car window and shows the impact point where it struck the driver.

laser shoots a straight beam to the point indicated. A laser pointer for lecture purposes is a good example. We describe how to show the beam, because it does not normally show. There are a few methods of accomplishing this task.

First, the trajectory must be determined as described in the text. We are interested in this section in being able to document the laser beam. To begin, let's assume you have set up your laser on a tripod or similar device. You have the terminal impact point illuminated by the laser and it has passed through a point of penetration prior to terminal impact.

The laser (a pointer is fine) is turned on and left on. A camera is set up on a tripod to show the terminal impact point and moving back in the direction the projectile came from to a point you desire. The photography is done much the same as for luminol.

1. The laser is turned on. (It has been aligned).
2. The camera has been aimed to include the desired area.
3. The camera has flash mounted and aperture is set for a normal photograph. The shutter is set to bulb or time.
4. The lights are cut off and the scene is preferably in total darkness (or as near as possible).
5. The shutter is tripped, firing the flash. The shutter remains open.
6. The aperture is then opened all the way, being careful not to shake the camera.
7. An assistant sprays something like powder antiperspirant. The laser beam is now illuminated. The assistant walks back and forth, spraying as necessary to keep the beam illuminated. If you spray above the beam, it remains illuminated for a much longer time.

   TIP: The assistant should not be in the photo area when the flash goes off. After, because it is dark and the assistant is moving, his or her image will not be recorded in the photograph.

8. The shutter is kept open for about 20 seconds. Be sure to bracket.

The finished photograph shows the scene as you normally see it, but with a laser beam indicating the flight of the projectile. A red laser works very well for this technique; however, a green laser shows a noticeable improvement in visibility and distance. The green laser is more expensive, but is still affordable for even a small department or private business.

PHOTOGRAPHS AND COURT

We mention several times concerns about court and admissibility. These concerns seem to vary widely, but must be addressed nevertheless. The photographs made from negative film must have the film placed in evidence. It does not have to be in the evidence room, but in a controlled, secure environment in locked files. They may be stored much the same as latent fingerprints, in an envelope or pocketed folder with the standard case information on it as well as a section for chain of custody. If the photos are of a digital nature, then the memory card or device is downloaded to a writable disc, *not a rewritable disc.* This disc is then placed in evidence with no alterations whatsoever. Another can be made for examination use. The original disc in evidence should also have an affidavit stating that the images were downloaded in their original condition with absolutely no manipulation or alteration. This should get the images into court.

The images printed on photo paper should be examined by the photographer and marked as to case number and the other pertinent information. These markings should also contain your evidence mark or signature. The markings are done on the back of the photographs. Nothing should be done to the image side of the photograph. The photographer should be able to state the images are accurate representations of what was observed at the scene. If any manipulation was done, such as special filters, lighting, and so on, that should be noted and offered freely. Like any other evidence, the chain of custody cannot be broken and must be kept at all costs. It sometimes comes down to everyone on the chain of custody being summoned to court to testify.

◢ SUMMARY

Photography is one of the most important documentation processes in forensic science. It can be extremely valuable when done properly, but can also be misleading when used by an untrained photographer or one with devious intentions. Photography, like chemistry, has applications in most forensic fields.

◢ REVIEW QUESTIONS

1. When photographing small items of evidence, why do we take two photographs and what are they?
2. In forensic and photography in general, what is considered the "standard" lens?
3. When photographing fingerprints, shoe print, and other pattern evidence, what is the rule for positioning the camera in relation to the evidence?
4. In forensics today, what is the standard for a photo scale?
5. What is meant by the term "film speed?"
6. What is the purpose of the aperture setting?
7. What is the purpose of a "barrier" filter?
8. What is the most common "film speed"?

◆ REFERENCES AND SUGGESTED READINGS

JAMES A. MCDONALD, *Close-up & Macro Photography for Evidence Technicians,* 2nd ed. (Photo Text Books, 1992).

STEVEN STAGGS, *Crime Scene and Evidence Photographer's Guide* (Temeculah CA: Staggs Publishing, 1997).

Eastman Kodak Company, *Guide to KODAK 35 mm Films* (Kodak Publication No. AF-1, Eastman Kodak Company, 1990).

Eastman Kodak Company, *KODAK Guide to 35 mm Photography,* 7th ed. (21 Jet View Drive, Rochester, NY 14624: Silver Pixel Press, 1998).

BARBARA LONDON and JIM STONE, *A Short Course in PHOTOGRAPHY: An Introduction to Black-and-White Photographic Technique,* 5th ed. (Upper Saddle River, New Jersey 07458: Pearson Education, Inc., 2003).

LARRY S. MILLER, *Police Photography,* 4th ed. (2035, Reading Rd., Cincinnati, OH 45202: Anderson Publishing Co., 1998).

JAMES A. MCDONALD, *The Police Photographer's Guide* (James A. McDonald, 1992).

DAVID R. REDSICKER, *The Practical Methodology of Forensic Photography,* 2nd ed. (Boca Raton: CRC Press LLC, 2001).

CHAPTER 6

Crime Scene Drawings

Key Terms

Crime scene sketch
Scale
Proportion
Crime scene drawing
Overhead line drawing
Elevation drawing
Exploded view
Triangulation
Court drawing

INTRODUCTION/OBJECTIVES

Drawing the crime scene is considered by many as one of the most disliked tasks in crime scene investigation. Much of the dislike is the result of misinformation and rumor and is underserved. We hope to convince you that it is not a task to fear, and in fact, it is actually not that difficult and can even be somewhat enjoyable if you understand the process. We want you to understand when to use each type to your advantage.

The drawing of a crime scene is referred to by various terms, each of which has different meanings to different people. For the purposes of this book, we use the following differentiations: A **crime scene sketch** is a depiction of the scene roughly sketched in a notebook or on a report form with no reference to scale or proportion. **Scale** is an exact representation, such as $1/4$ in. equals 1 foot. This means that each 12- $\times$ 12-in. tile square on a floor is represented by a $1/4$-in. $\times$ $1/4$-in. square on the drawing. **Proportion** means that although the drawing is not to scale, items drawn are in proportion to each other; for example, a person in the drawing is in relative proportion to a car in that drawing, or to a wall. The sketch is simply for the use of the officer to refresh his or her memory when working on the investigation. It is very rough and not in any way intended to be complete or to proportion. It contains only the information that the investigator considers important. A sketch may or may not have measurements, but if it is to be used for the construction of a crime scene drawing at a later time, it must have measurements included. This is a major problem with complicated cases in that there are so many measurements listed on the drawing that they become confusing and take attention away from the subject being drawn (Figure 6–1). A **crime scene drawing** is a view of the scene that is complete in detail and is drawn to proportion or scale, depending on your agency's protocol and, of course, your abilities. It is usually drawn by a crime scene technician or crime scene investigator with the use of a drawing board. Drafting is frequently done today on a computer using *computer-aided drawing* (**CAD**) programs. It is suitable as a final work for the investigation. A *crime scene diagram* is drawn to scale, with all information included. It is complete in all details and is usually completed by a crime scene tech or analyst using

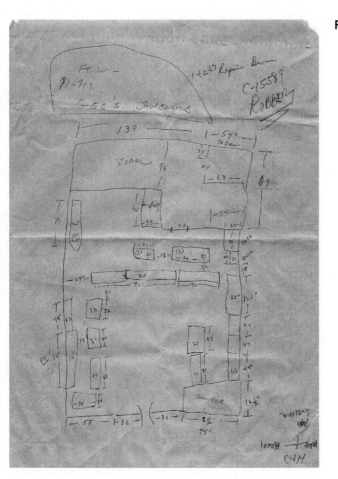

FIGURE 6–1   Rough sketch.

drafting techniques or a crime scene computer drawing program. These are usually completed for major cases where extreme detail is needed. Some agencies have crime scene draftspersons or a special *demonstrative evidence* unit that completes the work.

The purpose of these drawings is to record the scene of a crime accurately to complement the photography and narrative report of the event(s). As with the photographs, the diagram helps take the jury to the scene. It must therefore be easy to understand when listening to testimony in a court. The final product must be extremely neat, because the appearance of the diagram often reflects on how the jury places credibility on the maker's testimony concerning all matters in the case. A poorly made diagram can result in a lost case at trial.

You can learn to draw a very professional view of the scene with a little training and practice. A basic drafting course would be very advantageous. The returns are immense when considering how professional you will appear in court and to all those who view your work. People are less likely to challenge a drawing that is neat, complete, and professional. Remember, *we are judged by our work product.*

TYPES OF DRAWINGS

There are several types of drawings that we must address. These are the most common, but are not necessarily all inclusive.

1. *Overhead Line Drawing*. This drawing is by far the most common drawing found in law enforcement work. If the drawing is of a room or building, it is sometimes referred to as a *floor plan drawing*. It is a simple line drawing from directly above the scene, giving it its name. This two-dimensional drawing includes the walls of the building along with the contents and other pertinent items of evidence. It may be of an entire building or a house, or it may simply be a single room within the building (Figure 6–2). It may also be of a large outside scene (Figure 6–3).

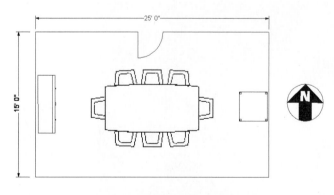

Conference Room

FIGURE 6–2   Overhead line drawing (bird's eye view).

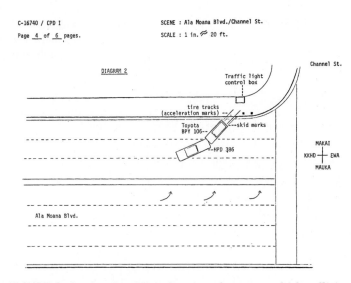

SCENE : Ala Moana Blvd./Channel St.

SCALE : 1 in. ⇆ 20 ft.

FIGURE 6–3   Overhead line drawing of a motor vehicle collision.

2. *Elevation Drawing*. This drawing shows height, such as a wall, the side of a vehicle (Figure 6–4), or anything with elevation. It could be a bullet hole in a window or wall or blood spatter patterns on a wall. It may include other interior furnishings if they are important to the case. On occasion, one might see an elevation view of a exterior wall with a *cutaway* portion showing interior features of the room.

3. *Exploded View*. The **exploded view** is a combination of the first two drawings in combination. The overhead line drawing is completed and the walls are then laid down and drawn in (Figure 6–5). In this manner, all four walls can be included in the same drawing as the floor plan. This drawing style is very valuable when showing the interior of a room and the lanai and

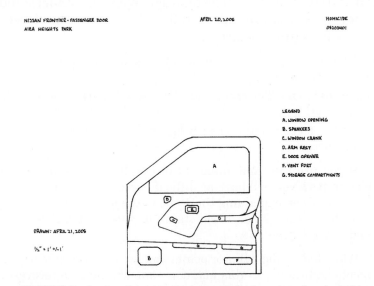

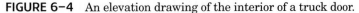

FIGURE 6–4   An elevation drawing of the interior of a truck door.

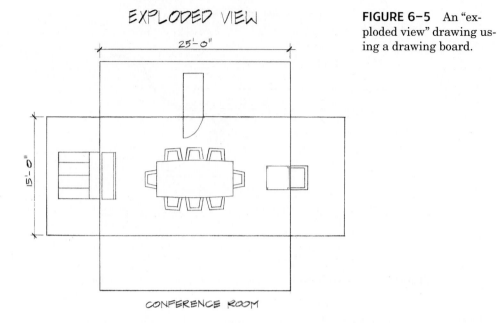

FIGURE 6–5 An "exploded view" drawing using a drawing board.

railing where someone might have jumped, fallen, or been pushed or thrown over a railing. An additional elevation view of the side of the building from the railing to the ground might be added to indicate the path and height of the fall.

4. *Cutaway Drawing.* This is often used when illustrating such topics as the interior mechanical workings of a firearm in questions of operability of the weapon.

There are many more styles or types of drawings, but for our purposes these are the most common ones we encounter or are required to draw. There is also some basic information required on all drawings used for official purposes in the investigation. With the understanding that your agency may require additional information, the most common requirements for a drawing are

- *Title.* The title might be the scene address, or the name of the building or the room in the building.
- *Compass direction.* The traditional "North" with arrow or direction such as "Up," or "Front."
- *Legend.* The legend contains such information as evidence and other items of importance.

TIP: If you use the same numbers in the diagram as those used in your evidence report, you will have no difficulty in court relating your evidence to the diagram when explaining the scene to the jury. If there are any symbols used, such as bullet holes, blood stains, or shoe prints, these should be explained in the legend as well.

TIP: When indicating items or points that are not recovered as evidence, use alphabetic indicators. In this manner, numbers indicate recovered evidence and alpha designators indicate points of interest that are not recovered.

- *Case Number.* This is usually your agency number, but included might be the number(s) of other participating agencies such as federal agencies and other local or state agencies.
- *Classification.* This is where you enter the classification or type of case being investigated.
- *Scale and **disclaimer**.* This indicates the scale or approximate scale of the drawing. For example, you might have the following indicator: "Scale: ¼ in. = 1 ft, +/−1 ft." This indicates your drawing is to a scale of ¼ in. equals 1 ft, plus or minus 1 ft. It gives you an out when considering such things as wall thickness, which may not be of importance. It also allows you to round off to the nearest 6 in. For example, a door that is 3 ft 2 in. can be 3 ft. Another way to put this is "Scale: Proportion, ¼ in. = 1 ft, +/−1 ft." It could also be "Scale: Proportion," or "Not to Scale." If the measurements are critical to the case, then of course you should indicate the exact measurement.
- *Signature Block.* This can include the date and time as well as the typed name and title of the maker, along with appropriate title. For example:

> *John Doe, ID#123456*
> *Crime Scene Technician*
> *07-06-2004 1605 hrs*

EQUIPMENT REQUIRED

A crime scene drawing can be very elaborate or very simple. Likewise the equipment used to accomplish this task can be very simple or very elaborate. We should remember that all the drawing instruments in the world will not make a drawing. It is a person who must use those instruments. For that reason, it is wise to base the instruments used on your skill level. It is suggested further that you work constantly on improving your skill, because you will be judged on your final product. We discuss some simple instruments for crime scene drawings with the understanding you do not have a computer-aided drawing program. We suggest many of these supplies in our discussion of kits. For starters, your list should include

- Two 100-ft steel tape measures. Tapes measuring 50-ft will work, but you will soon wish you had purchased 100-ft tapes. We use steel because other tapes stretch and can cause problems in court. If your jurisdiction does not question the use of cloth tapes, you might want to consider them. They are much easier to use and less prone to damage. If a steel tape is run over by a car or is bent, you have just lost a tape. They are also susceptible to rust and paint loss.
- One 25- to 30-ft steel tape measure. Again, two are better.
- One 12-in. ruler. Good quality with a raised edge so ink does not flow under the edges.
- A set of two drafting triangles. The first should be at least 8 in. long and is a 45° and 90° triangle, and the other is a 30°, 60°, 90° triangle that should be 10 in. These are considered standard for architectural drawings.[1] There

---

[1]DONALD E. HEPLER and PAUL I. WALLACH, *Architecture: Drafting and Design*. McGraw-Hill, 1987, p. 141.

FIGURE 6–6   A field drawing kit with case at top, drawing board with drawing machine attached, and a selection of house and office templates in both 1/8- and 1/4-in. scales. The template at right is a traffic template from Northwestern University Traffic Institute.

are also adjustable triangles that are able to make angles of varying degrees.

- One protractor. A half circle but an additional full circle would be good.
- A civil engineer's or architect's scale (Figure 6–6). This instrument is an individual choice. Look at them and determine which you prefer. They are very reasonably priced. Most are a standard size with a triangular cross section resembling three blades. They are also available in smaller and flat versions that are quadruple bevel, and others that are ideal to carry in your coat for court use. The *architect's scale* has 6 sides and 11 different scales.[2] The *civil engineer's scale* is constructed the same as the previous scale, but each inch is divided into decimal parts of 10, 20, 30, 40, 50, and 60.[3]
- A compass or two for different size circles.
- ***French curves*** are instruments allowing you to draw irregular curved lines. These are valuable for drawing roads. You can also use a *flexible ruler* for these kinds of irregular lines.
- One drawing board about 12 in. × 16 in.
- One T-square long enough to extend slightly over the longer side of the drawing board. Some drawing boards or tables have a "parallel slide" attached to the drawing surface and takes the place of the T-square. These are very handy both in the office and in the field.
- Graph paper with ¼- in. squares and light blue lines. You might prefer velum that comes plain and with light blue lines.

---

[2]Ibid., p. 132.
[3]Ibid., p. 134.

TIP: Graph paper often comes with light blue lines that do not copy well on a photocopy machine. If you are very neat with your drawing on the graph paper, it can then be copied and the result is a copy without the grids. This can then be overdrawn with ink to make an "original" drawing or you can put it on a drawing board/table with paper/velum over it and trace the diagram in ink to make your "original" drawing. The others then are simply draft or working copies.

- One or more mechanical drafting pencils with 0.05 mm lead; HB or other soft lead.
- Drafting eraser and erasing template.
- Brush for dusting off eraser particles. This is more of a convenience.
- Drafting tape or, better yet, drafting dots to attach the paper to the board.

TIP: Do not leave the tape or dots on the board for extended periods of time or they will damage the board and your drawing.

TIP: You can purchase a small drafting set in a case with board, built in T-square, with a two triangle set and protractor included for about as much as the separate items cost. All of these items are available at business supply houses, art stores, and college book stores. A decent set will run about $80.00 (Figure 6–6). Remember, these are instruments, not plumber's tools. They are delicate and are fairly easily damaged. Take care of them and they will last for many years.

TIP: When drawing with ink, *always wipe the instruments after each line.* If you do not, you get smears and smudges on your drawing. Likewise the instrument that is not kept clean damages subsequent drawings from the very beginning. These instruments must be kept exceptionally clean at all times.

Suggested Additional Items

- Traffic template. Northwestern University Traffic Institute has an excellent one that can also be ordered from some of the forensic supply houses such as Sirchie, Kinderprint, Lynn Peavey Co., and others. There are also traffic templates made by some of the drafting supply companies that are adequate.
- A selection of architectural templates that are office and house templates available at office supply houses and art stores in ¼-in. and ⅛-in. scales. They are also available in ½-in. and 1-in. scales, but quickly become very expensive, as they are about $10 or more per scale. The ones suggested here suffice for most report drawings. The templates save you time and make your task easier, not to mention give your drawings a professional appearance.
- A selection of templates for squares, circles, ovals, and the like. These are also available at office supply houses and art stores.

MEASUREMENT METHODS

There are numerous methods used for measuring a crime scene. The four most common are described next, all of which use some form of triangulation to plot evidence.

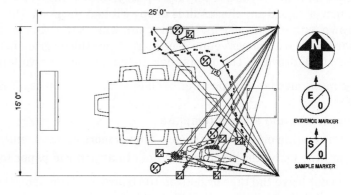

TRIANGULATION METHOD

Conference Room

FIGURE 6–7 "Triangulation method" using a computer with all measurement lines displayed. (This can get rather complicated.) A scale drawing can eliminate the need for the lines.

Triangulation

The first step in all methods is to determine the boundaries of the drawing. This also gives you an idea of what scale you want to use. The vast majority of drawings can be ¼-in. scale to make use of architect's templates.

Next, determine some known permanent or recorded points from which to take measurements. Examples would be road boundaries; street light or electrical poles, which are numbered and documented; corners of buildings; and so on. If you are in the field where there are no such points, a GPS reading establishes a point.

After determining two known points, a measurement is taken from each point to the item of evidence. This forms the legs of the triangle, with the line between the two points the base of the triangle (Figure 6–7). This procedure is repeated for each item of evidence until all are recorded. It is not necessary or even possible to always use the same reference points. The interior of a room is done by drawing in the walls, and the known reference points can be the corners of the room.

Right Angles or Rectangular Measurement

This method is used more commonly in buildings or on roadways. The first step is to draw in the outer walls of the scene. This is done simply by drawing a single wall. This can be accomplished by using the graph paper and drawing a line for the wall. If the wall is 27 ft long, then you simply draw a line of 27 squares on the graph paper. The second wall is done the same way, at a right angle from the first, and so on until all are recorded. Make marks at the location of each window and door. A 3-ft window is 3 blocks and a 3½-ft door is 3½ blocks. This is done until all interior walls are completed.

Next, items of evidence are plotted in the following manner. A pistol located 3½ ft from the north wall and 6 ft from the west wall is plotted by counting 3½ blocks down, or south, from the north wall and then 6 blocks east, or to the right, of the west wall. Each piece of evidence is plotted in the same manner until all are recorded.

When plotting furniture or bodies on the floor, to place them in their exact position, plot corners diagonally across from each other. This provides you with an exact position of the object. This is the same for either of the drawing methods. You can now draw in each piece of furniture and interior features of the room, house, office, and so on.

TIP: Use the template of the appropriate scale and position it on your reference marks and trace it in. This can be done with stoves, toilets, urinals, desks, tables, and so on. These templates include the vast majority of furnishings as well as variations and models of each.

It is recommended that you make your drawing to scale in the field, because this allows you to avoid writing in measurements. If you need to write in measurements and draw lines, the scene drawing (field copy) rapidly becomes so cluttered it is sometimes next to impossible to work with after returning to the office (Figure 6–7). With the scale field drawing, you need only pull out your scale and measure items to provide measurement to anyone.

TIP: If graph paper was used and it has pale blue lines, you might be able to copy it on a photo copier and have the drawing come out with no lines. Remember to make it 1:1 ratio, or the copy you make will not have the correct measurements.

TIP: When you need to make a drawing of a large, irregularly shaped area such as a cemetery parking lot, it is possible to take an aerial photograph from directly above the area. Then take some simple measurements on the ground for known references. Take the width and length of the parking stalls and a few other references. Then take the photo negative to your photo dark room or even a closet, where you can set up an enlarger or similar projection device. Enlarge the image until you have the scale of the measurements you took on the ground. Then simply put a piece of paper on the enlarger stand and draw in the image as it is projected. You have a scale (or at least a proportional) drawing. If it does not entail too large an area, you could substitute the photograph for the diagram.

Baseline Method

Another useful method in large areas with few reference points is to locate an object on opposite sides of your scene, such as trees, and run a baseline from one to the other. If possible, take GPS coordinates on both objects. Measure the distance at right angles from the baseline to your evidence.

You then have the distance from one tree to the point on the baseline where it is at a right angle to the evidence. Then measure from the baseline to the evidence, thereby providing you with two measurements.

Grid Method

The **_grid method_** has many advantages in that it is excellent when used for recovery of small evidence, such as trace evidence. It is also very useful when working small areas at a time, such as using the vacuum. Each grid block can equal one vacuum filter or tape recovery. The only difficulty with this method is that measuring from the boundaries of each block can become very cumbersome and can complicate court testimony, as well as causing more difficulty for those twelve jurors who have no experience in crime scene investigation. That said, we believe it is still the best method for those subjects we have discussed.

SYMBOLS

As you construct your crime scene drawing, try as much as possible to use standard map symbols; for those objects not found on maps, use standard, easily understood symbols. Be sure to include these symbols and definitions in your legend.

TIP: Standard architectural symbols are very good for structures, as they are readily understood by many people. They are available in books and can even be found on drawing templates such as those we describe in this book.

MOTOR VEHICLES

Motor vehicles tend to be drawn from the overhead view when investigating accidents. CSI staff in smaller agencies might draw these, but in the larger agencies there are specialists trained in reconstruction of motor vehicle cases. CSI staff tends to get involved when the vehicle is used in a major crime. They usually draw their vehicles from the same perspective, unless, of course, they need to show bullet holes, blood spatter patterns, or evidence related to height. In this case, the vehicle tends to be viewed in a series of elevation drawings of the front, back, and both sides, as well as from inside and outside (Figure 6–8). The reason for drawing vehicles is not only to show the locations of such objects as guns and drugs, but also to indicate bloodstain patterns, bullet holes, and the locations where latent prints were found. Your latent print card should also have a small drawing of the location from which the print was recovered. Be sure to indicate interior or exterior of vehicle and put an arrow on the latent print card indicating the position of the print; for example: Latent print located on the interior surface of the right front passenger door. Vehicle License (2005) Hawaii ABC-123, VIN #123K456LMN789.

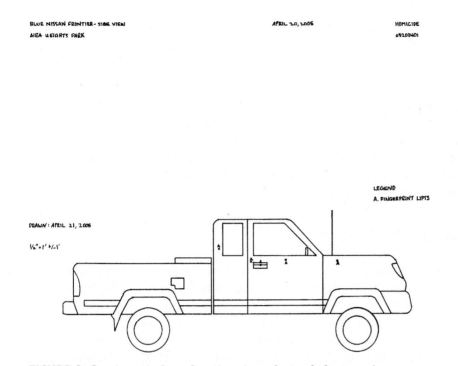

BLUE NISSAN FRONTIER- SIDE VIEW   APRIL 20, 2006   HOMICIDE
AREA HEIGHTS PARK   0420341

LEGEND
A. FINGERPRINT LIFTS

DRAWN: APRIL 21, 2006

1/2"=1' +/-1'

FIGURE 6-8   A vertical, or elevation view, of a truck drawn using a drawing board.

TIP: When recovering latent prints, after placing them on the lifters, leave them affixed to the car and then photograph the car with the cards in the photos. Draw the car with the cards and appropriate measurements.

SIZE OF DRAWING

The size of the drawing depends on the use and the scale. The vast majority of case drawings are of a scale to fit on the standard $8\frac{1}{2}$- × 11-in. typing paper. It is very easy to fit a room or even an entire house of this size paper. However, if the area shown is very large, then even this drawing may well be very large. Another option is to make a series of drawings that are a continuation of the previous drawing. There are cases with a primary and several secondary scenes that might each require one or more drawings.

MAPS

There are instances where a very large area may need to be drawn, and it is possible to draw a fairly decent drawing using a good road map or possibly a **_topographic map_** available from map stores, outdoor sports outlets, and the US Government. These are available in a number of scales. Remember, the scales can seem confusing, because a map of a very large area is referred to as a *small-scale map* because the scale is small, and conversely, a map of a small area is a *large-scale map* because it uses a large drawing scale.

NARRATIVE REPORT

The diagram is most often fairly self-descriptive, but in your narrative report there should be a section for the description of the drawing(s). It is here that you can go into detail about items included in the drawing and the significance of these items.

COURT DRAWINGS

Court drawings must be large enough for the jury to see without difficulty. It should also be made to scale when feasible. The drawing usually consists of the scene with furniture and appliances included. Items such as evidence, blood stains, bullet holes, and so forth should not be marked on the diagram prior to trial unless instructed to do so. The evidence might not be allowed and your drawing might not be available to the jury because of prejudicial issues. The items indicated might negatively influence the jury.

TIP: When you make a court drawing, you can make very light soft pencil marks where the evidence is located. This is visible only to you. On acceptance of the evidence by the court and when the witness is instructed to draw in the evidence, it can be done easily because the marks are present. This makes the presentation run smoothly, and makes the witness appear professional.

TIP: A large courtroom drawing can be placed on an easel and photographs of the scene can then be placed on the board around the drawing, with line designations to relate the point on the drawing with an actual photograph of that portion. This is the ultimate in drawings and photographs complementing each other.

Many agencies now have a demonstrative evidence unit or graphic artist unit that can assist with these court exhibits. They are sometimes enlarged and printed or drawn on large paper stock by a plotter. This is a very fast and efficient method that looks very professional, and tends to be cost effective in that it is much cheaper to have a machine draw the diagram instead of an employee who may require many hours to complete each exhibit.

COMPUTER-AIDED DRAWING PROGRAMS

Next we address computer-aided drawing (CAD) programs. There are many available today and they run the gamut from mediocre to outstanding. Study them and ask for a demo disc of the program prior to purchase.

Ask questions to determine if the program addresses your department's needs. You must also determine the learning curve for the program. Is the cost of the program justifiable considering your needs and skill level? They can be wonderful additions to your work aids, or they can be an awful waste of money.

ARCHITECTURAL MODELS

Architectural models are not often used in our cases, but when they are, they become a very valuable tool in the court room. These may not be practical for you to make, and therefore you might want to contract out to have one made. However, some agencies have a demonstrative evidence unit or graphic arts unit that could assist you with this effort. It is something you should consider in cases where complicated movement within a building on one or more floors might be necessary for the jury to understand what happened. The International Association for Identification has some outstanding classes at their annual educational meetings that greatly simplify the task.

Computer Modeling

Computer modeling could be a viable option to the architectural model, and some drawing programs have these built in as a part of the program. This allows views of the scene from different angles and vantage points as well as for plotting bullet trajectory and blood-spatter patterns and plotting. Because projectors and large-screen monitors are now fairly common, it might be a viable option for courtroom presentation. Some of these programs, commonly referred to as *3-D drawings,* allow the viewers to "walk through the scene," and the programs can take "camera views" from any location you may desire.

Actual Object

Still another option is bringing in the actual object in question. In Chapter Seven, we discuss a case involving fingerprints on a tub. In that case, an actual tub was brought to the courtroom. If the objects are of manageable size and not too numerous, they can be brought in as the ultimate piece of demonstrative evidence, and a drawing for court might not be required.

 SUMMARY

The diagram and models are extremely important in assisting the jury in understanding what is being discussed. Although photographs take the jury to the scene, they are two-dimensional and therefore sometimes not that clear. The drawing, even though usually two-dimensional, can show three dimensions, and the model, of course, makes it even clearer.

REVIEW QUESTIONS

1. What is the crime scene drawing used for in reference to the documentation process?
2. Which type of drawing is most commonly used to document scenes?
3. What are the major components of a crime scene diagram?
4. With reference to evidence, what do we recommend you use to designate individual items of evidence?
5. Why do we suggest you carry at least one or two pieces of graph paper in your notebook?
6. When diagramming a scene, what is generally a good scale to use?
7. What is one of the reasons for graph paper being made with light blue grid lines?
8. What is the main advantage to drawing the scene to scale?

REFERENCES AND SUGGESTED READING

DONALD E. HEPLER and PAUL I. WALLACH, *Architecture: Drafting and Design* (McGraw-Hill, 1987).

HENRY C. LEE, TIMOTHY M. PALMBACH, and MARILYN T. MILLER, *Henry Lee's Crime Scene Handbook* (Academic Press, 2001).

Fingerprints

Key Terms

Fingerprint
Latent print
Inked print
Automated Fingerprint Identification
    System (AFIS)
Bichromatic powder
Magnetic powder
Superglue fuming
Ninhydrin

INTRODUCTION/OBJECTIVES

Fingerprints are undeniably one of the best and most dependable methods of identification of an individual. A fingerprint is a distinctive pattern found on the palmar surface of the palms and fingers of the human. Also included is the distinctive pattern found on the plantar areas of human feet. These patterns consist of a series of ridges and valleys that flow in a pattern. These unique patterns are formed at about 4 months (120 days) of fetal life. The patterns remain unchanged, except for explainable reasons throughout life and until the body decomposes. The changes that come about are the result of injury, such as being cut, or other causes of deformation. To date, no two prints with the same exact characteristics have ever been detected. This chapter provides you with the material needed to perform most of the fingerprint duties generally needed for most crime scenes. Most of these can be done in the field, and are usually the responsibility of the crime scene unit.

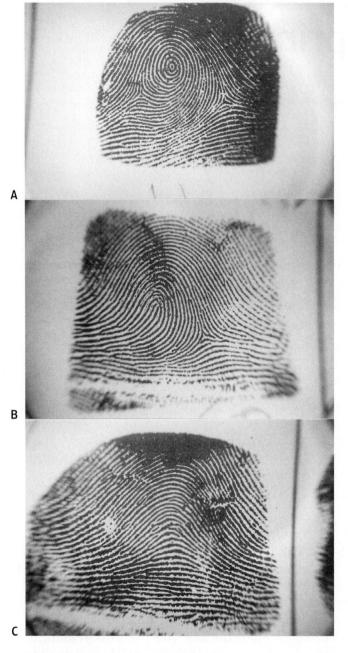

FIGURE 7–1 Basic fingerprint patterns. (A) A whorl; (B) a loop; (C) an arch.

TYPES OF FINGERPRINTS

When examining fingerprints, we can include them in three types of patterns. They are the *arch, loop,* and *whorl.* These are in turn broken down as follows:[1]

---

[1]Federal Bureau of Investigation, The Science of Fingerprints. US Government Printing Office, Washington, DC.

Arch (Figure 7–1a)
- Plain arch
- Tented arch

Loop (Figure 7–1b)
- Radial loop
- Ulnar Loop

Whorl (Figure 7–1c)
- Plain whorl
- Central pocket loop
- Double loop
- Accidental whorl

It does not matter if we are looking at ink to ink prints or ink to **latent** (usually unknown) ***prints***, it all begins with a good set of **inked** or ***known prints***. Inked prints are the result of lightly inking the ridge surface and then pressing or rolling the pattern surface on another surface, such as card stock. Later, identifications can be made with another set of inked prints from a subsequent arrest or latent prints recovered from a specific location, such as a crime scene. We discuss this later in the chapter.

INKED OR KNOWN PRINTS

The most common method of obtaining ink prints (*known prints*) is with black printer's ink rolled onto a smooth slab such as glass. The fingers are both pressed onto the slab for "flats" and rolled from one side to the other for "rolled" prints. These are then placed on preprinted card stock. These prints are the foundation of fingerprint examination. Ink prints are being replaced with electronically recorded scanned prints, but the purpose is still the same: to provide a set of known prints with which to later identify a person. It is for this reason that the inked prints must be of excellent quality. They must be clear and contain as much of the friction ridge pattern surface of the hand and/or feet as possible. For fingerprints, the pattern area must include the core and delta(s), if that pattern includes one (Figure 7–2). The arch pattern has neither a core nor a delta. The more ridge pattern recorded, the better your chances of later completing a successful identification. The rolled prints should include the fingerprint ridge pattern from as close to the fingertip as possible to below the first joint crease, and include both sides of the fingertip as well as the major pattern surface. A good rule of thumb is to roll from nail to nail (Figures 7–3a, 7–3b)

The most common mistake made when recording inked prints is using too much ink (Figure 7–4). This results in the furrows filling with ink and thereby recorded as the ridges, which is known as a ***reversed print***. Other problems include allowing the finger to slip or twist while printing. This problem is usually a result of the awkwardness of rotating the arms of the subject being printed. Still others are a dirty ink slab, too much or too little pressure, or not rolling the digit completely from nail side to nail side. Extremely clear prints are even more critical if the agency is using

FIGURE 7–2 This is a whorl. Whorls have two deltas and a core, whereas a loop has one delta and core, and an arch has no delta or core.

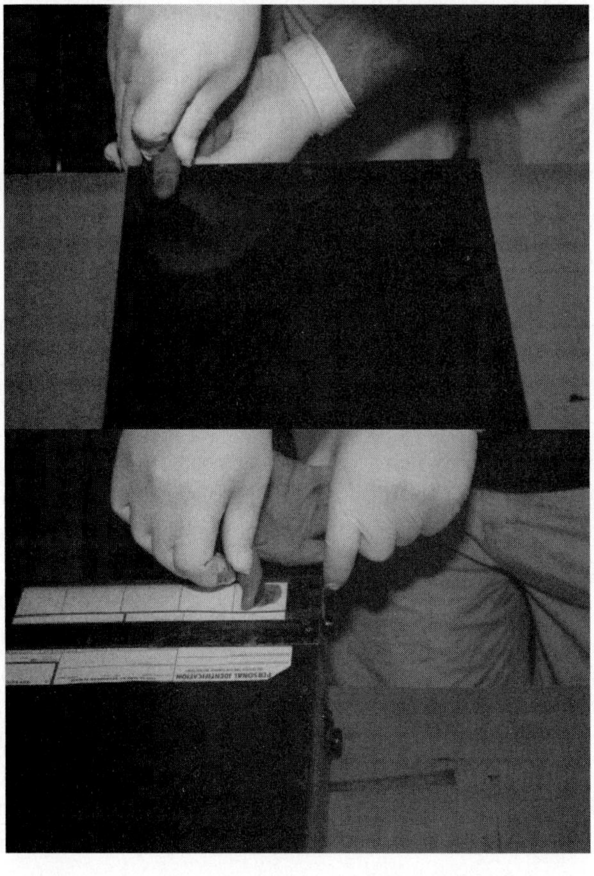

FIGURE 7–3 Using ink to fingerprint a person. (A) Rolling the finger on an ink slab. (B) Rolling the finger on a print card.

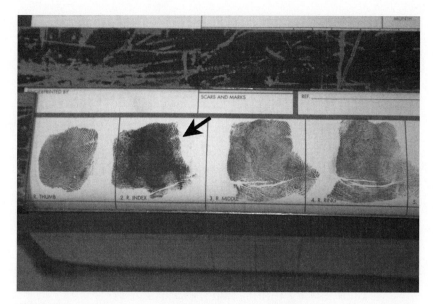

FIGURE 7–4 The print on the left (*arrow*) has insufficient pattern recorded. The print second from the left has too much ink; and the print second from the right is a good print. The right print has uneven inking in center.

the **Henry Fingerprint Classification System,** which is a method of classifying all ten fingers in a filing and search system. For this reason, the Henry System is also referred to as a **ten-print system.** Sir Edward Henry invented this system in 1899. The Henry System requires that values be given to various portions of the print patterns. These values are recorded in the form of a fraction, with the right hand being on top and the left hand on the bottom. Therefore, the proper designations cannot be completed without those portions of the prints. This is a ten-print manual system of filing prints. The implication here is that one must have all ten digits to complete the classification, with amputations being noted. The Henry System is rapidly being replaced with the **Automated Fingerprint Identification System (AFIS).**

AFIS is a **single-print system** that uses a computer-based classification and search protocol. For this reason, it may be slightly more forgiving when it comes to patterns. It not only stores the prints for future use, but also automatically searches the existing ink files as well as latent print files. It is extremely fast. A manual identification may take hours or days to complete; AFIS searches can now be done in a matter of minutes. It has made possible the ability to determine positive identification and relationship to other cases prior to a person being released from custody after the booking procedure. Even though this is a computer search engine, a human examiner must still confirm the results. The computer obviously cannot testify in court. As mentioned earlier, prints are also being recorded more often as "live scans," which makes the task easier and more efficient as time passes.

Let's begin with a step-by-step approach to the inked or known prints, because that is the real beginning.

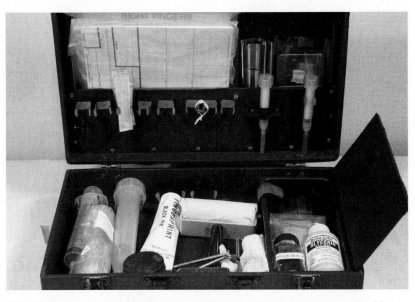

FIGURE 7–5   A postmortem fingerprint kit with glycerin, tissue builder, ink, spoons, and syringes.

Necessary Equipment

Following is a list of the equipment necessary for the recording of fingerprints:

- *Black fingerprint ink.* This is printer's ink and if you have no source for forensic supplies simply go to an art store and get printer's ink for wood block printing. *Do not use a stamp pad.* The weave pattern of the cloth pad will be transferred to the print card and make it extremely difficult to compare.

- *White card stock.* It is best to obtain preprinted fingerprint cards, which can be ordered from a number of sources. The FBI furnishes the DC cards, which are the cards for their records. You need an ***ORI number,*** which your agency must apply for from the FBI. The ORI is a number assigned for the originating agency. For example, Hawaii ORI numbers begin with HI and a series of numbers, such as HI000123. Each agency in that state has its own number. The cards you obtain are standard, as far as ten-print cards go. They have certain information at the top of the card and two rows of blocks below for the rolled prints. Under that are the blocks for the flats, or simultaneous four fingers of each hand, and a separate block for the thumb on each hand (Figure 7–6). An additional advantage to the FBI cards is that they are color coded to preclude criminal cards from being mixed with applicant cards, personal identification cards, and so on.

- *An ink roller.* This can also be obtained from a supply house for law enforcement or forensic equipment, which is nice because they have them designed to lay with the roller slightly off the slab so you do not end up with a flat spot.

   TIP: You can also go to any art-supply house and purchase a wood block roller that works just as well.

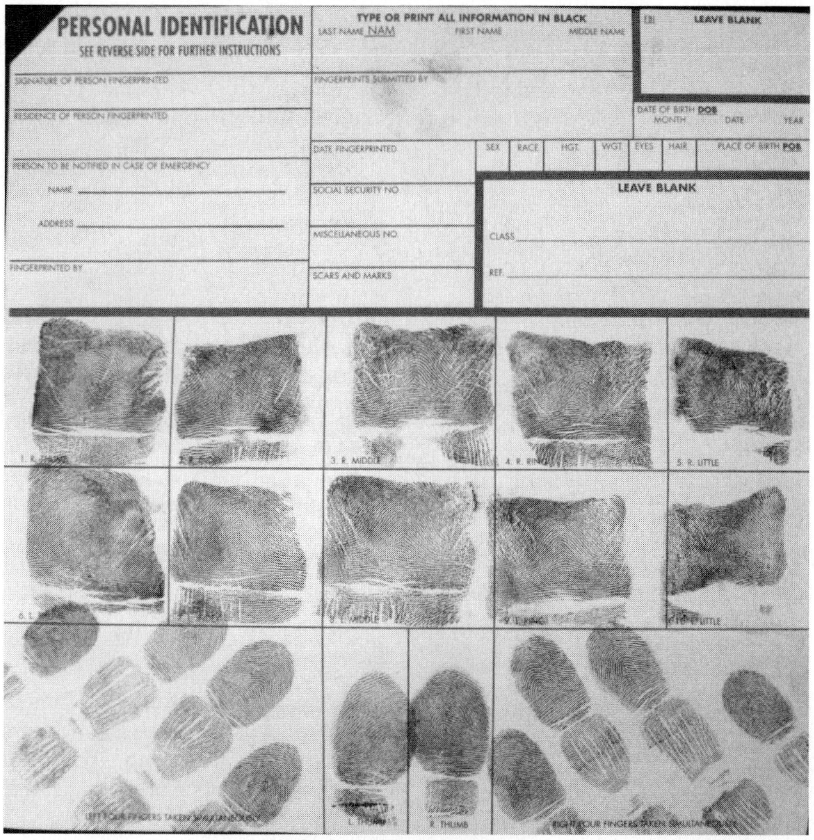

FIGURE 7–6 A properly inked ten-print card.

- *Ink slab*. The ink slab can be chrome, stainless, or glass. The glass is nice because it takes the ink better, and because of its transparency, it is possible to see the surface below the glass. There is a reason we want the transparency. We want to be able to see through the glass to determine the amount of ink to put on the glass. A good-quality optical glass large enough to take both full handprints is best.

  TIP: If you do not have access to an ink slab, in a pinch you can use a glass louver or other sheet of glass. Make sure the edges are smooth so that no one is injured. Tempered glass is best because it is difficult to crack.

- *A Card holder*. This holds the fingerprint card in place. These are commercially available and it is highly recommended that one be used. They can be permanently affixed to the table or temporary fixtures held in place by simple rubber legs that resist sliding. These card holders come in both wood and metal combinations as well as plastic and metal configurations.

  TIP: If there is a need to set up a portable inking station and you do not have portable card holders, you can tape the permanent holders to a table. There is a lip on either side of these holders with holes for screws. Simply place the tape over these lips and press onto the table.

- *Hand cleaner.* Just about any good hand cleaner, including those designed for mechanics, is sufficient. It is used to remove the ink from the hands. There is a new ink on the market that can be wiped off with water.
- *Paper towels.* These are used to remove ink and dry the hands.

Procedure

Following are the steps for recording fingerprints:

1. Place white paper (typing or copy paper is fine) on the table or counter and place the glass over the paper. The glass should be secured to the table surface, which can be accomplished with tape in the field and a three-sided wood frame in the office to allow for cleaning the glass and changing the paper under the glass.
2. Place two or three dabs of ink on the glass at intervals (Figure 7–7). You do not need more than this or you run the risk of too much ink.

    TIP: If you have too much ink, simply take a piece of paper towel and rub it across the surface one or two times, and then reroll the same ink again.

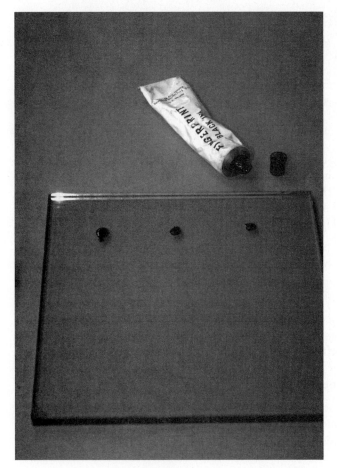

FIGURE 7–7 This is enough ink to cover this glass. The biggest mistake made is too much ink.

3. Roll the ink over the surface going in different directions, such as vertical and horizontal, to evenly spread the ink. Finish by rolling horizontally to avoid lines in the ink and thereby in the prints.

   TIP: When the ink is spread properly, you should be able to see the paper beneath the glass. This results in the proper amount of ink being applied to the glass.

4. Place the print card in the holder.
5. Begin with the right thumb and work to the little finger. This is repeated on the second row for the left hand. The third or bottom row has a block for the left hand, four fingers and then the left thumb. Next is the right thumb, followed by the right four fingers.

TIP: Do not roll or place fingers on the glass surface that has already been used. Your ink will be uneven, and as a result, hard on the fingerprint examiner's eyes (Figure 7–8). Always roll the ink evenly over the glass again prior to reusing any surface on the slab. Always use light pressure when rolling or pressing for flats. Too much pressure results in ink building up in the furrows, possibly resulting in a reversed print or at least a distorted print.

TIP: Always clean your slab and apply fresh ink at least every shift or 8 hours. This task might be warranted sooner in heavy load situations such as booking facilities. The ink picks up dust and other debris that can alter or distort your prints.

TIP: There are fingerprint cards, commonly referred to as *major case cards* (Figures 7–9a, 7–9b), that are a very advantageous. These cards are used in addition to the standard ten-print cards and they contain flats as well as fingertips and the sides (*writer's palms*) of the palms. These

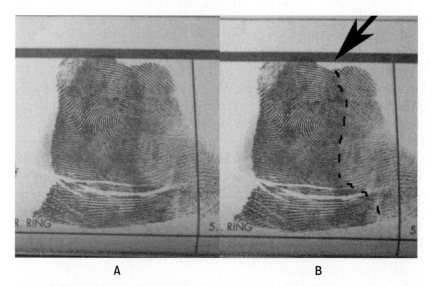

A   B

FIGURE 7–8   (A) An inked print that was rolled on ink slab that has had a digit already rolled on the glass. (B) The ink line.

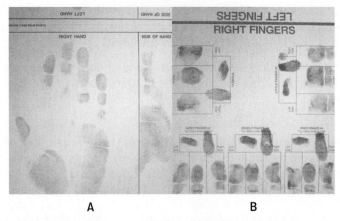

FIGURE 7–9 Major case card with side of palm (writer's palm, A) and fingertips (B).

prints are very important, especially for document cases where the writer holds the paper with the secondary hand with the heel or side of the palm and the fingertips and the predominant hand writes with the palm touching the paper. These portions of the ridge surfaces might not be captured on the standard ten-print card.

Take your time and do the prints properly, or your entire effort may well be wasted. Large agencies cannot waste time with poorly taken prints and will send them back. This, of course, can make the difference between solving a case or not.

With cooperative adults, you can ink an entire hand and then put the prints on the card. If you have an unruly person or a young child, it might be a good idea to do one finger at a time. If you attempt to ink an entire hand, you may have more ink on you than on the fingerprint card. You cannot go wrong if you ink one finger at a time as a standard procedure.

DECEASED PERSONS' FINGERPRINTS

The fingerprinting of deceased persons is not as difficult as one might imagine. If the person is not in rigor and is recently deceased, then the method is very simple. It is done much the same as it would be done for a live individual. The traditional method is to use ink and a "spoon" to place the card on to obtain the print (Figure 7–10). When you use this method, the fingerprint card is cut so that the row for each hand is inserted into the spoon. Each finger is inked and then pressed onto the card using the spoon. There is another method that is just as good if not better and certainly easier to do. This method uses latent print powder, tape, and cotton swabs or gauze pads.

Equipment required:

- Black latent print powder
- Cotton-tipped swabs (the longer wood-shaft swabs are better)
- Celluloid print blocks made from overhead projection sheets. Celluloid fingerprint cards are made using a copy machine by making a copy of a fingerprint

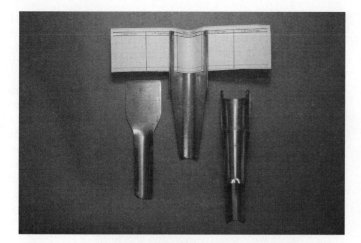

FIGURE 7–10   Spoons used to fingerprint deceased persons using ink and a fingerprint card.

card. The copy is then run through the same machine just as if you were making overhead projections. You can make two celluloid cards with one overhead transparency sheet.

- Latent fingerprint tape
- One ten-print card for inked prints

The process is as follows:

1. Dip a cotton swab in a jar of fingerprint powder and rub it over the finger to be printed (Figure 7–11a). The entire hand is done in the same manner.
2. Latent fingerprint tape is then used to lift the print from the finger (Figure 7–11b).
3. The print is then placed on the back of a celluloid fingerprint card.

   TIP: Once you get good at this, you will be able to take the prints from an entire hand on a single intact strip of fingerprint tape and then affix it to the card with the proper spacing (Figure 7–11c). A nice advantage to this method is that you can press on the finger to make sure the entire print transfers to the tape without distortion.

4. The prints are placed on a regular fingerprint card. It now has a white background, and the tape is sandwiched between the card and celluloid card.

TIP: By using a *Mylar sheet*, it is possible to lift the entire simultaneous impression of the hand. Two hands fit on a single 8½- × 11 in. sheet.

TIP: With wrinkled fingertips, you often hear about injecting water into the fingers to return them to their original shape. Often the water simply shoots out when you press on the finger. Another suggestion is to use glycerin or embalmer's tissue builder and inject in the same way. These remain in the fingertip. Glycerin can be purchased at any drugstore, and of course, embalmer's tissue builder can be purchased from a mortuary supply house or you can obtain some from your local mortuary. The tissue builder has the advantage of hardening, and provides a better surface for printing.

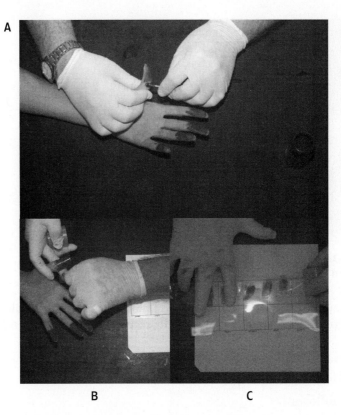

FIGURE 7–11
Fingerprinting a dece-
dent (or live person) us-
ing fingerprint tape and a
celluloid fingerprint card.
(A) Apply latent print
powder with cotton-
tipped swab. (B) Lift the
print with fingerprint
tape. (C) Place all five
left-hand fingers simultaneously on card.

Latent or Unknown Prints

Latent prints, a generic term for the prints recovered at crime scenes and elsewhere as the result of scene investigations, are the ***unknown prints***. Latents include a few different types of prints:

- Actual latent or hidden prints which are the result of persons touching objects with sweat, body oil, or any number of contaminants on their hands and feet (Figure 7–12).
- ***Plastic*** or ***patent prints,*** which are three-dimensional prints, are the result of the print surface being impressed into putty, such as window putty, wet paint, grease, and (for whatever reason) human skin.
- ***Visible prints*** are two-dimensional prints that are the result of contaminants on the friction ridge surface being transferred to another surface. These may be the result of touching very wet paint or grease, as with plastic prints, but then touching another object, thereby leaving the second two-dimensional print. For this reason, you might find a finger impression in paint that is plastic and then another next to it as a direct result of the first.

These latent prints make up the evidence that is sent to the fingerprint examiner for comparison with the known prints. Advances in the recovery of latent prints have been rapid over the past several years and are so numerous that it becomes quite a task just to keep up with them. We discuss many and (hopefully) the most valuable to you as a crime scene investigator. The

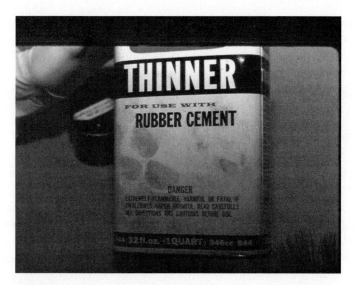

FIGURE 7–12 Latent prints on a can recovered with black powder and an ostrich feather.

most common method of recovering latent prints is with the use of a fiberglass filament brush and black fingerprint powder of various formulas.

Necessary Equipment

There are so many very good pieces of equipment available to the crime scene investigator that we discuss the most important first, and then address those other items that make your job more efficient, but something you might be able to get along without. Those critical items for everyday dusting are as follows:

- *Fiberglass filament latent print brush*. There are also camel's hair brushes sold for this purpose.

  TIP: Cosmetic brushes also make outstanding fingerprint brushes.

- *Black fingerprint powder*. A true black or **bichromatic powder**. A bichromatic powder is one that although being black, shows up on black or dark surfaces as a lighter shade. This makes recovery of prints a much simpler task because it is possible to avoid using color powder.

- *Latent print tape*. It comes in clear and frosted. Many fingerprint examiners prefer frosted tape because it is easier on the eyes, but either suffices. Do not use regular office tape. If you are in a bind, then you use what you have access to, but this type of tape is extremely unsatisfactory and makes the examiner's task very difficult.

- *Latent print cards*. These are available commercially and if your agency does not have its own cards, it is recommended you use the commercial ones.

  TIP: In a pinch you could use 3 × 5 index cards.

- *Magna brush*. This is a ***magnetic wand*** that allows one to spread magnetic powder.

- ***Magnetic powder*** *in black*. The Magna Brush system produces wonderfully clear prints under difficult conditions. It is great for prints on surfaces such as styrofoam beverage cups and human skin. It is a powder, either black or colored, but with metal filings as a base.

The following items are very useful to have and should be acquired as soon as feasible:

- Gray latent powder, both regular and magnetic.
- White powder, regular and magnetic.
- Extra fiberglass brushes for the different powders. Do not mix brushes, as this contaminates the powders.
- Blue light, of which there are several types and of various prices. The new blue light-emitting diode (LED) lights work well. It is recommended that it have at least four bulbs.
- Orange glasses (filter) you use with blue light (as well as the same filter for your camera lens).
- Orange powder with brush.
- Larger print tape and/or lifters. Sheets of adhesive Mylar can be cut to size for oversize prints such as palm prints.

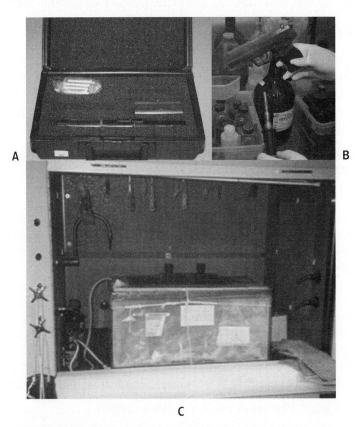

FIGURE 7–13 Cyanoacrylate ester fuming. (A) A fuming kit. (B) A pistol being fumed with a fuming wand. (C) A fuming tank in a fume hood for safety.

- A "superglue" gun, wand, or device for fuming (Figures 7–13a, 7–13b, and 7–13c). This can be accomplished without the gun, and we discuss the technique later in this chapter.

PROCESSING EVIDENCE FOR LATENT PRINTS

An object to be dusted for latent prints is first examined with the unaided eye and with the aid of a flashlight or other *alternate light source (ALS)*. Holding the light at an oblique angle often makes it possible to visualize the prints with little difficulty. It may also be necessary in some cases to use other ALSs to visualize prints. These include the laser, xenon light, and blue light.

Once the latent prints have been located, they may be treated by *dusting*. When latent prints are located and there is any question as to the success of *lifting* the print, do one or both of the following. Photograph the latent print, and then, if possible, bring in the actual object. At this time you may process the print. If no prints are found, the object can be dusted to determine if any true latents develop. The general method used to develop latents is to use a brush, typically a fiberglass filament brush that has been dipped in latent print powder. It is then carefully brushed in a circular motion across the desired area. The tip of the brush should barely touch the surface. Heavy brushing can destroy your latent prints. As prints develop, the brush is maneuvered to fully develop the print. This is a matter of practice and experience. Usually, a general area is dusted prior to any recovery being attempted.

MAGNETIC VERSUS TRADITIONAL POWDER

Most surfaces can be dusted by using the traditional latent print powder and fiberglass filament brush, but quality comes in to play. There are some surfaces that are difficult if not impossible to recover latent prints with the standard powder. Styrofoam containers are a good example. The magnetic powder can develop extremely good latent prints from Styrofoam. The Magna Brush can develop exceptional prints on raw wood. However, it is difficult (although not impossible) to lift prints off a vertical surface or ferrous metal with the magnetic powder. Another very important advantage to using magnetic powder is that it is very clean to work with when compared to standard powder.

Once prints have been visualized, they can be recovered. Remember, if there is any question, photograph the prints prior to lifting. (Photographic techniques for latent prints are covered in Chapter Five.) If you are not using a 1:1 ratio fingerprint camera, include a reference scale, such as the ABFO#2. Latent print tape is used for most recovery, and the placement of the tape is important. The tape can be either placed to one side of the print and then smoothed over the print or, in some instances, it might be better to place the tape directly on the print and work outward, depending on the individual circumstances. Be careful to work out any bubbles if possible.

TIP: Cool a car or other hot object prior to dusting. If the car has been sitting in the sun for some time, you might find that as you lift your fingerprint tape from the surface, the glue and print remain on the car and the tape comes off. Or even worse, you might lift part of the print with other parts remaining on the car. Cooling prevents this from occurring.

TIP: Pull the amount of tape off the roll that you are going to use. By pulling a little tape off the roll and then a little more, you leave lines on the tape that make it more difficult for the examiner.

TIP: When you place your tape on the object being dusted, put a little more than is required to leave an anchor point. When this method is used, it is possible to place the tape on your latent cards without completely removing them from the object. This is a distinct advantage in the wind and also allows you to take a photograph of all the latents together on their cards prior to removal. This may be a good technique to use when describing your actions to a jury. It also allows you to make your sketches on the latent print card prior to removal. If the cards are on a relatively flat surface such as a wall, counter, or even an automobile, you can proceed to place information on the card. Depending on the card, the information varies slightly. We next discuss a typical card.

SIMULTANEOUS IMPRESSIONS

The investigator often comes across simultaneous impressions left from the same hand. These can sometimes be lifted with a wider tape or, if you are so equipped, large lifters or Mylar sheets. Many investigators do not have access to these supplies, but there is still an option. You can place standard fingerprint tape on the prints, such as an entire handprint. Following is the procedure:

1. Leave a tab on the ends and run the tape the length of the print, from finger tip to wrist if that much is present. This should begin on one side of the print, such as thumb side or little finger side (Figure 7–14a).
2. Run a second tape alongside the first tape, being careful to barely overlap the tapes. You can run your fingernail along the overlap crease to ensure the entire print is present.
3. Continue the process until the entire print is covered. All of your tabs should be at one end (Figure 7–14b).
4. Carefully slide a pencil or pen under the tabs of the tape, lifting slowly so as not to separate the joints. Stick the pen to the tape.
5. Carefully lift the tapes using the pen as a lifting bar until the entire ridge surface has been lifted, but the tape is still attached to the surface where the print was found (Figure 7–14c).
6. Slide a white paper sheet or a fingerprint card (blank reverse side) under the tape until it stops where the tape is still attached to the surface (Figure 7–14d).

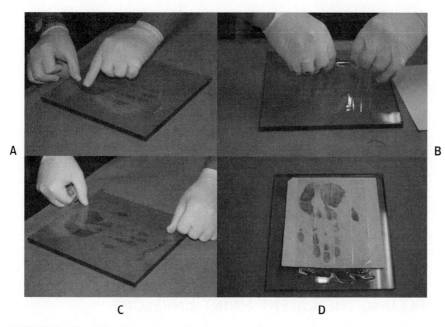

FIGURE 7–14 Lifting a palm print using overlapping standard fingerprint tape attached to a ballpoint pen to lift the tape simultaneously.

7. Now slowly slide your palm or another pencil over the surface of the tape, proceeding to stick it to the paper or card until the print is completely on the card. The tabs and excess tape can now be cut off. The lift can now be placed on an oversize card or paper for filing.

COMPLETING THE LATENT PRINT CARD

One side of the ***latent print card*** is typically for the placement of the latent print. The opposite side is for placement of specific information that is not only important, but in some instances may be critical to your case (Figure 7–15). Let's look at that information.

- Case number and classification of the case.
- Date and time of lift.
- Location where prints were recovered (scene).
- Object from which latents were recovered. This should be in some detail, such as, "Interior window glass at point of entry."
- Prints lifted by: Your name and ID number. ID numbers are used because they are issued to only one person, but a badge number has most likely been issued to someone before and many persons after you leave or are promoted.
- Diagram of lift location. This is an extremely important bit of information.
- The print side of the card should have an indication of "up, down, front, rear," and so on.

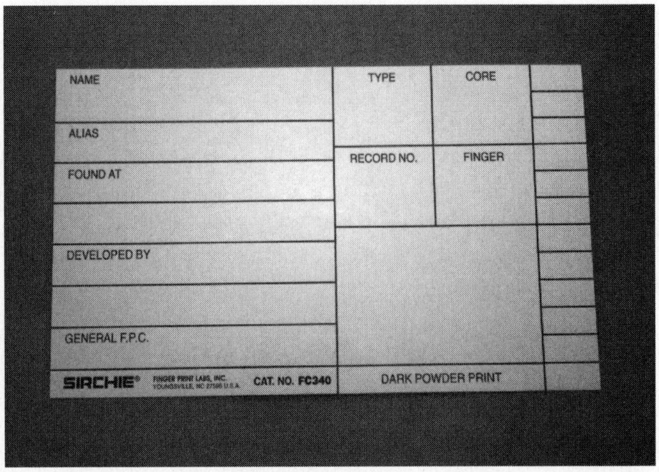

FIGURE 7–15   Latent fingerprint card.

COMPLETING THE LATENT PRINT ENVELOPE

Latent print cards are placed in a fingerprint evidence envelope that has basic case information as well as a "chain of custody" portion. These are for the most part self-explanatory, but there are a few items that justify discussion (Figure 7–16).

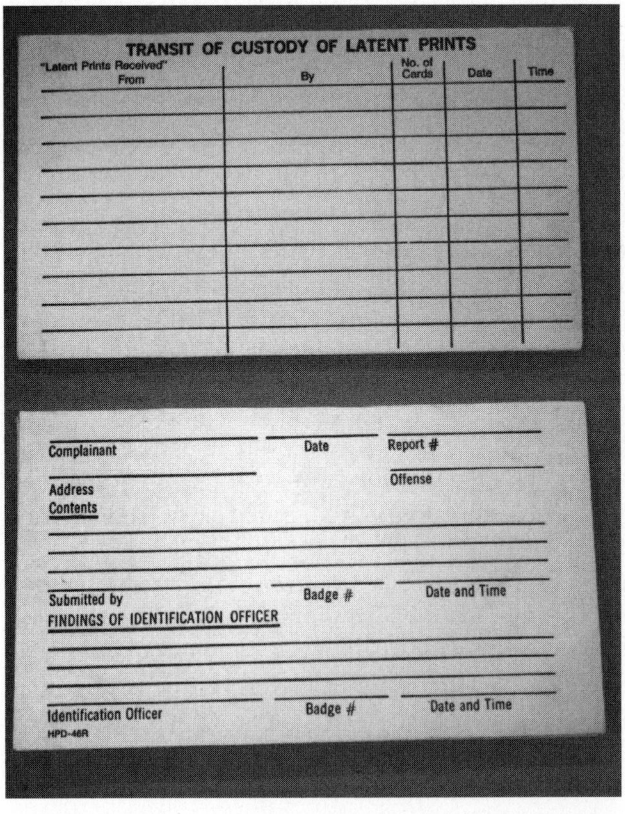

FIGURE 7–16   Latent print card custody folder.

- If there is a section for "number of latents," always put the number of cards, not latents. Most of these envelopes state "cards" and not "latents" because you might be questioned in court as to the number of latents being different from that of the examiner. Always let the expert determine the actual number of latent prints. A card may have more than one latent print and often does.
- If you are unsure of the quality of a latent, submit it anyway and list it. Let the expert decide what is identifiable and what is not identifiable.
- "Second lift" cards are counted as another card.
- If the envelope is being used for an oversize latent print, you can fill it out as usual and then attach the envelope to the larger one holding the lifts. Some agencies have special envelopes for "oversize prints."

CASE STUDY

A female was raped and murdered on the floor of a bathroom and her body was found where she died. The top of her head was against the side of the tub, with her body straight. It appeared that she was attacked in this position.

The tub was dusted for latent prints and entire palm prints were recovered. These were positioned with the fingers on the inside of the tub facing down and the palms on the sill of the tub. Also visible were the creases at the wrists. These were photographed and diagrammed, with very precise measurements noted. The prints were then recovered.

The suspect in this case denied that he had anything to do with the murder and related his prints were on the tub because he had washed his feet in the tub as he was standing outside the tub.

When the case went to trial, a tub was used as a display with photocopies of each of the prints being attached exactly where they were recovered (Figure 7–17). The jury was then able to see the tub with the prints in place.

FIGURE 7–17 Photocopies of handprints attached to the tub exactly where they were recovered, as described in the case study.

The latent print examiner explained that had the accused washed his feet as he had said, at most there might be fingertips on the tub. In this case there were no footprints found. The examiner went on further explaining that the position of the prints and the wrist creases indicated the person was on a very low plane, as if prone, and was in line with the body. This indicated the suspect was possibly holding on to the tub to brace himself while attacking the victim. On appeal, it was found the examiner, being an expert, could offer his opinion, and the conviction was upheld. By the way, the water in the bathroom was turned off. The room was used as a utility storeroom.

SPECIAL FINGERPRINT TECHNIQUES

Decomposed Bodies

We often work with bodies that are either decomposed or mummified and sometimes they are a combination of both. Let's begin with the decomposed body. As the body begins to decompose, it bloats and becomes wet. If this process is not too far advanced, it is possible to dry the surface with towels and use latent powder in the same manner described earlier of deceased persons. The skin can also be flushed with acetone and then printed. As the process of decomposition continues, skin becomes detached from the body and begins to slip. It is possible at this time to remove this "glove" and print it.

Removal of the "Glove"

The remaining technique, should the previous one fail, is the removal of the digit in one form or another. We look at skin slippage first, because that is actually the easier technique to use. With this technique, the body is in a fairly advanced state of decomposition and the skin is sloughing or coming off. In this case simply slip the skin off the hand or finger (Figure 7–18a). If the skin has not completely released, the process can be expedited by very careful scalpel work (Figure 7–18b).

After the "glove" or skin is removed, it is possible to slip this "glove" over your gloved (examination) hand and print the finger as if you were rolling your own finger (Figures 7–18c, 7–18d). If the skin is very wet or slimy, it can be flushed using acetone from a laboratory squeeze bottle.

Removal of the Digit

This method is useful with both decomposed and mummified bodies. Should the finger be decomposed or mummified and not sloughing, then the digit can be removed in one of two ways. The first requires cutting off the digit at the first joint and removal of the entire appendage. The other method is to use a scalpel and cut in front of the fingernail and along the sides above the pattern area. Then cut through the finger just below the bone and remove the friction ridge surface. This can then be powdered or inked and recorded as described previously.

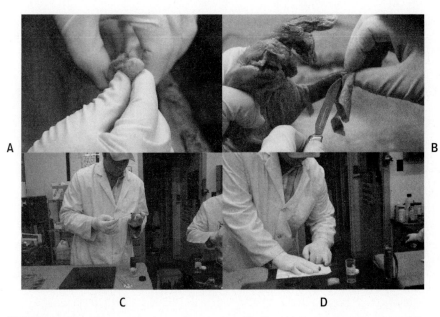

FIGURE 7–18 Fingerprinting a decomposed body. (A) Removing the skin. (B) Using a scalple to remove the still-attached skin carefully. (C) Placing the skin on a CSI's finger. (D) Rolling the finger.

Mummified Bodies

With badly mummified fingers, it might be necessary to remove all tissue from the underside of the dermis (Figure 7–19a). The skin is more pliable. Another option is to mount the remaining skin between two pieces of glass and transmit light through the skin, much like a photographic slide (Figure 7–19b). Then the illuminated print pattern is photographed.

Palm Prints for Deceased Persons

The equipment required for this task is the same as that for fingerprints, except the tape is replaced with a sheet of Mylar or a large print lifter.

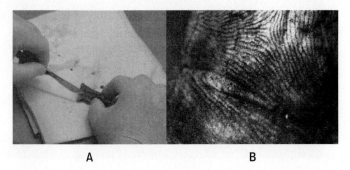

FIGURE 7–19 (A) Removing skin from a mummified finger. (B) Projecting light through the skin to photograph the ridge pattern.

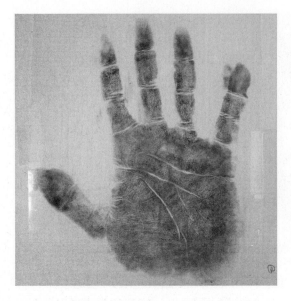

FIGURE 7–20 Lifting the palm print of a decedent using latent print powder and a Mylar sheet.

The hand is powdered in the same manner, although we prefer a gauze pad when recording an entire hand. The Mylar is simply pressed onto the hand, including fingers, and then placed on a Mylar or clear cover (Figure 7–20). These prints are examined with the lift on the bottom and the cover on top. In this way, you do not have a reversed print. If you do not have Mylar, you can use standard fingerprint tape. When placing the tape over the palm, the edges of the tape must slightly overlap to make the tape into a single sheet for lifting (Figures 7–21a, 7–21b). The tape can then be placed on the back of even a clear plastic bag if nothing else is available (Figure 7–21c).

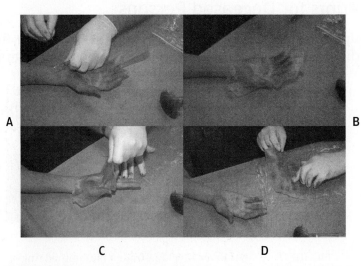

A
B
C
D

FIGURE 7–21 Recovering a palm print using overlapping latent print tape and then placing tape on plastic bag to view properly.

Burned Body

It is possible to obtain prints from a burned body simply by having another person work with you (this can be done alone, but is much more difficult to manage) who holds paper towels around the digit to soak up the body fluid that comes from the burned area. The paper is removed and then powered very rapidly, after which the latent print tape is applied as described previously and quickly removed. The tape is then placed on the acetate just as quickly. This method produces better quality prints than using ink. The skin can also be treated with acetone as in the decomposed body procedures described earlier.

If the burned area is dry and brittle, photography is used with oblique lighting, and then you can use silicone to mold the ridge characteristics. Be very careful not to press too hard as you can destroy the skin. It is sometimes better to remove the outer layer of burned skin and print what is beneath. These techniques are used on a case-by-case basis after careful evaluation. Always photograph first, and if you are not confident with the techniques, then you can always request assistance from someone with the right experience.

To Soften the Skin

1. Soak the finger in dishwashing liquid for a period of time determined by checking the finger every few hours until it softens. It can then be printed by either the ink or the powder method.
2. Should this procedure fail, the fingers can be soaked in a 1% to 3% solution of sodium hydroxide or potassium hydroxide. Care must be taken with this procedure to not destroy the tissue, because these are destructive in nature. Another important factor is that these procedures are hazardous and should be conducted in a fume hood to avoid inhalation of the caustic fumes.
3. The fingertip can also be carefully thinned from the rear with a scalpel until the skin can be pressed between two pieces of glass, and then photographed with a camera and lighting from the sides or the rear, based on experimentation to get the best contrast.

Latent Prints from Human Skin

There are several different methods used to recover latent prints from human skin, including using silver plates, photographic film, bromide photo paper, and superglue. Each of these has had some success, but limited at best. There may not be a "best method." The latent prints recovered from human skin included in this book were processed with standard black fingerprint powder that was dusted on the skin surface of the abdomen. Three latent prints were visualized and photographed. Two prints were successfully lifted using standard fingerprint tape (Figures 7–22a, 7–22b). At the 2004 IAI Educational Conference in St. Louis, Missouri, a presentation was

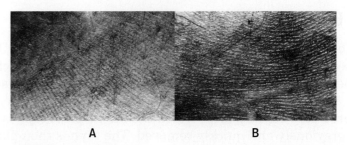

FIGURE 7–22   Latent fingerprints from human skin. (A) A two-dimensional and (B) a patent print (three-dimensional). Both were recovered from the abdominal area of the same decedent.

made in which 67 cases of latent prints were documented as having been recovered from human skin. Of these, 40% were recovered using the direct (traditional) method, 16% were recovered using chemical methods, and 12% were recovered using superglue. Also, 60% of the prints recovered were palm or partial palm prints.[2] For this reason, the use of the traditional method is suggested here. Superglue is hazardous and cannot be used on live persons. Chemical methods are also problematic for the same reason.

Chemical Processing for Latent Prints

Processing evidence for latent fingerprints follows a hierarchical process shown in a chart provided by the Armor Forensics/Lightening Fingerprint Company (see Figure 7–1), available from their catalog and at the Forensic Academy and Association meetings. It is highly recommended it be kept in the laboratory as a reference.

Processing evidence for the presence of latent prints often includes methods requiring chemical reagents. There are obviously two ways by which you can acquire these chemical reagents. If your agency has a laboratory or access to one, it is possible to have them mixed for you. The advantage to this method is that you always have fresh chemicals and can mix them as required. The problem with this method is that some courts require the chemist mixing the reagents appear in court to describe the process. The second method is to buy the reagents already mixed, or at least the basic stock solutions. Although this method is more expensive and requires you to have a specific amount on hand, along with the fact that many of these have a fairly short shelf life, you have the advantage of not having to produce the chemist, in most cases. It is definitely an advantage for smaller agencies and private companies to use the commercial route.

In this section, we discuss the process and source for each method, with the hope that smaller agencies understand the true value to using

---

[2]WILLIAM C. SAMPSON, KAREN L. SAMPSON, and LORENE MORE, "Recovery of Fingerprint Evidence from Human Skin." Lecture, IAI Educational Conference, 2004.

chemical processes and make use of them properly, thereby solving more cases in the end.

We discuss the most oftenly used processes, although there are many more, and it is suggested that you obtain either the *Processing Guide for Developing Latent Prints,* published by the FBI and revised in 2001, or the *Scene of Crime Handbook of Fingerprint Development Techniques,* which is abridged from the *Manual of Fingerprint Development Techniques* (Scientific Research and Development Branch of the Home Office, London, England). These books list the formulae as well as how to use them and in what order. They belong in every fingerprint office.

As a general rule, all examinations should start with a visual inspection, followed by examination for ***fluorescence***. These are nondestructive in nature and therefore can be used in all cases. For this section on chemicals, we assume you have already conducted the visual and fluorescence inspection and begin each one at the next step.

Any prints discovered should be photographed. For smaller agencies, you might want to use the blue light and/or a xenon variable frequency light source. The former is extremely cheap and the latter a few thousand dollars, but the variable frequency makes it a better purchase than a laser, as a general rule. Fluorescence should be conducted after each use of fluorescent dyes and DFO (1, 8-Diazafluoren-9-One).

Disposal of Chemicals

Please remember that along with using these chemical processes goes the responsibility and requirements for properly disposing of the chemicals. Observe all environmental requirements, including federal, state, and local regulations.

Chemical Sources

There are many chemicals used in the development of latent prints, and they can be purchased from supply houses, such as Armor Forensics/Lightening Fingerprint Company, Kinderprint, Lynn Peavey Company, and Sirchie Fingerprint Laboratories, Inc. Company. If your agency has a laboratory or access to one, they know where to purchase their chemicals. An advantage to buying from supply houses is that they are often premixed or partially mixed. This means you have little or no mixing to do, and what does have to be mixed is relatively simple. Appendix A provides a list of some of the supply sources for your convenience.

Safety

Always use these chemicals in a safe manner, using fume hoods, respirators, gloves, and/or any other necessary safety equipment. Some of these chemicals are carcinogenic, flammable, and explosive, among other safety concerns. Remember to ask for ***Manufacturers' Safety Data Sheets (MSDS)***. They are required and your staff must have access to them.

Follow all safety instructions as well as disposal procedures. Do not take shortcuts with these processes.

The following procedures are not all-inclusive. For more complete lists of procedures, please refer to the books mentioned earlier or to procedural charts provided by various supply houses, such as Lighting Powder Company's catalog. The following material may vary somewhat from those sources mentioned. The sources mentioned may also vary somewhat from source to source.

Smooth, Nonporous Surfaces[3]

1. *Cyanoacrylate* (superglue) **fuming**
2. Latent print powders
3. Dyes can be used. Among these are **sudan black** or **small particle reagent** (SPR)

Paper Products

1. If smooth or glossy, use fingerprint powder. (If not glossy, proceed to no. 2.)
2. *DFO*
3. *Ninhydrin*
4. *Physical developer*

Plastic and Cellophane

These containers seem to defy traditional powder techniques, but do react well to the magnetic powder.

1. Magnetic powder
2. Cyanoacrylate fuming (superglue)
3. Dye stains, such as **crystal violet** and **rhodamine 6G**.

Tape and Adhesive Surfaces

NOTE: A major problem when working with tape and other adhesive surfaces is that they are often stuck to something or themselves. **Un-Du** is an adhesive release agent that may be used to release the materials from the adhesive. It does not hurt the adhesive and it remains sticky after the chemical has evaporated. You can remove the item and then treat it as described here.[4] Simply allow this chemical to come in contact with a corner you have lifted slightly and then lift the tape away as you add more of the chemical (Figures 7–23a, 7–23b). If necessary, you can wet the paper from

---

[3]*Processing Guide for Developing Latent Prints,* FBI, rev. 2001, p. 6.
[4]M. Dawn Watkins and King C. Brown, "Make Your Case with Un-Du." Presentation at IAI Educational Conference, 2004.

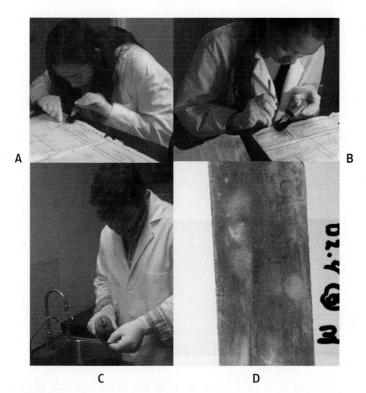

FIGURE 7–23   Using Un-Du to remove tape and recover latent prints on the sticky side of the tape. (A) and (B) removing tape. (C) Treating the sticky side with gentian violet. (D) Photo of the latent print recovered.

the back, allowing the chemical to penetrate the paper entirely. After the tape has been lifted, use a dye stain such as ***gentian violet*** (Figures 7–23c, 7–23d).

Nonadhesive Side

1. Superglue fuming (Do not superglue the sticky side. The tape should be attached to something during the process.)
2. ALS
3. Powder

Adhesive Side

Sticky-side powder or dye stain, such as gentian violet.

Wet Surfaces

Wet surfaces can be treated with ***molybdenum disulphide*** (small particle reagent, or SPR).

NOTE: If the object was touched *prior* to becoming wet, this technique works. It worked even in the rain. However, if the person handles the object *after* it has become wet, there is little to no chance that prints will be found.

SPR is mixed per instructions or used as a ready mix. It is simply sprayed onto the wet surface and then rinsed off with water or rain, as the case may be. This can be photographed and is lifted with standard latent print tape by drying a spot to one side of the print to stick the tape on. Then the tape is pushed over the surface and then lifted off and placed on a latent print card.

Raw Wood

1. Magnetic powder
2. ***Iodine fuming***
3. Ninhydrin
4. Physical developer

LATENT PRINT PROCESSES

Magnetic Powder

Magnetic powder comes in about as many variations as regular powder, including fluorescent and even black. Using the powder is very straight-forward. It is used on many different surfaces, but is outstanding on paper, raw wood, Styrofoam, and cellophane.

The powder is "brushed" with a magnetic brush or wand. The wand has a magnet inside and when it is dipped into the powder that contains metal filings, the powder sticks to the wand. A loose lump comes out and it is simply pulled over the area to bring out the print. The wand is then held over the powder container and the magnet release is pulled, allowing the powder remaining to fall into the container. The wand can be waved over the print to pick up any excess powder and it is also put back into the container. As you can see, this is a very neat and clean way to process latent prints.

TIP: When picking up the magnetic powder, it comes out as a loose clump, for lack of a better term. Pull the end of this lightly over the search area. Do not allow the wand to touch the surface, as this may damage your latent print.

TIP: Magnetic powder should not be left in the vehicles, especially in a humid climate. Remember, the powder consists partially of metal filings. If this is left in a vehicle, you will have a lump of rust within a short period of time.

Sticky-Side Powder

Sticky-side powder is very simple to make. It is also simple to use. The sticky side of the tape is subjected to having the powder brushed on the glue surface; after 1 minute, it is flushed gently with cold water. This process can be repeated.

Solution One
1. One teaspoon of standard black powder in a Petri dish.
2. Liqui-Nox liquid detergent is mixed 50:50 with water.
3. Mix the two items until you have a slurry mixture (about like pancake batter).
4. Using a camel hair brush, paint the solution on the tape and rinse.

Solution Two
1. One teaspoon of gray powder in a Petri dish.
2. Photo-Flo solution.
3. Combine the first two items in the Petri dish until you get a loose, pancake-like batter.
4. Using a camel hair brush, paint the solution on the glue; after about 1 minute, rinse gently with cold water. You can repeat as necessary.

Superglue (Cyanoacrylate Ester)

Equipment Needed
- A 10–15 gallon aquarium with a wood, plastic, or glass solid (nonvented) top. You can make this yourself.
- Cyanoacrylate ester (superglue) that can be purchased in the usual tubes or in bulk containers of about 1 pound from suppliers.
- Coffee-cup warmer
- Aluminum to put glue in for heating.
- Various chemicals and reagents for developing latent prints. (Again, we discuss this in detail later in the chapter.)

Superglue is one of the most often used "special techniques." There are various methods for processing superglue, but all have in common the need for a fuming chamber. A 10- or 15-gallon aquarium is ideal for this purpose, and certainly a lot less expensive than some of the other options. It should have a top of glass or Plexiglas or even plywood is appropriate. A good, heavy glass cut to fit is great and can be drilled with a ceramic bit to take a handle. The fuming tank should have a venting apparatus or be used in a fume hood certified for that use. It must be vented after use, and the fumes are hazardous. Do not open the top and breathe the fumes.

A method for heating the glue is also needed. There are fuming wands available today for this purpose, but here are a few substitutions. One method is to have a 40-watt light bulb in the tank and place an inverted paint can over the bulb. The bulb heats the can and you can use some aluminum foil to make a small dish in which to place the glue. You can also buy ready-made dishes from supply houses. Still another method to heat the glue is by chemical reaction. This is good in the field where you might not have electricity. Cotton pads that have been soaked in sodium hydroxide can be placed on the foil and the glue poured directly on the pad. This immediately begins to fume. Still another method is to use a coffee warming plate (the kind you use on your desk) to heat the glue.

Humidity is also needed, and if you do not have an apparatus for this, a dish of water in the fuming tank suffices. Of course, a steam iron provides its own humidity, and the best option is a humidifier attached to the tank.

The evidence is placed in the tank, either hung from clothes pins or something similar, and the items fumed. You must watch the progress in order to avoid overdeveloping the evidence. The fish tank is good for this, as you can see through the glass.

TIP: The tank builds up superglue residue. This must be cleaned off at regular intervals in order to avoid diminished effectiveness. This is easily done with a single-edge razor blade in a scraper handle. There is also a chemical cleaner available, but the scraper works very well.

TIP: To avoid buildup of superglue residue in the tank, clear plastic bags can be placed in the tank and simply removed as they become contaminated. These bags still allow you to see into the tank to observe your progress.

Safety

Fuming with superglue is not a technique to take lightly or carelessly. It should never be used on live persons. Your fuming tank must to be vented. If you use the portable tank, placing it in a fume hood is highly recommended. Avoid breathing any fumes.

Ninhydrin

Ninhydrin is a commonly used reagent that reacts to amino acids in the prints. It is used on porous surfaces such as non-glossy paper and is very effective. There are various formulae for this, but if your agency is not going to do a lot of work with it, you might want to consider ordering it premixed.

Ninhydrin comes in a spray bottle and can be sprayed or dipped, depending on the formula being used. The formula is important to consider, in that it can cause ink to run. It usually "flashes" or evaporates very rapidly.

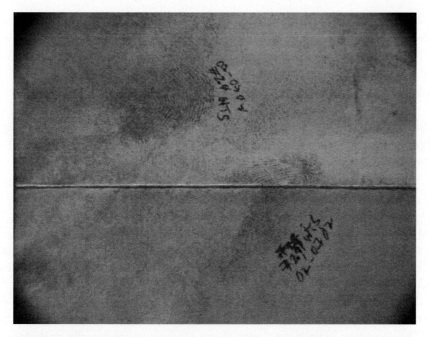

FIGURE 7–24 Latent fingerprints developed with ninhydrin. Note the evidence marks.

Procedure

The paper is either sprayed or dipped in a dish containing ninhydrin. It is removed immediately and hung in the fume hood to dry. It begins to show latent prints in about a day or so (Figure 7–24). Using a humidity chamber or iron to bring out the prints can speed this up. The prints show up purple and eventually fade, so they must be photographed.

TIP: If there is a need to speed up the process, an old steam iron is useful to heat the item as well as provide humidity. We say an "old" iron because the iron corrodes and cannot be used on clothing.

Safety

It is extremely important that ninhydrin be done in a fume hood. It is carcinogenic and causes irritation to the throat, not to mention turning your skin purple. Heavy, long gloves should also be worn and the evidence handled with forceps or something similar if it is not being hung in the chamber. The evidence will take a day or so to cure. Be patient.

DFO

DFO is also excellent for use on porous surfaces, and like ninhydrin, it reacts to amino acids. The prints developed with this process fluoresce when illuminated with a laser or other ALS.

DFO can be used by dipping or spraying and then dried using heat. A clothes iron can be used, but the steam feature should be turned off for this procedure. A humidity chamber can also be used.

Physical Developer

Physical developer (PD) is commonly used after treatment with either ninhydrin or DFO. It is very effective when used to develop latent prints on paper currency, and is a four solution process, as follows:

1. Maleic acid solution. The items are placed in this solution for about 5 minutes and then removed.
2. The specimens are then placed in a tray containing Redox solution combined, then the detergent solution, and then the silver nitrate solution. (These solutions are added in the order named here and stirred as each is combined.) The items remain in this tray for 5 to 15 minutes. The more specimens in the tray, the longer they take.
3. The specimens must be washed next in a water rinse to remove the excess chemicals that would otherwise result in the specimens becoming brittle.
4. The specimen is then air dried. It can be dried more rapidly with heat, such as a dry iron.

Dye Stains

There are various dye stains that are commonly used, and most can be either sprayed or the evidence dipped into a dish of the dye. Your specific conditions dictate which method to use. Simply place the dye in a Petri dish (or a larger container such as a casserole dish) and dip the evidence in the dye. Then rinse or flush with water or methanol, depending on the specific dye stain used. The directions with your specific product should advise you what should be done.

Some stains react immediately and provide you with a result that can be photographed. Still others may be fluorescent and require an ALS and photography of the prints for collection. The photography portion is discussed in Chapter 5.

Gentian Violet

Gentian violet is an excellent method of obtaining latent fingerprints from the sticky side of tape. It works on any of the various tapes. This is a particularly good process because the shelf life of the solution is indefinite.

Gentian violet is simple to use. It can be placed in a glass dish, such as a casserole dish, and the tape simply dipped into the dye and then rinsed off with water. Another method is to use a laboratory wash bottle to rinse the tape with the dye and then rinse the tape. Keep the used dye as it can be reused.

Solution

1. 1 gram gentian violet
2. 1000 mL distilled water
3. Combine the gentian violet with the distilled water, stir, and place in a dark bottle.
4. Pour as much as you need into a shallow dish and dip the tape in this dish. Let the tape remain in the dish for about 2 minutes, and then rinse it gently with cold water.
5. This solution can be reused.

Sudan Black

Sudan black is a good dye to use on surfaces that are greasy or oily. It will result in a blue–black image. Simply place the specimen in a glass tray for about 2 minutes, rinse with water, and allow the object to dry.

Solution

This is another solution that is convenient in that the solution has an indefinite shelf life.

1. 15 grams of Sudan black
2. 1000 mL ethanol
3. 500 mL distilled water
4. Combine the Sudan black and ethanol and stir. Then add the distilled water and agitate.
5. Place in a dark bottle.
6. Pour just enough solution to work.

There are other useful dyes, but for the purposes of this book, you are well advised to obtain them from a supplier. They are used in combination with ALS, and some require more complex mixing procedures.

◢▲ SUMMARY

Fingerprints are the most valuable form of evidence we have. It is the only form of evidence that is regularly individualized. This fact alone places fingerprints at the forefront of forensic science. Although it is not without controversy, it has withstood the challenges consistently.

The science of fingerprints is in constant flux, as are the other forensic sciences. With each forensic journal printed, new methods are discovered or improved. We can look forward to many breakthroughs in this discipline.

This chapter describes some techniques that are part of the laboratory side of crime scene investigation, but are included here because they are usually conducted by the CSI staff who are scientifically trained to do so.

▨■ REVIEW QUESTIONS

1. What is a fingerprint?
2. At what stage of life do fingerprints develop?
3. What is the most common method of obtaining known fingerprints?
4. What is the most common method of recovering latent fingerprints?
5. What is the major use for ninhydrin?
6. Name some of the health/safety concerns associated with fingerprint chemicals.
7. Briefly discuss the use of the magna brush and magna powder.
8. In a few words, describe one of the methods using superglue.

◆ REFERENCES AND SUGGESTED READING

T. KENT, ed. *Fingerprint Development Techniques.* Heanor Gate, Derbyshire, 1988.

Processing Guide for Developing Latent Prints. FBI Laboratory Publication, FBI, Washington DC. 2001.

The Science of Fingerprints: Classification and Uses. Federal Bureau of Investivation, U.S. Dept. of Justice, 1978.

Pattern Evidence

Key Terms

Impression evidence
Definitive markings
Gunshot residue (GSR)
Trace metal detection test (TMDT)
Tool marks
Weave pattern
Indented writing
Dental impression

INTRODUCTION/OBJECTIVES

There is a lot of overlap in forensic science, and **impression evidence** is a perfect example. Impression evidence is a form of pattern, as are fingerprints, shoe prints, tire prints, bite marks, tool marks, and *firearms*. The forensic community seems to break each down into a specialty, which makes sense from the standpoint of accountability and certification, but there has been discussion of making *pattern evidence* a specialty. Patterns are extremely important in forensics and critical to the crime scene investigator (CSI). Part of our discussion concerning "letting the scene talk to you" refers to patterns. What stands out as being missing, out of place, not belonging, and so forth? A lot of the ability to see patterns and apply meaning to them is developed through experience. After working cases over a period of years, one seems to gain the ability to notice these things and use them to their advantage. We hope you build an understanding of just what pattern evidence is and how you can use it to solve cases. Once you have the basic understanding, it is just a matter of experience.

CHAPTER 8

A unique characteristic of pattern evidence is that it often allows the examiner to identify the object to the exclusion of any other. This is our ultimate goal. Pattern evidence is much like putting a puzzle together. We look for the pieces that fit, as well as those pieces that do not fit, and the pieces that are missing; to include and exclude. They can all tell a story, if we understand how to read it. Like all forensic sciences, this overlaps into several other topics, such as fingerprints, impressions, blood, glass, and just about any physical evidence. It is very closely related to impression evidence, but deserves attention as a unique class of evidence.

DIRECT AND INDIRECT METHODS

Two methods are used when looking at pattern evidence. The first is the most common. This is simply putting the "puzzle pieces" in their respective places, as in putting together a broken window pane. The second method is quite rare, with possibly only one actual example of this method being used. In the Lindberg kidnapping case, wood from the ladder used at the Lindberg residence was matched to wood rafters in the attic of suspect Bruno Hauptman's residence. By looking at the grain (growth-ring patterns) on two pieces of wood, it was possible to project the probable pattern for the missing connecting piece.[1] Although this worked in the Lindberg case, it is advisable to be extremely careful with this sort of opinion testimony.

FIREARMS

Possibly no other subject can be associated with pattern evidence more than fingerprints, but next in line are firearms. Our concern in this text is the recovery of firearms and related evidence, with emphasis placed on their potential as physical evidence in our investigations. We proceed with the understanding that utmost safety precautions must be taken for all concerned.

It is also advisable that a certain protocol be worked out with your firearms examiner and serology unit prior to processing any firearms so that you have an understanding as to the order of processing that they desire. For example, some firearms examiners do not want you to unload the firearm or cycle it, and the serology unit may be concerned about blood and tissue that could have been ingested into the muzzle in a contact or near-contact shot.

External Examination

A firearm has the potential of providing some excellent fingerprints and must be examined carefully. It should be handled by the checkered portion

---

[1]R. Saferstein, *Criminalistics: An Introduction to Forensic Science.* Prentice Hall, Saddle River, NJ, 2004, p. 193.

of the *pistol grip* and similar areas on long arms. You cannot get prints from these areas. *Do not put anything into the muzzle of the firearm.* There is entirely too much evidence you can ruin by doing this. As just mentioned, in contact or near-contact wounds, blood and tissue is sometimes ingested into the muzzle. Also of concern is that the striations found on the bullet are imparted for the most part in the end 1 in. or less.

TIP: After recovery of prints on the firearm, you can use your fingerprint brush to dust the *serial number* and other markings on the firearm and then place these lifts in your notes or notebook. By following this procedure it can never be insinuated that you might have recorded the number incorrectly, because you have the actual impression. Likewise, the *cylinder* of a revolver can be dusted with the *cartridges* in it to record the order of cartridges, their *head stamps,* and if the *primers* show firing pin impact. This too can be attached to your notes.

Internal Examination

The internal examination covers several different topics that may or may not be done by the CSI. With a revolver, the firearm is unloaded after recording the *cylinder rotation* and placement of cartridges within the cylinder. The cartridges are each dusted. Cartridges in a revolver typically yield fingertip prints of the thumb, index, and middle fingers because this is a common way to hold the cartridges while loading them. On an automatic or semiautomatic *magazine,* one often finds the thumbprint as the result of the cartridge being inserted into the magazine.

By taking the firearm apart (determine whose responsibility this is) and processing the covered parts for fingerprints, maintenance of the object can be shown. By this we are referring to the *barrel* beneath the slide or on other internal parts of the firearm. This eliminates any claim of a suspect that his or her prints were placed on the firearm by simply picking it up. These can be very valuable prints for your case.

Patterns on Projectile and Cartridge

The *bore* of the firearm has rifling marks referred to as *lands* and *grooves* used to impart a spin on the projectile, thereby providing stability in flight. Individual firearms have a distinct number of lands and grooves as well as a direction and rate of twist. Remember, they are imparted as a mirror image, the lands in the barrel are grooves on the projectile; likewise, the grooves in the barrel are lands on the projectile. These are *class characteristics* that aid in the identification of the firearm. Identification is also aided by the more **definitive markings** made in the barrel as the result of fouling by bits of lead, copper, and other debris from the firing process (Figure 8–1). These markings can be definitive in nature, which is why we do not want anything placed into the *muzzle* of the firearm. It is the last ¾ in. or so of the bore that imparts the majority of

FIGURE 8–1   Revolver being fired. Note projectile, burning powder, soot, smoke, and flame, all of which leave gunshot residue (GSR). (Photo Courtesy of the FBI Laboratory, Washington, DC.)

these marks on the projectile, and anything placed in the bore to pick up the firearm can alter these marks. As a matter of interest, placing something in the muzzle and picking up the firearm is not only terribly wrong, it is extremely awkward, because the full-size firearm is very heavy when lifted in this manner.

The firearm also leaves many other patterns on the cartridge and/or projectile.

- Be aware that it is possible to have the magazine lip marks on the cartridge cases as it has slid in or out of the magazine.

FIGURE 8–2   View of a rifle bolt. Note the orifice for the firing pin, which is retracted here.

FIGURE 8-3 Breech face or bolt face.

- Also know that the ***firing pin*** (Figure 8–2) on a firearm can leave a unique signature, so this must be preserved undamaged.
- When an automatic or semiautomatic firearm cycles, it pushes a cartridge from the magazine into the chamber, which can leave ***chamber marks***.
- Likewise, at the moment of discharge, when the cartridge is blown back on the breech face for recycling, a ***breech-face*** or ***bolt-face signature*** (Figure 8–3) can be impressed into the primer. Again, this is a unique signature.
- As the ***bolt*** travels rearward, an ***extractor*** (Figure 8–4) hooks the lip or rim of the cartridge casing, thereby leaving its signature on the inside of the rim.
- At the rear-most point of travel of the bolt, an ***ejector*** (Figure 8–5), which may be as simple as a small protrusion from the bolt, ejects the casing from the firearm. Again, this also leaves its unique marking on the cartridge casing.

Remember that the items discussed here leave their marks on either the projectiles or the spent cartridge casings that are often found at the scene. Take care in recovering and preserving them to protect this valuable evidence.

FIGURE 8-4 Rifle bolt showing the extractor.

FIGURE 8–5 Rifle bolt showing the ejector.

Patterns on Target or Shooter

A muzzle held in close contact with the body or a cloth can impart the muzzle design in soot and singeing on the surface. This can sometimes be clear enough to identify the specific kind of handgun responsible for the markings.

Sometimes the size, pattern, and number or pellets making penetration can tell us a lot. For example, a circular pattern of nine .32-caliber pellets can indicate 12-gauge .00-buck shotgun round. The same kind of information can be learned from the shot cup (Figure 8–6) or wadding from a shotgun round. Be careful about making these judgments.

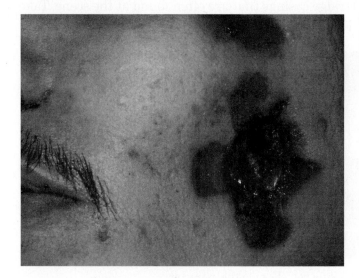

FIGURE 8–6 A close-range shooting. Note the "wings" of the shot cup from shotgun.

When shot at close range, the target, a person, clothing, and other objects may have patterns that consist of burned and unburned powder, burns, and other residue in the target. This is commonly referred to as *tattooing* or *stippling.* Be sure that the subject's clothing is recovered, along with anything else that might bear the pattern. On dark or bloody clothing, this may not be readily visible, but it can be brought out chemically or by x-ray. When recovering the clothing, do not just crumple it up and throw it in a bag. It should be placed flat on paper and then covered with paper and taken to the laboratory for drying and processing. If the exact firearm is recovered, it is possible for the crime lab to determine the distance from which the object was shot.

Also in shooting cases the shooter may have *primer residue,* also known as **gunshot residue (GSR)** on his/her hands. This residue consists of barium, lead, and antimony. The hands should be bagged with paper bags that can simply be sealed at the wrists with tape. Do not allow the possible shooter to use the hands to relieve himself or herself, because an old trick among "con-wise" suspects was to urinate on their hands in order to defeat these tests. This was very common when the dermal nitrate (paraffin) test was still in use.

TIP: A police officer or anyone who is armed or works with firearms should not administer the primer residue tests. These tests include *atomic absorption analysis (AAA), neutron activation analysis (NAA),* or sampling for *scanning electron microscopy (SEM)*. Remember that these persons are most likely contaminated because their holsters and other equipment are contaminated from wearing the equipment for practice and qualification shooting and other related activities. Avoid cross contamination at all costs.

Trace Metal Detection Test

The **trace metal detection test (TMDT)** consists of a reagent (8-hydroxiquenilene) in isopropanol. The test is rather simple to perform, but the results are not always used to their ultimate advantage. The TMDT is sprayed on a person or an item, such as a clothing pocket, and if there was a metal object in contact with that surface for any time, it may provide positive results. "Positive results" is somewhat debatable in that just showing trace metal may be of no real value to the successful investigation of your case. There are many reasons a person may test positive for trace metal. Where this test is really valuable is with patterns. For this reason, the traditional testing of the hands is not always that productive. Even if a person held a gun, it may not have been long enough to establish metal traces. It is often very successful with patterns in a person's pockets, where a gun may have been carried for an extended period. Another place a person may carry a gun is in their pant waistband. In this location, the firearm is held tight to the body and can therefore provide a very clear image of the firearm (Figures 8–7a, 8–7b).

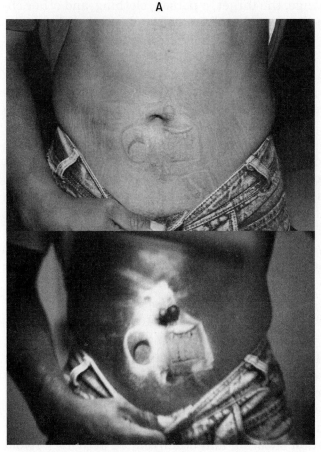

FIGURE 8–7 (A) An impression on a male's stomach showing where he carried a pistol. (B) The image brought out with the TMDT process.

Necessary Equipment
- Shortwave ultraviolet light (Woods lamp)
- Spray bottle
- TMDT solution, which can be purchased from supply houses

Procedure
1. Spray lightly the surface you want to test. Allow it to dry, then spray another coat (or two), allowing each coat time to dry.
2. Use the shortwave ultraviolet light to illuminate the surface in total darkness.
3. The image should appear and be one of several colors, supposedly relating to the type of metal it represents. It is hoped that you see a pattern you can distinguish.

Recording TMDT Results

Necessary Equipment
- Camera with adjustable shutter speed
- Tripod
- Cable release (shutter release)
- Flash

Procedure

1. The object must be steady (still).
2. Spray the object.
3. Illuminate with shortwave ultraviolet light.
4. Focus the camera on the object (this can be done earlier with the light on).
5. Set the flash on its minimum power, or cloth can be placed over the flash to cut back on light.
6. Using shutter release, shoot the object with 400 ISO color film. Set the shutter on time or "bulb" so that it stays open. Lock the shutter in the open position.
7. After flash has gone off and without closing the camera lens, carefully open the aperture to its widest opening. Leave open for 1 minute.
8. Bracket the photo one step up and one step down.

Tool Marks on Firearms

As in the case of firearms, tools impart their signatures on surfaces with which they come into contact. As a matter of fact, **tool marks** are the reason firearms and their assorted paraphernalia leave so many individualizing marks. For example, it is the grinding of the bolt's face that results in the breech face signature.

Obliterated Serial Numbers on Firearms

Before we leave firearms, we must address a very important aspect of pattern evidence as related to firearms: the ground-off serial number of a gun. When the serial number is imparted on a gun, it changes the structure of the metal, and as a result, even though the serial number has been ground off, it is still often possible to restore the number. This is accomplished by a fairly simple procedure, as follows:

1. Clean and degrease the surface. Remove any paint.
2. File the surface until it is smooth and polished. Care must be taken if using a motorized polisher that heat is not generated, which might change the molecular structure of the metal. It is best not to use these devices.
3. Etching is accomplished with either gel or liquid reagents. These may be specific to certain metals if you are using a commercial kit, such as the Sirchie number restoration kits. When using these kits, be careful to follow the directions very carefully.
4. Build a clay dam around the area where the serial number was removed. Put the reagent, such as Turner's solution, within the dam's center. Watch the process very carefully so that the process can be stopped at the proper time.
5. An electric charge can be used to accelerate the process, and once again these are available such as the Sirchie unit. Again, follow the instructions included with the unit.
6. In any case, after etching has been completed, you must neutralize the acid. Photograph the restored number, and this would be a good time to use the fingerprint-tape lift method to recover an impression of the actual number, if possible.

TOOL MARKS

Firearms and tool marks are considered a specific discipline, and rightly so. They are examined in the same way. Tool mark evidence is unique, and it can make a case under the right circumstances. Let's look at some examples of tool mark evidence that are commonly found at a crime scene, and then briefly consider how the evidence is examined in order to make the relationship and process clear. Some of the commonly recovered tool marks are

- Doorknobs that have been broken by using slip-joint or water-pump pliers
- Doorknobs that have been broken with a plumber's or pipe wrench
- Cashboxes pried open with a screwdriver or similar tool

    TIP: Sometimes the blades break, and a portion of the blade might remain at the scene. The fracture point is a unique pattern in itself. Look for these portions of broken tools.

- Doorjams broken by prying with a crowbar or wrecking bar
- Wire may have the signature of the plate orifice it was extruded from during manufacture
- Wire cut with wirecutters, electrician's pliers, or other similar tools can be compared with the tools
- Fencing and lock hasps cut with a bolt cutter can be compared with the tool (Figure 8–8).

There are many other ways to determine tool marks and their evidence, and you can use your imagination to add to this list. How do we address

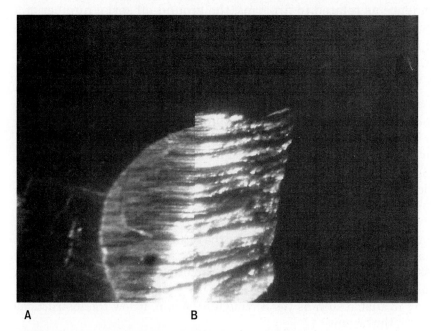

A   B

FIGURE 8–8   Photomicrograph. This image is viewed with a comparison microscope. (A) A piece of chain-link wire. (B) The bolt-cutter blade that cut the wire.

the evidence? Again, there is a hierarchy in the recovery and documentation process. Consider the following:

- Always photograph the entire door or other object of attack. Then take close-up photographs of the damage. These should include ***photomacrographs*** (not to be confused with ***photomicrographs***, which would be taken by the examiner through the microscope) where possible, although this can be accomplished in the field if necessary, but are best done in the laboratory.

- Cast or mold the damage with a silicone-type casting material, such as Mikrosil or other dental silicone. These casts can be very useful to the tool-mark examiner.

- Recover the article. If it is a doorknob, remove the entire knob and submit it. It is of no value to the victim; it's broken.

- If it is a door jam, it can be cast and then that portion cut out and submitted to the laboratory. Striker plates on the door jam can simply be unscrewed and sent to the lab.

- If the door was kicked open, do not forget about shoe marks (Figure 8–9). These may be found on walls or doors that have been kicked in.

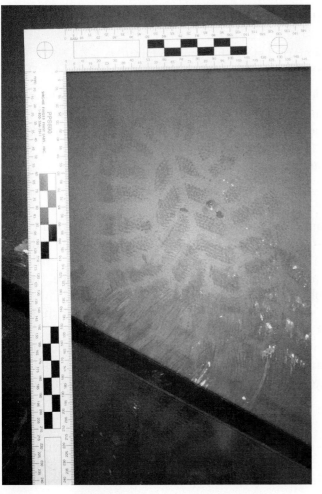

FIGURE 8–9 Image of a shoe print on a glass door.

- If the tool has been recovered, submit it to the lab and make sure it has been processed for latent prints.

When the laboratory receives the evidence, it goes through the processes we have described if you have not completed them already. The photographs, casts, and actual damaged materials can be compared with the suspect tools, if located.

A good material to use for this is Mikrosil or Permlastic by Kerr. These are very easy to use and provide extremely detailed impressions of the tool marks. They can be used on both horizontal and vertical surfaces. This two-part mixture is simple to use.

Necessary Equipment

- *Mikrosil,* which consists of two tubes, one of catalyst and one of base material
- *Spatula,* which can be a tongue depressor or other flat object
- *Mixing tray,* which can be a piece of cardboard, plastic, or glass

Procedure

1. Squeeze out equal portions of catalyst and base material. Use enough to cast the area you desire.
2. Mix the material on the mixing board with the spatula until you obtain a uniform color.
3. Spread on desired tool mark. Let dry for about 5 minutes.
4. Recover by lifting off the impression. Place in a safe container.

The tool suspected of making the tool mark or impression should be recovered and packaged in a manner that does not damage the marking surface. It should then be transmitted to a crime laboratory, where standards can be made for comparison. This should not be attempted by anyone other than a tool-mark examiner.

Other Surfaces

Impressions are often found in window putty, partially dried paint, and many other substances that allow for such impressions. These impressions can be recovered in the same manner as tool marks using Mikrosil or similar silicon-type material. As with all types of this evidence, the impression should first be photographed with and without a scale. The extra effort you take with this evidence pays off in many ways, the ultimate of which is reaching a successful solution of the case.

A common method used for an exemplar is to slide the tool over a sheet of lead, thereby producing the tool's unique signature, and then comparing it with the damaged material under a comparison microscope.

GLASS

Glass provides valuable evidence because we come in contact with it so often. We use glass for containers, windows, filters, reflectors, mirrors, and so on. Glass can fit in to many different "class" groups, such as clear glass, optical-quality glass, window glass, tempered glass, or safety glass, each of which is a class characteristic that narrows down the parameters of the search, but unless we can put two pieces together, as in a broken glass, we cannot analyze it to the point of identification, individualization to the exclusion of all other existing pieces of glass in the world. If we were to analyze a piece or pieces of glass, we might look at it by asking certain questions, such as

- Can you place that piece of glass into the original source? Putting the puzzle together (Figure 8–10).
- Are the broken edges smooth? If so, this may be a ***thermal fracture*** that is the result of heat; however, it could be ***tempered glass*** (Figures 8–11a, 8–11b).
- Do the edges of the fractures exhibit L-shape curves, or ***hackle marks*** (Figure 8–12)? These are stress points that can indicate which surface of the glass the pressure originated from. For example, on the ***radial fracture***

FIGURE 8–10 This louver shows the typical meandering of a thermal fracture.

A

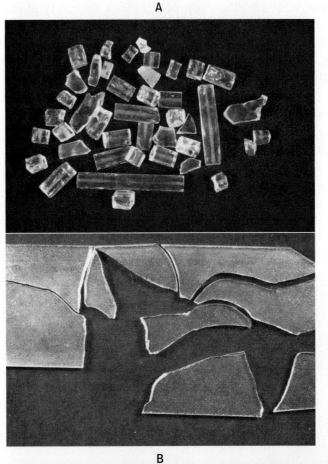

FIGURE 8–11   (A) Broken
safety glass. None of the
edges are sharp. (B) A thermal fracture in the process
of being reconstructed. Note
the lack of soot.

B

FIGURE 8–12   The edge of a piece of glass showing the stress marks that
can aid in determining from which side the force originated.

edges, the top portion of the L is perpendicular to the surface from which the force came. It is the opposite surface from that line.

- Do the fractures form a "spiderweb" pattern of *radial* and **concentric fractures** (Figure 8–13)? This is an indication that the fracture is mechanical in nature.
- If this is a bullet hole, the smaller hole is the entry and the larger crater is the exit. (Incidentally, this is also true of the human skull.)
- It is possible to determine order of penetration because fracture lines do not cross existing fracture lines. If a fracture line stops at another fracture line, then it came after.
- Is the glass broken into small, fairly uniform rectangular pieces with no indication of hackle marks? This is tempered glass, and determination of force is difficult. This glass is also capable of being rolled in the hand without cutting you as it is a safety glass, *but it is not advisable to test it in this manner.*
- When you observe glass in a fire scene, is the soot baked on? If so, it was most likely a slow moving fire. If, however, the soot is readily wiped off the glass, then you have a fast moving fire and should look for an accelerant.
- Does the fracture just meander instead of spiderweb, as in a **mechanical fracture**? This is possibly a **thermofracture**, also known as a **heat fracture**.
- A broken window at a fire scene may imply that someone broke into the building. Determine if the window was broken from the inside or outside. Burglars break into a building and leave by the easiest method, which is usually the door. A window broken from the inside might imply the window was broken to make the fire seem to be the work of a burglar. This fire could be for insurance purposes or any number of other reasons.

FIGURE 8–13 A typical mechanical glass fracture on a car windshield with laminated glass.

Cloth

Cloth and other woven material can vary in its levels of value. Cloth has a specific **weave pattern** and *thread count* in some instances, and even the color of the material may have a specific indicator or *dye number.* These are class characteristics of value. In one case, a police officer was investigating a case when a motorist passed by, striking the officer and then fleeing the scene. The officer made contact with the front fender and broke off the car antenna. The side mirror of the vehicle then hit the officer. There were several pieces of valuable evidence left behind as well as taken away, as explained by the Locard principle. The car fled, leaving behind

- Broken car radio antenna
- Chrome bezel from the antenna base
- Paint that flaked off the fender

The car also took away

- The weave pattern of the uniform
- *Fibers* from the uniform
- Black dye from the leather gear

These individual pieces of evidence can be examined in different ways:

- The broken radio antenna can be matched via fracture marks to the base remaining on the car.
- The chrome bezel can be matched to the impression left on the fender.
- The flaked paint might be matched to fracture patterns on the fender. The paint might also be linked to the car by instrumental analysis. This might be unique, if the paint was not factory paint.
- The uniform was custom made—a standard practice for the agency at that time—and all uniforms were therefore made with the same cloth, weave, thread count, and dye number. All of these things were class characteristics for the material used by the tailor.

Another example of *fabric pattern analysis* involved the investigation of a serial bomber. He made a series of pipe bombs and used material torn from a bed sheet for wadding in each of the bombs. Because the bombs did not destroy the material completely, it was later matched by tear patterns with the remainder of the sheet, which was located in his house (Figure 8–14).

Transmittal to Lab

Because tool-mark evidence can be damaged if not handled properly, it is critical that you package this evidence with extra care. The surfaces should be padded with paper, cardboard, or cloth and the tool placed in a box. Bubble wrap offers excellent protection for such evidence.

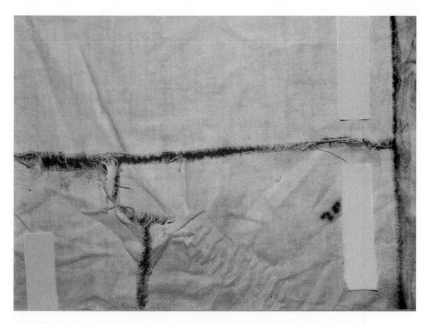

FIGURE 8–14 These pieces of cotton originated from the same sheet. Each was used as wadding in pipe bombs.

DOCUMENTS

Documents fall under the general category of pattern evidence and impression evidence as well. Documents are common at crime scenes, and care should be taken in searching for as well as recovering and protecting them. When you recover documents, you must take care to avoid any contamination that would limit or destroy the ability to analyze it. Some of the examinations possible are

- **Indented writing** that results from both the pressure of the writing instrument, such as a pen or pencil, or that from the printing device, such as a typewriter or printer (Figure 8–15)

  TIP: Be aware that the impression often penetrates one or more pages, and therefore you may have a tablet with nothing written on it, but subjecting it to analysis by an ***electrostatic detection apparatus (ESDA)*** to bring out indented writing, you may end up with valuable evidence.

  TIP: Always complete your evidence envelope prior to placing the evidence in it. A well-meaning officer can place document evidence in an evidence envelope, and then complete the information required on the envelope. Now, that information is part of the document contained therein.

  TIP: If you do not have access to an ESDA, you can sometimes use oblique lighting to bring out indented writing, which can then be photographed.

- ***Ink analysis*** that can indicate alterations, obliterations, and other modifications to a document
- ***Instrument analysis***, such as the copy machine or printer producing the document.

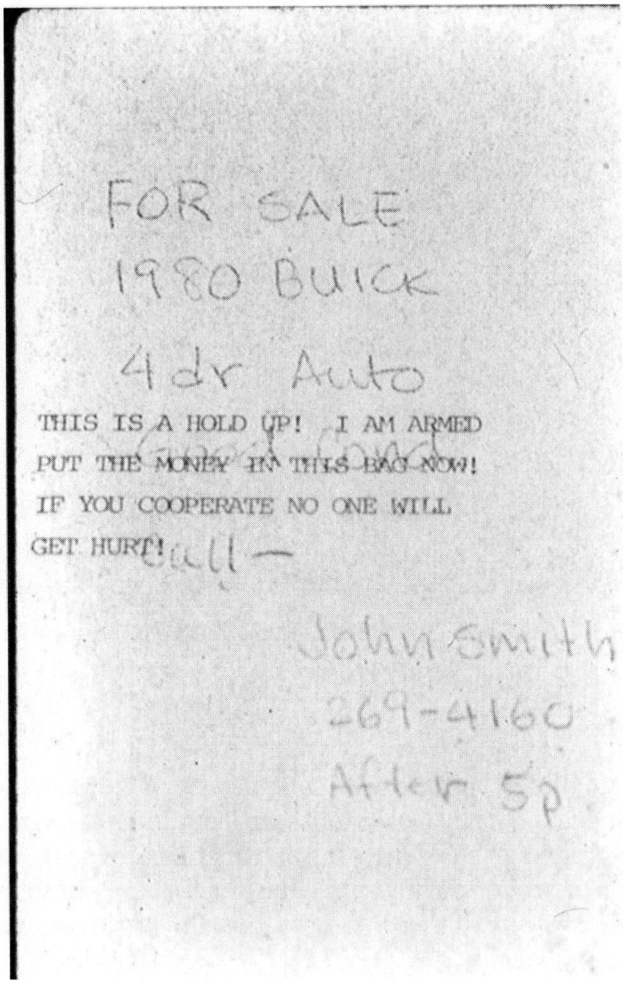

FIGURE 8–15   A copy of a hold-up note with indented writing brought out by an electrostatic detection apparatus (ESDA). The indented writing is a note advertising the sale of a car.

- **_Writing style_** that is often unique. There are still many people who use specific writing/printing styles, such as the once taught **_Palmer Method_**. There are some persons who prefer to write with a fountain pen, whereas others might prefer a felt-tip pen. These persons differ from the vast majority who write with a ballpoint pen or some variant.

Burned Documents

Documents may sometimes be burned. If the document is still in one piece or large pieces where printing can still be seen, it is possible to recover these (Figure 8–16a). One method is to use spray lacquer to solidify the ashes. Simply get a can of spray (aerosol) clear lacquer. (Do not get enamel or polyurethane, because they dry slowly.) The method is as follows:

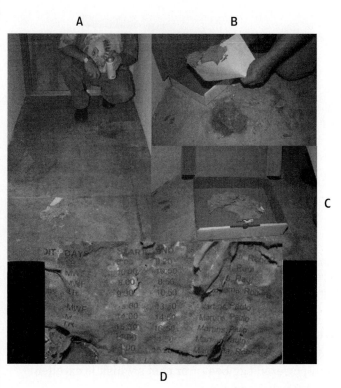

A   B

C

D

FIGURE 8–16 (A) Burned paper on the floor. It is sprayed with lacquer to stabilize the ash. (B) Removal of the ash, which is put into a box. (C, D) The ash from the burned paper. The contents of the document are easily read.

1. Spray the lacquer over the ashes, spraying parallel to the plane on which the ashes are positioned (Figure 8–16b). The spray should be a short burst at about 20 in. above the document. The lacquer settles as a light mist over the document and dries rapidly. It "flashes" where you can see the vapors leave.
2. After the lacquer has flashed, repeat this procedure. *Do not rush. Do not spray directly down onto the object.*
3. After you have put several coats on the document, you can gently lift it and place in a box or other suitable container (Figures 8–16c, 8–16d). It is then covered and transported to the laboratory for analysis. You must be very careful not to jar the container. Several coats are far better than one or two. Provide enough body to the ashes to prevent it from collapsing.

TIRE PRINTS

Tire prints are one of the common types of impression evidence we come across. They are found in different physical environments, such as sand, dirt, mud, and concrete (Figure 8–17). Many of these can be cast for recovery and comparison purposes. Prior to any attempt to cast prints (or any impression, for that matter), photography of the impression must be completed both with and without a measuring device. Photographs should include location reference photos, identification photos, and examination quality photos where possible. Use of an L-shape ruler, such as the ABFO #2 ruler, but larger. These are also available from forensic equipment supply houses.

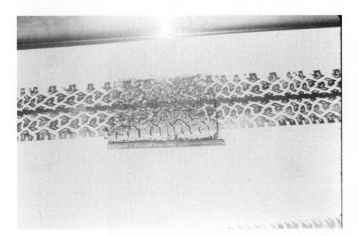

FIGURE 8–17   An inked tire exemplar. A transparency of a plaster cast from a homicide scene is placed over it to show the match. There is a scale in the image of the cast to enable its being enlarged to 1:1 ratio.

Necessary Equipment

- Mixing container—nylon mixing bowl that is easy to clean
- Measuring container, such as kitchen measuring cup
- Stirring device—a hand-powered egg beater or chef's whisk is excellent
- Water container (at least 2 gallons in size)
- Casting frame—aluminum is very versatile
- Casting material—dental stone appears to be better than plaster of paris
- Spray lacquer or hair spray

TIP: Dental stone comes in a 25-lb box. It is a good idea to place 2 lbs of material in large zip-top bags for easy use and eliminate the mixing bowl. You can just add water to the bag, seal it, and then squeeze the bag repeatedly to mix the contents, after which you pour directly from the bag (Figure 8–18). The material can also be mixed in a mixing bowl. Use the chef's whisk to mix the material. Either way, mix it well.

TIP: When mixing the material, add the material to water, and not water to the material. It is helpful to stir with the whisk or egg beater as the material is poured into the water. You want the consistency of pancake batter.

Once the material is mixed, pour the mix over the impression being cast. Do not pour directly onto the print. Break the fall of the material with something like a putty knife to avoid collapsing your pattern.

After the cast has dried to the early stages of a solid mass, use something like a pencil or scribe to mark the cast with your evidence mark, as well as the date, report number, and cast number. It is helpful to use the putty knife to smooth the surface prior to inscribing information.

Do not wash the cast after it has been removed (Figure 8–19). Let it dry for 1–2 days, and then you can use a fairly soft brush to remove any dirt. Be careful not to damage the print. The cast should be removed from

FIGURE 8–18 The first pour of plaster in a shoe impression. Gauze is placed in the plaster to reinforce it. A second pour completes the cast. If dental stone is used, the reinforcement is not required.

the scene. You should also recover soil samples from under the impression and from the general area around the impression for analysis.

If the impression is in very fine dirt or fine sand, it is advisable to first mist the print with a fixative such as hairspray or lacquer. Do not spray directly at the impression. Spray the lacquer parallel over the impression, allowing the mist to gently fall on the impression. Several coats can be made using this method, after which the pattern is stable and capable of holding up to plaster casting material.

Casts should be stored in a cardboard box or some other protective container. It is also a good idea to photograph and print the cast in 1:1 ratio for comparison purposes. It can also be made into a transparency for overlay comparison.

Exemplars

If the tire or shoe that possibly made the print is available, it should be recovered. If the party is not willing to provide the item, then you should consider seeking court action for their recovery. The tire or shoe should be photographed in the manner previously discussed for tire and shoe impressions. Then one of two methods can be used to print the tire. The vehicle can be jacked up and the tire inked with standard fingerprint ink. The car is lowered so that the wheel is on a piece of white poster board or similar material and then rolled forward to record the entire circumference of the tire tread pattern. The tire should remain on the vehicle to allow the tire to be "under load," thereby providing a realistic pattern. Another method is to use latent print powder instead of ink and have the car roll over a plastic or Mylar film to record the prints. Be sure to indicate the time, date, location, and case classification of case, along with report number and your evidence identification mark. Please note that we said to print the entire circumference of the tire.

FIGURE 8–19   The cast of a shoe print.

This is very important, because the impressions you recover at a scene match the subject tire in only one place. The pattern, although appearing the same, actually varies completely around the circumference of the tire. This is a result of the attempt to eliminate "road noise" when the tire is rolling.

SHOE PRINTS

Shoe prints may be two dimensional, such as on paper, cardboard, or in dust, or three dimensional such as in mud, sand, or dirt. Recovery methods vary with the circumstances.

During your investigations you sometimes come across shoe prints on walls or floors that are the result of muddy shoes. In these cases, photograph the print and then, if possible, remove the print by cutting out the wallboard (Figure 8–20).

For shoe print exemplars, a good source for impressions is a product known as Bio-Foam, which produces an extremely good replication of both

FIGURE 8–20 A shoe print on a wall that has been cut out and recovered as evidence. It took about 1 hour to determine the make and size of the shoe.

foot and shoe impressions by simply stepping into the box that contains the product (Figure 8–21).

Recovering shoe prints at a crime scene is done in the same manner as the tire print. Be aware that shoes, like tires, have distinct wear patterns. Where a tire print can indicate alignment, balance, and inflation characteristics, shoes can provide the examiner with information as to the walking style and condition, such as physical abnormalities, of the wearer.

Styrofoam

A case involving suspects who kicked holes in walls and otherwise damaged a building under construction left very good two-dimensional prints on the walls. Some prints were on sheets of Styrofoam that was used for packing material. These prints were photographed in place and then close-up

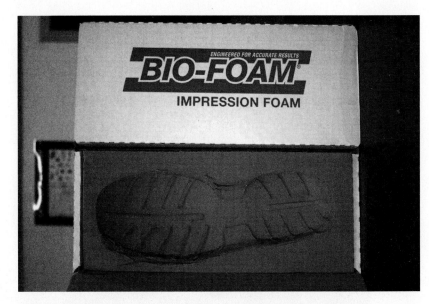

FIGURE 8–21 A Bio-Foam exemplar of a shoe-tread pattern.

photographs were taken with oblique light to enhance the three-dimensional pattern. The impressions were then cut out and placed in evidence.

FOOD WITH DENTAL IMPRESSIONS

At one time or another, you may come across food that has been bitten or partially eaten (Figure 8–22). You might come across a bite mark on a body as well. These are photographed and molded with Mikrosil or a similar material. There are some serious considerations however. Among them are

- Photograph the bite mark immediately.
- Photograph should be perpendicular to the mark and with oblique lighting to enhance the pattern.
- Photograph both with and without a scale.
- The food must be taken to a laboratory immediately. It should never be transported or stored in a hot vehicle or delayed in shipment.
- Some food, like candy, might melt, and the pattern can be lost.
- Cheese and similar foods shrink and alter patterns.
- Apples and other foods of that sort dry out or become moldy, thereby altering the pattern.
- If you cannot get the material to the laboratory within a reasonable time and preserved as needed, then you must cast the marks after photography.
- Cast the patterns with Mikrosil following the instructions provided earlier.
- Qualified medical staff, such as a dentist or an odontologist, should do casts on live persons.

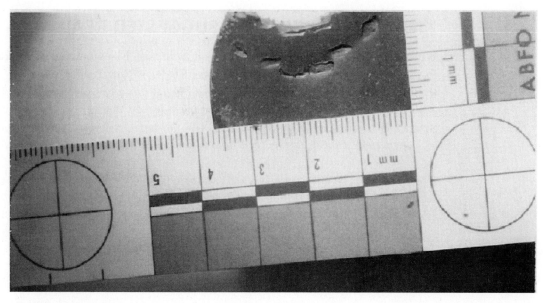

FIGURE 8-22

◤ SUMMARY

Pattern evidence encompasses and overlaps several specialties with forensic science. It involves patterns that are both two and three dimensional. Regardless of which specialty area we may be involved with, we are looking for the same result—*individualization*. Pattern evidence can be part of a *class characteristic* or an *individualizing characteristic*. To be successful in this field, you must strive to be very aware of patterns and their possibilities of being both similar or unique. You must understand light and how it can aid and hamper your investigation.

◼ REVIEW QUESTIONS

1. Briefly describe the process of casting a shoe print. Be specific.
2. What do we mean by the term *individualization?*
3. What can the *lands and grooves* on a projectile tell us?
4. What is the purpose of lands and grooves in a barrel?
5. Briefly describe how to recover a burned document.
6. Why do we always take one photograph of these patterns with a scale?
7. How do we handle food with teeth impressions?
8. Name two uses for lacquer spray.

◆ REFERENCES AND SUGGESTED READING

WILLIAM J. BODZIAK, *Footwear Impression Evidence.* Elsevier, New York, 1990.

PETER MCDONALD, *Tire Imprint Evidence.* Elsevier, New York, 1989.

RICHARD SAFERSTEIN, *Criminalistics: An Introduction to Forensic Science.* Pearson Prentice Hall, Upper Saddle River, New Jersey, 2004

STUART H. JAMES and JON J. NORDBY, eds. *Forensic Science: An Introduction to Scientific Investigative Techniques.* CRC Publishers, Baton Rouge, Florida, 2005.

HENRY C. LEE, TIMOTHY PALMBACH, and MARILYN T. MILLER, *Henry Lee's Crime Scene Handbook.* Academic Press, San Diego, California, 2001.

BARRY A. J. FISHER, *Techniques of Crime Scene Investigation.* CRC Press, Baton Rouge, Florida, 2004

Property Crime

Property crime is one of the most common offences investigated by police, and yet one of the most neglected cases with regard to evidence. Unless the crime involves an extreme amount of monetary loss, property crime does not seem to get much attention. Property crime involves a vast variety of possible scenarios, and that alone makes it a very interesting crime to investigate. Some of these crimes seem to have absolutely no reason for having been committed, whereas others are very obvious from the moment you see them. Regardless, they are important to the victim and deserve attention. The evidence is not really that different than that of other crimes, but there are some variations that we hope you become aware of after studying the following chapters.

Property crime related to graffiti is possibly one of the most costly, because it is so expensive to restore the property that has been vandalized, only to have it happen again. Some targets seem to have immense popularity and are subjected to repeated attacks. We must not look at only the damage, but must also look for the instrumentalities of the crime. It is often there that we find the answers and evidence we are looking for, such as paint cans with fingerprints on them.

Types of Property Crime

Key Terms

Vandalism
Method of operation (MO)
Signature
Graffiti
Extortion
Burglary

INTRODUCTION/OBJECTIVES

Property crime covers a wide variety of subject matter, but can be discussed in mostly general terms. Unfortunately, too many investigators look at property crime as being relatively unimportant in the overall scheme of things. This is far from true, because property crime can result in thousands or even hundreds of thousands of dollars in losses from a single incident. One case involved the investigation of a property crime in which about $250,000.00 (CD) damage was done to windows alone. The entire building, which was still under construction, ended up being demolished. We must give these crimes the attention they deserve. You should be able to look at the various types of property crime and determine just what kinds of evidence are most valuable to your investigation, and then take advantage of those items. Remember, you are looking for evidence that will eventually put a name to the object or damage.

VANDALISM

Vandalism is most often opportunistic in nature, making it more difficult to investigate. Vandalism involves damage done to property of another, which may be intentional to "get back" at someone, or it could be simply the culprit's desire to "tag" or put his or her "art" on property that may simply be what was available, with no ill intent. From the CSI standpoint we are looking not at the motive, but the **method of operation (MO)** of the perpetrators. It is fortunate that so many offenders commit their crimes in the same way, thereby leaving their **"signature"** at the crime scene. These crimes still are not simple. You must possess an extremely open mind in addition to having or developing an ability to notice similarities in signatures and associate various types of evidence.

In this book, we can provide you with only ideas and examples, such as the following:

- **Graffiti** is usually done with the same medium, such as canned spray paint (Figure 9–1). Although the "tag" is in itself a signature or moniker for the "artist," there might be a particular paint used or a particular object of

FIGURE 9–1 Graffiti on a column in a building. Note the cut out in the wallboard where a shoe impression has been removed.

attack, such as street signs or buildings. Photographing the tags and creating a database of them might be very valuable. Do not overlook the possibility of discarded paint cans and their resulting latent fingerprints.

- Broken car windows are the result of some mechanical action. You should look for evidence of that device, such as a baseball bat, center punch used in carpentry, or pellet gun. Are all the cars hit from the front, street side, or rear? Are they drive-by, or is the person walking? The latter situation could yield latent prints.
- What kind of building was vandalized? Was it a building under construction, an office building, or a government building?

INSURANCE SCAM

This type of scene is usually limited to one object of attack, such as a specific business or car, but could be multiple vehicles belonging to the same company. These are sometimes possible to detect by looking at the business records of the company, if that is the "victim." A business that is doing poorly and has little chance of success and likewise little chance of being successfully sold might find the "logical" way out is to destroy the business and make up the losses from the insurance company. A typical method is fire. You are obviously going to look for evidence of arson, which could include

- *Forced entry.* Is the door forced open or the window broken? Broken windows can be very telling in themselves. Was it broken from the inside or the outside? Criminals break in, not out. If the building is burned, is the broken window the result of a mechanical fracture or a thermo fracture? The mechanical fracture has the spiderweb fracture pattern, whereas the thermal fracture has a meandering fracture pattern. Likewise, the thermal fracture does not have "hackle" marks on the broken edges, but is glossy (see Chapter Seven for more detail on the fractures).
- *Use of accelerant.* Are there "trails" where an accelerant was poured? Is there a gas can or other container either inside or outside the building?

We now turn to vehicles. Cars can fall victim to various scams, including *"keying,"* in which a sharp object is used to damage the paint on a car. Although this may be the result of someone unhappy about a traffic incident or some other believed wrongdoing, it could also be the doing of a car owner who wants to have some dings fixed or accidentally scratched surface repainted. Instead of having the small portion fixed and possibly paying for it because of deductible, it may be advantageous to scratch up the entire car so that the entire car is repainted. If a large area is damaged, it might be sufficient reason to suspect possible insurance fraud. Look at the type of scratching. Document anything that might equate to a signature, including words and patterns. Furthermore, you might want to look at the depth of the scratches. Are they just enough to ruin the paint, or do they cause real damage to the metal or fiberglass? Again, use your imagination here. If there are words, are they slang, racial, or gang-type graffiti? Are they appropriate for the location? Are any misspelled? If so, does the victim also misspell the same words?

Another scam in which it is helpful that the CSI be knowledgeable is the burning of a car with "high-end" electronics and after-market parts. Be careful to take extra effort in documenting the remains of the equipment. Are the remains consistent with the brands and models that were supposed to be in the car? Some people remove the expensive parts and replace them with cheap equipment that they then burn. They then collect insurance from the expensive equipment and sell the real things, thereby collecting twice the money for the same equipment. However, it is difficult to destroy the equipment to the degree that a determined CSI cannot find some evidence. There is no crime that leaves no evidence. If we do not find any, it simply means we missed it. This is not necessarily a negative indication of your work. It is possible that we do not have the technology at this point in time to detect it. You cannot find what you aren't aware of at the time.

The investigation of these crimes depends a great deal on the efforts and skill of the detectives as well. CSIs cannot do everything. There is a lot of information, such as bank records and other business dealings, that can lead to successful closure of the case. We will not discuss these, as they are beyond the scope of this book.

EXTORTION

Extortion involves threat of physical or property damage done either very explicitly or by inferring something "bad" will result if something is or is not done. Extortion is sometimes referred to as "insurance," a reference left over from the 1930s, when businesses were advised to pay for "protection" to keep their business for suffering from an "accident," such as fire. Extortion may have exactly the same kinds of evidence as the insurance scam category. Extortion evidence may indicate a less complete burning or the lower amount of effort than put into an insurance scam, such as evidence of a quick drive-by fire bombing instead of a lot of time spent entering and spreading around an accelerant. If the desire were to extort protection, then little would be gained by destroying the business. The damage would fall short of that, but be enough to convince the owner that they need this protection. You as the CSI will be able to look for only physical evidence at the scene; determining the intent may be completely up to the detective. There is sometimes documentary evidence in the form of notes or "warnings," but more often these are transmitted by word of mouth to avoid leaving evidence.

BURGLARY

Burglary is the unlawful entry into the dwelling or business of another with the intent to commit a theft or felony therein. Note we say "dwelling." This means if a person lives in a car, then that car could qualify as a dwelling under the intent of this law. Burglary is an interesting crime because there is so much potential for evidence. It is a felony that is unfortunately seen by many investigators as a minor crime and viewed as troublesome and time consuming, often resulting in little effort being put into the investigation of this "property crime." Quite the contrary, burglary is a crime that hits home (no pun intended) for so many of us. Burglary costs society enormous amounts of money each year in losses. Possibly more important, it is the invasion of our private space and the loss of objects of personal value, often our history. Burglary is also interesting to CSIs in that it is often a crime with immense amounts of potential evidence.

Photography

Photography is somewhat straightforward in that we photograph the entry point of a crime scene, the evidence of activity within the scene, and any objects of interest. The fact that photography can tell a story is very important here, as we are able to tell so much about the suspect if we know what to look for and then document it properly.

- The entry point is important because it can provide such information as the MO of the suspect, such as a "cat burglar" who specializes in entry via hotel balconies. The number of window louvers removed may provide us with indications of the stature of the suspect. Is the suspect careful and neat by not breaking glass? Does the suspect enter by visually obstructed windows?

- Activity within the scene can be important because a suspect may eat or use the telephone. Food can be very important for the recovery of impressions left on cheese, candy, apples, and other foods that may possibly provide dental impression evidence.

  TIP: Food with impressions of teeth must be taken to a laboratory immediately. It should usually be refrigerated, and if there is no chance of getting the food to a laboratory rapidly, impressions can be made with a dental casting material (see Chapter Eight for materials and methods). These items can be ruined by heat and dehydration.

- While we are discussing impression evidence, this would be a good time to remind the reader about latent fingerprints. Even objects like apples and bananas are good surfaces for the recovery of latent prints. Do not forget the telephone, toilet, and rubbish cans for cigarette packages and other evidence that may have been thrown away.

- Are there certain objects of attack, such as cabinets and drawers? Are only certain ones searched and little or no attention given to others? This may be another part of the MO. Do they search the pockets of clothing in the closets? Do they look under the mattress? Do they look in shoes under the bed and in the closets?

- Another area to check is the refrigerator. Sometimes property and drugs are kept in the refrigerator or freezer. If the burglar searches these areas, he/she might possibly be looking for drugs. Photograph all of these areas if there is any sign of a search.

- How about the floors? In some instances people might be barefoot or leave impressions of the shoe or footprints. Window sills are a good surface for impressions of weave patterns of trousers as the suspect sits on the sill. Such patterns can indicate type of cloth, style of trousers, and, in some rare instances, definitive patterns such as the unique pattern resulting from seams sewn in jeans.

Latent Prints

We already discussed latent prints in Chapter Six, but we must address this subject as it applies to burglaries. Burglars handle objects with their hands, and this is important even if they are wearing gloves. Glove prints are important because they are associated with MO. A CSI can also sometimes determine the type of gloves used and possibly identifiable prints from the gloves.

TIP: Again, remember that gloves thrown away at the scene may well provide prints on their interior. Careful examination of gloves found at a scene can provide you with valuable prints. The gloves can be turned inside out and inflated or even placed over another hand and then dusted. Photograph the resulting latent prints prior to attempting any other recovery. A good starting technique might be cyanoacrylate fuming, although other techniques such as a Magna brush can be used.

A logical pattern of searching for latent prints would be from the outside prior to processing the inside. This means beginning at the entry point and then into the scene. Latent prints tell a story as well. Key questions and considerations include the following:

- Are prints on the inside or outside of the windows? In the case of louvers, it is sometimes possible to determine if someone removed the louvers from inside or outside the house. This can provide evidence of a staged burglary, possibly for insurance purposes or to cover another crime.
- You can see prints but cannot seem to lift them. This does happen sometimes and the obvious answer is to photograph the prints, or if warranted, bring in the object, even if it means cutting a portion of the wall away.
- Remember, when it comes to latent prints, the position of the prints on a specific object may provide you with information, such as the exact location of the person depositing them as well as information regarding the activity itself, such as climbing in, out, or even over an object. It may also provide you with the dominant hand of the depositor. Always provide a sketch on the latent card indicating location and manner in which deposited, such as facing in, out, up, or down.
- Do not forget the exit. Burglars may enter a window but may exit by the easiest and fastest way if it provides cover (and sometimes when it does not). A person simply exiting a building as if he or she belonged there does not attract much attention. Sometimes the safest method of being inconspicuous is not to hide!

Safe Burglary

Safe burglaries provide some excellent evidence, among which are

- Shoe prints, which may be found in insulation material.

- Tool marks from tools used for punching, peeling, cutting, or whatever other method was used to gain entry.
- Welding slag has been analyzed in Japan and identified to that found in the trousers of a suspect. If you get a suspect, recover the trousers and shoes.
- Look around and recover eating and drinking material at the scene. Entering a safe takes time.
- Recover any cigarette butts found.
- Some safe burglars use specially modified tools. Look for evidence of these, or, if a suspect is stopped with tools, look for modifications such as leather or rubber on the tools to muffle pounding (Figure 9–2).

Burglary Tools

Burglar's tools are usually ordinary tools, although sometimes altered to render them relatively silent during use by sewing leather or rubber covers over the impact point. Then what are burglar's tools? It has to do with *modification* of the tools, or the possession of certain tools in their *totality,* with consideration being given to the *location, time of day (or night),* and other circumstances. For example, a briefcase containing a hacksaw, water pump pliers (slip joint), plumber's wrench, hammer, chisels, punches, police radio scanner, flashlight, and so on (Figure 9–3) should raise the concerns

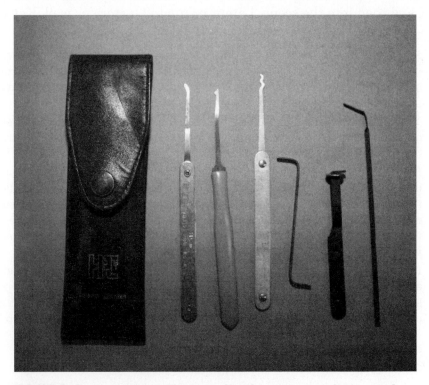

FIGURE 9–2 Lockpick set. These are illegal in many jurisdictions and may be deemed "burglar's tools." The middle pick is a diamond pick, the right pick is a rake, and the angled bars are tension bars.

FIGURE 9–3   A set of burglar's tools used by a safe burglar. Note the modifications to some of the tools to silence them during use.

of a competent investigator. There are some other tools that can be carried alone that, when found under the right circumstances, can be considered burglary tools. Examples would be persons walking around a residential or business district late at night carrying a pipe wrench, slip-joint pliers, slide hammer, or similar tools, including lockpicks (Figure 9–4). You are limited only by your imagination when looking for evidence at a burglary scene.

FIGURE 9–4   Common burglar's tools: (top) A slide hammer or dent puller; (middle) a water pump or slip-joint pliers; (bottom) a plumber's wrench. None of these are illegal, but are great at defeating locks.

 SUMMARY

Property damage is a very broad field, ranging from damage done by the "victim" to insurance scams and extortion and even that of totally unrelated graffiti "artists." Whereas some of these cases are fairly simple to solve, others, such as extortion, may be extremely difficult, and you must be very observant to detect physical evidence that can be used in the prosecution of these cases.

■ REVIEW QUESTIONS

1. Give an example of what physical evidence one might find related to extortion.
2. What are some examples of property damage for insurance purposes?
3. How might evidence differ in an insurance scam as compared to extortion?
4. What might we want as evidence in cases of vandalism, such as graffiti?
5. Does the law enforcement agency in your jurisdiction keep records of the "tags" used in your area?

➤ REFERENCES AND SUGGESTED READING

STUART H. JAMES and JON J. NORDBY, eds., *Forensic Science: An Introduction to Scientific and Investigative Techniques.* CRC Press, Boca Raton, Florida, 2005.

HENRY C. LEE, TIMOTHY PALMBACH, and MARILYN T. MILLER, *Henry Lee's Crime Scene Handbook.* Academic Press, San Diego, CA, 2001.

BARRY A. J. FISHER, *Techniques of Crime Scene Investigation,* CRC Press, Boca Raton, FL, 2004.

CHARLES R. SWANSON, NEIL C. CHAMELIN, and LEONARD TERRITO, *Criminal Investigation.* McGraw-Hill, NY, 2003.

Fire and Explosion Investigations

Key Terms

Point of origin
Alligatoring
Pour patterns
Low-order explosive
High-order explosive
Secondary device

INTRODUCTION/OBJECTIVES

The fire scene is one of the more difficult scenes to investigate because it is in such disarray (Figure 10–1). Firefighters broke windows, punched holes in the roof, pulled down portions of walls, and so on. To make things worse, everything is wet, there is no electricity to power lights to see, and the scene is hot; to put things in perspective, life at a fire scene is basically miserable. Where do we begin to take measurements? How do we find evidence? What is the procedure for photography? There are answers to all of these questions, but the answers do not make it any easier to accomplish. After completing this chapter, you should have an understanding of what to do at a scene, and just as important, what not to do. We want you never to forget that these scenes can be very dangerous environments in which to work. Do not attempt to do anything you are not qualified to do. Your actions in these scenes can put not only your life in danger, but the lives of others as well.

FIGURE 10–1 A fire scene. Note the "alligatoring" on the wood at bottom of photo. The far wall has burned out, and the right concrete wall is chipped, "spalling" from the heat.

FIRE SCENES

Photography

Fire scenes are dark and everything is black. Black absorbs light. This means you must use artificial light sources and your exposures should have a wider aperture (*f*-stop) opening. You need more light or your photographs will be underexposed. This is your main consideration with photography. Use a flash unit in all photography. If using floodlights, consider using either battery-powered units or outdoor waterproof electric lines to avoid possible electric shock.

TIP: Waterproof cameras, some of which are priced very reasonably and are classified as disposable, may be the way to go. These are less likely to cause explosions in explosive environments, and can be decontaminated in clandestine laboratory scenes.

Diagram

Your diagram will not be as neat and to the point as it would be under normal circumstances. It is more difficult to determine walls that no longer exist, as well as much of the furnishings. Do the best you can, and that is all that can be expected of you. You may have to rely on a floor plan provided by the contractor or owner. Be aware, however, that blueprints are not very friendly to crime scene investigators in that they are very cluttered, and often contain much more information than you would ever require.

Evidence

Evidence in fire cases is rather difficult to find and process in that the evidence is wet, not in its normal location or condition, and may have been walked on or any number of destructive happenings.

The evidence to look for pertains to the fire's **point of origin** (Figure 10–2). This is not easy to determine, as there may be more than one point of origin. Some arson cases have several. You are well advised to seek the assistance of the fire investigator or the police arson investigator at the scene, who can provide you with ideas of what to photograph and recover, and are worth their weight in gold at these scenes. However, there will be times when they will not be available, and you are on your own. The following can assist you with your investigation:

- **Alligatoring** is deep charring that actually looks like alligator skin (see Figure 10–1), indicating that the fire burned long and hot at that location,

FIGURE 10–2 Typical arson case with multiple points of origin.

and may in fact be the point of origin. Take overall photographs of this area and close-up photographs of the pattern.

- Cut away some of the pattern as deep as you can and put it in an unlined paint can (about 1 quart to 1 gallon in size). Seal it tightly with a lid.
- Residue at the floor level, even with water flooding, should also be scooped into a can and sealed.
- Any water you see with a sheen on it that resembles the sheen of oil or other petroleum products should also be placed in a can and sealed.
- If there is a strong smell of something resembling gasoline or other similar product, an air sample should be collected. Take a plastic garbage bag, whip it open like a grocery store bagger, and simply knot the bag closed. This provides you with the desired sample.
- Do you see any patterns that look like the fire burned downward? Document and photograph these areas. Recover samples as well. Fire usually burns up, and a downward burning pattern may indicate an accelerant.
- Do you see **pour patterns** or "tracks" on the floor and/or walls? These may be pour patterns from an accelerant, with the trail leading out of the scene.
- If there are glass windows, see if you can rub off the soot. If you can, this may be indicative of a fast-moving fire in which an accelerant was used. Baked-on soot that cannot be rubbed off is indicative of a slow-moving fire.
- Is anything melted? By examining what melted and determining the melting point for that material, you may get an indication of the speed of the burn. *Melting point* is that temperature at which a specific material turns to a liquid, and *freezing point* is that temperature at which the material turns to a solid.
- Although broken windows may mean a break-in, they could be there to make you believe that a break-in occurred. Check the glass for mechanical fracture patterns and determine if they were broken from the inside or the outside. Burglars do not break out, they break in. This broken glass should exhibit the typical characteristics of a mechanical fracture.
- Does the broken glass have a meandering fracture with no distinctive pattern and smooth edges? If so, you have the characteristics of a ***thermal fracture.***
- Is there a gasoline can or similar container that could have contained an accelerant? Check it for fingerprints and residue that could be sampled in the laboratory.
- Sometimes fingerprints can actually be etched into an object, such as a gas can. Also, be aware that soot is a good method of developing latent prints. At one time, camphor was popular as a method of producing soot to bring out latent fingerprints.

All of the evidence recovered as a result of the techniques or suggestions described here should be submitted to a crime laboratory, where they will be tested for the presence of accelerants. This is usually accomplished with the use of instrumentation, such as the gas chromatograph. These samples are heated and air samples taken with a hypodermic needle and/or a carbon strip placed in the can and then heated.

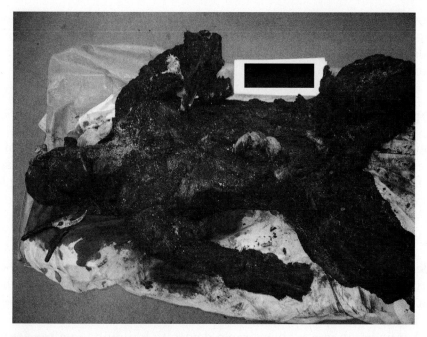

FIGURE 10–3   A fire-related death with a pugilist pose. (Photo courtesy of the Honolulu Medical Examiner.)

BURNING DEATHS

Victims of burning (Figure 10–3) are very difficult to work with for many obvious reasons. We discuss printing fire victims in Chapter Seven. Visual identification, although sometimes possible, is often difficult and might be very traumatic for family members. Some decedents are so burned that there is noting left for visual or fingerprint identification. In these cases, we must rely on other methods, such as

- Identification by dental records, comparing them with the teeth from the body
- Sometimes there are dentures that may have a name or an identification number on them
- Replacement joints made of metal have a manufacturer's identification number that can be traced to an individual
- Implants also have a serial number (these are more valuable in decomposed bodies, for obvious reasons)
- Jewelry may be of assistance, but not for a positive identification
- Previous injuries, such as broken bones, are also valuable in these cases

Safety

Protective boots or firefighter's boots should be worn in fire scenes. A construction-type hardhat (not of metal) should be worn at all times, and it is advisable to also consider gloves and coveralls. These scenes should always have the electric service stopped, but never take any chances. Work as if the electricity were still on, and consider the possibility of materials falling on you or that you might fall through a floor. Safety is a major consideration.

EXPLOSIONS

Explosions share some similarities to fires, such as the burning of evidence and surroundings. They are part of the same event in some cases in that fire may result from an explosion, such as at a clandestine drug laboratory, or just the opposite, where an explosion may occur as part of a fire.

Evidence

Evidence is often elusive without special knowledge. If the case is a bombing, there may well be evidence specific to the type of device used, and this in turn may tell you something about the abilities of the person(s) responsible for the bomb.

A pipe bomb is a rather simple device to build and is often found in cases of property damage by juveniles around New Year's and the Fourth of July. These are often made with the materials from celebratory explosives like fireworks. They may be initiated by a simple fuse such as a firecracker fuse, or a fuse designed for model airplane jet engines, sometimes referred to as a *jet-x fuse*. With this type of bomb, you most likely find that

- The pipe or pieces of the pipe used for the body of the explosive device (Figure 10–4)
- The end caps used in the manufacture of the device to seal each end of the pipe body

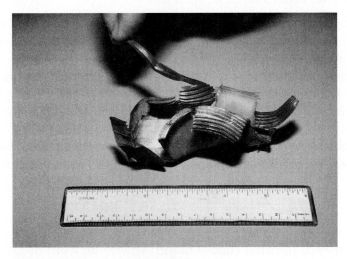

FIGURE 10–4 Portions of a pipe bomb.

- A hole in either the tube or one of the end caps for the fuse
- Wadding material, such as sheeting, found in the scene

Each of these is very important as evidence. It may be possible to take the wadding material from a bomb and match it to that used in other bombing cases, thereby linking bombs to an individual serial bomber.

More sophisticated devices may be the work of a "professional" who is well versed in the art of bombing and the science of explosives. In these cases, the device may have a very complicated timing device or initiator and may involve the use of various explosives that require the use of an initiator, a booster, and a main explosive. With these cases, it is important to look for

- The bomb container
- An explosive container, such as a paper wrapper for dynamite, a cardboard tube from TNT, or a plastic bag from plastic explosives
- The remains of the "*squib*," or *blasting cap*, a small cylindrical tube with either wires or fuse protruding from one end
- "*Leg wires*," the small copper wires leading from the electric blasting cap
- A *time fuse*, often a plastisized cloth tube containing the fuse material that burns at a specific rate
- A timing device, such as a watch, clock, or something more crude and imaginative, such as a pressure or pressure-release device that is tripped by stepping on something; lifting something, such as a book; or opening a door, trunk, hood, or even by placing the gear shift of a car in drive or reverse
- **Low-order explosives** are compounds such as black gunpowder, flashpowder, and others that require only heat to initiate. Think of the "crackerball" poppers that you can step on or throw down and they explode. These are the best examples of this level of explosive.
- **High-order explosives** are explosives like dynamite, C-4, or TNT. These are somewhat safer to work with but offer a higher explosion level. These can burn and not explode, and are used with an *initiator*, such as a blasting cap or squib. They are usually manufactured commercially, and often their use is the result of a theft from a construction company or other source of these explosives.
- **Quarrying explosives** are used as the name implies. They are a mixture in either slurry or wet granular material that can be dropped into bore holes in plastic tubes that look like sausage or pumped from a truck. They can explode with such force as to move tons of rock at a time. This is basically a three-step process in that there is an initiator (blasting cap) that sets off a *booster* (TNT), which in turn boosts the mixture to critical mass and sets off the *explosive charge*. This is particularly destructive and is the type used to cause destruction on the order of the Murraugh Federal Building in Oklahoma City.

Safety

Like fires, bombing scenes may involve unsafe structures and other considerations. There are some very specific concerns with bombing, however.

- A **secondary device** *or a second bomb*. This may be a real concern, and is a common consideration in terrorist-type bombings. Always keep this in mind.
- *Electric triggers*. These are a concern, especially with reference to the use of telephones and radios at a bombing scene. The rule of thumb here is, *Do not use a radio or telephone at a bombing scene.*
- A *booby-trapped scene*. Sometimes something might be very obviously wrong or out of place. Do not attempt to correct these obvious things at scenes. Notify an expert who can determine if what you found is, in fact, a booby trap.

◤ SUMMARY

Fire scenes are very difficult to investigate because the structure is no longer in its original form. It is very hot and dirty, as well as wet. Even with the difficulties, there is plenty of evidence if you know what to look for and how to interpret what you find.

When investigating a bombing, there is an old saying: "The only thing that limits a bomber is imagination." You are well advised to commit this to memory. Remember that at a bombing scene there is always the possibility of a secondary device. Both fire and bombing scenes are very dangerous places to work.

◼ REVIEW QUESTIONS

1. What is *alligatoring* and what is its significance?
2. When considering burn patterns, in what direction do we expect the fire to burn?
3. Why is melted material important?
4. Describe a thermal fracture.
5. What is so important about broken windows in a fire case?
6. Why is the direction of the force that caused the break so important?
7. What is meant by the term *secondary device*?
8. What is the general rule concerning telephones and radios at bombing scenes?
9. With regard to photography, what are the lighting considerations, and what are some solutions?
10. Why should we consider underwater cameras?

◆ REFERENCES AND SUGGESTED READING

RONALD F. BECKER, *Criminal Investigation*. Jones and Bartell Publishers, Sudbury, MA. 2005.

CHARLES R. SWANSON, NEIL C. CHAMELIN, and LEONARD TERRITO, *Criminal Investigation*. McGraw-Hill, New York, 2003.

DAVID R. REDSICKER, *Forensic Photography.* CRC Press, Boca Raton, FL, 2001.

STUART H. JAMES and JON J. NORDBY, eds., *Forensic Science: An Introduction to Scientific and Investigative Techniques.* CRC Press, Boca Raton, FL, 2005.

HENRY C. LEE, TIMOTHY PALMBACH, and MARILYN T. MILLER, *Henry Lee's Crime Scene Handbook.* Academic Press, San Diego, CA, 2001.

BARRY A. J. FISHER, *Techniques of Crime Scene Investigation.* CRC Press, Boca Raton, FL, 2004.

Assaults

Key Terms _____

Assault
Battery
Incised wound
Lacerated wound
Stab wound

INTRODUCTION/OBJECTIVES

Assault is a rather complicated group of offenses in that there is often no physical evidence and the suspect may not even have made physical contact. We, of course, are going to be concerned with the more serious assaults in which **battery** (physical contact) was made or a weapon was involved. We begin this discussion with the weapon, and then move to the injury. Each of these has specific requirements to establish an assault has taken place, and these may vary somewhat from jurisdiction to jurisdiction. As the CSI, you must determine what evidence is essential, and then document and recover that evidence.

WEAPONS

Weapons used in an assault are not limited to a firearm, knife, or fists. Just about anything that is sharp or has a little weight behind it can serve as a weapon when used as one. Recover that weapon if possible and determine if it is consistent with the one reported being used. Determine if there are any latent fingerprints on the object and, of course, who deposited them on the weapon. There are two ways to determine the nature of the weapon, other than the accused readily informs the investigators of its identity. The intended victim or witnesses can advise you of the identity of the weapon, or you can determine its identity by examining all likely candidates at the scene. Look for blood, tissue, shape corresponding to the injury, or shapes consistent with the injury. Some weapons used in these cases include

- Knives, swords, and letter openers
- Firearms
- Fists and feet
- Ashtrays
- Cue sticks; broom and mop handles
- Chairs
- Dishes, bottles, and eating utensils
- Animals
- Cars and other motor vehicles

INJURIES/DAMAGE

There may be injuries to victims, including the intended target as well as other persons in the path of the weapon. Injuries should be determined and the following steps taken, with the understanding that these are not exclusive and other steps may be necessary, dependent on the circumstances:

1. Photograph of the injured party for identification
2. Photograph of the injury alone
3. Photograph of the injury with ABFO scale

   TIP: Injuries, such as bruises, change over time. It is a good idea to photograph the injuries over a period of 3 days. This should allow you to get the injuries as seen almost immediately after the incident and then the injuries that show as time progresses.

4. A mold of injuries, such as teeth marks. This can be accomplished with medical casting material, such as that used by dentists.

   TIP: When possible, have the casts done by or at least monitored by medical personnel to avoid accusations of improper testing, resulting in infection. Bite marks change over time, as does any other wound. If you photograph and mold the bite mark too late in the process, it might not be feasible for the odontologist to make a definitive determination.

   TIP: If the wound is healed prior to you being called in, it is possible in some instances to document the healed injury by using a camera with *infrared film* and an *infrared bypass filter* over the lens. Another method is the use of a camera, such as the Sony cameras with Nite Shot infrared capability. Simply place the bypass filter over the camera lens and place the camera on Nite Shot or super Nite Shot and film with incandescent light. There is another method that sometimes works and is better than nothing. If you get the injured portion of the person cold, sometimes the injury can be visualized and then photographed with standard photography.

5. Medical reports of the treatment sometimes provide the investigator with a wound description and a possible weapon or type of weapon.

6. Do not overlook blood stains on the weapon and at the scene. You can determine the identity of the person depositing the blood, and the stains may assist you in reconstructing the offense.

7. Look for any property left at the scene that may aid in identifying the participants. This is not an uncommon occurrence.

INJURY TYPES

There are various injury types that may provide you with information that can provide answers to many questions, such as weapon type or type of injury. Some are

- **Incised wounds** are wounds that are cut with a sharp instrument and usually longer on the surface than deep
- **Lacerated wounds** are those that are torn or separated by crushing or tearing, such as when hit with a blunt object
- **Stab wounds** are those wounds that are deeper than they are on the surface; instead of a slashing movement, a stabbing or thrusting motion was used

TIP: The depth of a stab wound is not an accurate method to determine blade length.

The scene is documented as any other scene with regard to photography, diagram, latent prints, and so forth.

 ## REFERENCES AND SUGGESTED READING

STUART H. JAMES and JON J. NORDBY, Eds., *Forensic Science: An Introduction to Scientific and Investigative Techniques.* CRC Press, Boca Raton, FL, 2005.

HENRY C. LEE, TIMOTHY PALMBACH, and MARILYN T. MILLER, *Henry Lee's Crime Scene Handbook.* Academic Press, San Diego, CA, 2001.

BARRY A. J. FISHER, *Techniques of Crime Scene Investigation.* CRC Press, Boca Raton, FL, 2004.

Blood and Body Fluids

Key Terms

Double gloving
Presumptive test
False positive
Phenolphthalein
Reconstructive agent
Luminol
Chemiluminescence

INTRODUCTION/OBJECTIVES

Blood and body fluids have come to the forefront in forensics as viable evidence. It was not too many years ago that the use of body fluids was limited to determining blood type. It can now provide you with the identification of a specific person. Furthermore, we can now obtain DNA from the flap of an envelope or the back of a postage stamp. The author has students working with DNA from disposable contact lenses. Remains from the American Civil War are being identified. We have truly come a long way, and all of this progress directly effects forensic science. You should be aware of not only the methodology of obtaining samples, but just as important, the safety concerns.

SAFETY PRECAUTIONS

There are basic precautions that must be considered when working any scene containing blood and other body fluids known as *universal precautions,* and are used in laboratories, hospitals, and other agencies working with trauma and death. Working outside at a crime scene is all the more reason to take precautions. You are not in a clean laboratory environment with the many controls and safety features encountered there. You are working on an environment in which you have relatively little control.

Gloves

Of all the precautions, gloves are the most basic, both from the standpoint of safety and to avoid cross-contamination of the evidence with which we come into contact. Quality is nothing to scrimp on when considering gloves. Paying a little more for better-quality gloves is nothing compared with the possibility of an employee contracting hepatitis and/or AIDS. There are just too many dangers to this occupation today to take any of this lightly.

Some crime scene investigators wear two pairs of gloves, **double gloving**. There are several reasons justifying the practice. First, wearing more than one pair of gloves eliminates the possibility of a glove breaking, thereby resulting in contamination. This is not a rare occurrence. Second, when wearing gloves and working with blood, decomposed human remains, or even working with fingerprint powder and ink, gloves can become so contaminated that they must be removed. It is simple to slip one pair off and then continue the task at hand without having to leave the scene for another pair. The dirty pair is simply removed and put in a rubbish container and the work continues uninterrupted. When considering cross-contamination issues, a new pair of gloves should be taken from the box or container and put on between each task. Another consideration with properly fitting gloves, which are the best way to go, is that after some time they begin to conform to the hand, and by their picking up various contaminates, it is possible, although not common, to leave your fingerprints at a scene.

When removing gloves, there is a simple technique that may be used to avoid contamination of skin or the gloves beneath the pair being removed. Take the wrist opening of the first glove and pull it off. It comes off inside out. Hold the first glove in the hand that removed it, and then the hand with the fresh glove or no glove grasps the wrist of the second glove. By pulling the second glove off while holding the first glove, the first glove remains inside the second glove and can then be either thrown away on removal or knotted to keep the contents inside the now inside-out gloves. This results in the dirty sides being on the inside. When removing the glove, you can hold any other small contaminated article to be disposed of in the gloved hand, which results in it being contained inside the now inside-out glove package. The cuff of the glove can be knotted, and you can now dispose of the sealed "glove package" properly.

It should be obvious by now that in a large or very contaminated scene, an investigator might use quite a number of pairs of gloves. This should not be a consideration. Safety must come first, and right behind safety are contamination concerns.

Masks

Following gloves is the use of masks. A particle mask is usually sufficient for most crime scenes. Its purpose is to avoid inhaling both accidental splashes and more dried particles of blood, fingerprint powder, and the like. If there is a good chance of splashes, then a full-face mask is best. When working with dried blood we may have to scrape the dried stain, and it is possible to inhale airborne stray particles or have the powdered blood go into your eyes.

One often sees persons wearing charcoal "antiputrefaction" masks. If the purpose is filtration for safety purposes, then this can be justified. If, however, the purpose is to avoid the odor of decomposed body tissue, then the mask is a waste of funds, because although it might aid in cutting down the odor while wearing it, consider the fact that your clothing is absorbing the odor, as is your hair, and so on. When the mask is removed, you continue to smell the offensive odor. The additional cost is minimal, but be advised that it does not make the task at hand that much less offensive. Get used to it.

Safety Glasses and Goggles

These are not the same and do not provide the same level of protection. When working with dried blood, it is definitely recommended to use goggles. You do not want dried blood particles getting into your eyes, and goggles should prevent this. They are awkward and hot, and even more concerning is that they are not as effective when used with eyeglasses. They are often vented, however, and do not tend to fog up, as the older ones did. They offer excellent overall protection.

Next in consideration is safety glasses, which, although offering protection against most small flying objects and limited protection against some small splashes, are not recommended for blood use, except maybe in the laboratory.

Two other options that offer excellent protection are for the most part too expensive and limiting in nature. They are the full-face mask shield and the full-face mask with filters or with a positive airflow system that continually produces air flowing out of the mask. They are often used in clandestine drug labs and similar environments. When a mask is required, remember that a full-face mask is required for anyone with a beard. A respirator-type mask does not seal properly with a beard. Another consideration is that there may be requirements mandating a fitting test and certification. Employers should be aware of this.

Clothing

Disposable suits—often of Tyvek or similar material that are a one-use coverall, often with built-in booties or shoe coverings that can be worn with the pantlegs tucked into them—are warranted, especially for particularly bloody scenes or scenes with a lot of contaminates present. They are often used in conjunction with other protective gear, such as Nomex at fire and clandestine drug laboratory investigations. These suits offer protection from spills and splashes and are also great in addressing contamination/cross-contamination issues. These are also available with an attached hood. It might be advisable to require all persons working in major crime scenes to wear such equipment, both to ensure safety and to eliminate contamination problems.

Booties are important because what we walk on (or in, as the case may be) may end up in our vehicle or our homes and offices. This can be a very serious problem, especially with small infants and young children crawling and playing on the floor.

FIELD TESTING AND SAMPLING

In keeping with our goal of discussing field operations, we stress those areas here. Keep in mind that what you recover in the field must be submitted to a laboratory for further definitive analyses. If care is not taken in the recovery, storage, and transportation of the samples, the recovery was for naught. With that in mind, let's look at a basic recovery kit (Figure 11–1) and protocol. This can be almost as simple as you want, or, if your caseload warrants it, as complete as you want. We next look at something in the middle.

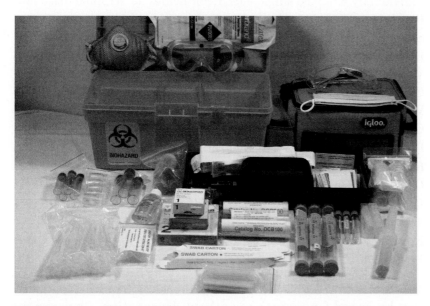

FIGURE 11–1 A blood kit with swabs, vials, mask, gloves, sharps containers, swab boxes, sterile swabs, blood reagents, glasses, filter paper, an insulated bag for samples, and some reagents.

Basic Blood and Body–Fluid Kit

We use a rather simple testing/sampling system.

TIP: The vast majority of reagents and related supplies can be ordered ready made from various forensic, law enforcement, or medical supply houses. Pay attention to shelf life and expiration dates on supplies, and always keep your Manufacturer's Safety Data Sheets (MSDS). This is not only a legal requirement, but is also critical should anyone need emergency medical attention. It is a good idea to keep a set in the facility as required as well as a copy in the lab vehicle. This allows someone who requires medical attention to take a copy along for the ER staff. Hospital medical staff advise that this practice makes their tasks both faster and easier.

A list of suggested supplies includes

- Plastic carrying case
- Insulated container for chemicals and blood/body-fluid samples
- Mask to cover both nose and mouth
- Goggles and safety glasses
- Fitted gloves
- Sterile, cotton-tipped swabs in packs of two
- Swab cartons that protect the swab and allow it to air dry
- Alcohol in jelled form
- Alcohol wipes or similar product
- Sharps containers for needles, etc.
- Filter paper for sampling
- Individually wrapped single-edge razor blades for scraping dried blood
- Purple-top (EDTA) blood-sampling tubes
- Saline solution for wet blood recovery (check your local protocol)
- Disposable eye droppers and capillary tubes
- Various glass containers for blood recovery
- Clear film containers (empty)
- Wax film for sealing blood containers
- Glass microscope slides in transport/storage containers
- Phenolphthalein test kits or Hemastix
- *Hematrace* (human/higher primate-specific) or
- *OBTI*, which is human-specific
- *Leucomalachite green* test kits
- *Acid phosphatase* kits
- Luminol test kits (spray bottle kept separately)
- Biohazard labels

This is a fairly complete system and is not expensive. Most of the supplies can be stored for some time without degradation. By using the commercial reagent kits, you can avoid having a chemist prepare your chemicals. The kits are simple to use and come with complete instructions.

Again, you must remember that these are presumptive tests, and therefore not definitive, except for OBTI and Hematrace; therefore, further testing is required.

Procedures

Prior to conducting sampling and testing, photography and drawings must be completed to document evidence. Then consideration must be given to goals. For example, the use of luminol for reconstruction must come after sampling for some other blood tests. There are conflicting reports on the use of luminol and other presumptive tests being detrimental to subsequent DNA profiling, with the latest evidence showing no serious concerns; however, it is better to be safe than sorry. Each procedure must be considered in light of its effect on other procedures. In general, it is a good idea to take your samples prior to other chemical procedures. Our next discussion bears this in mind.

Blood Sampling

There are two somewhat different methods of recovering wet blood at a scene. We discuss both, with the suggestion that you either determine from the laboratory that processes your evidence which method they prefer, or recover blood using both methods.

Wet Blood

1. Use an eyedropper to recover some blood and place it in a sterile glass container.

   TIP: Paraffin film comes in large rolls that have a blue design on the paper covering. The author cuts squares of this film along the blue lines and places them in a sterile container. The film is now in squares that are just right for sealing the glass blood containers. This glass container is then placed in one of the clear plastic 35-mm film containers and sealed with paraffin film. This insulates the blood container from breakage. In the unlikely case it somehow does leak or break, it is still contained in the plastic film container. Otherwise, you might return to you facility only to find your kit full of suspect-quality blood.

2. Add a small amount of saline solution to the sterile glass container and then an amount of wet blood recovered with either the disposable eyedropper or the sterile swab. This is then sealed in the same manner as described in step 1. The purpose of the saline solution is to keep the blood cells from lysing (the walls of the blood cells break).

The samples should be placed in the insulated blood container or in a refrigerator in the vehicle, if one is available. It should be taken to the laboratory within a reasonable time. Be sure to keep chain of custody logs on this and all other evidence.

Samples should be taken from representative areas throughout the scene. Never reuse eyedroppers, capillary tubes, or other sampling supplies. All should be one-time use and then disposed of properly in a ***biohazard bag***.

New Method

Today, the preferred method is to recover wet blood on swatches of test paper (some are available for this purpose) and allow the blood to dry. This method is better, as there is no need to carry as many different supplies. The blood recovered is dried, regardless of the method used because it is stored in a freezer at about −70° F. You are pretty safe by drying your samples, but check with the laboratory that services your team. The main consideration here is to be sure the blood dries in a manner that does not allow it to be cross-contaminated by anything else. Also, make sure that the blood is placed in an environment in which it will not putrefy. It must receive an adequate amount of ventilation. This can be accomplished in a "swab drying" box with a small ventilating fan circulating regular air. The box should also have a method of locking it, and it should be stored in a secure area. It is imperative that the box be cleaned and sterilized after each use. There is no reason to recover the blood if it will never be admitted into evidence.

Dried Blood

Dried blood poses some unique health hazards. A dust respirator and goggles should be worn when recovering dried blood to protect mouth and nose as well as the eyes.

If the dried blood is on a smooth surface, a single-edge razor blade can be used to scrape the blood off the surface. A new razor blade should be used for each sample taken. The blood is scraped or shaved and placed on filter paper, which is folded into a druggist bindle. It is then placed in another sterile container, such as an envelope. Be sure to place the used blades in a suitable sharps container for disposal.

If the dried blood is on a rough surface such as asphalt paving or concrete, you can wet a sheet of filter paper with saline and place this on the stain. If it is hot, a glass can be placed over the filter paper opening down. The rehydrated blood wicks into the paper, and this can then be dried and submitted.

Still another option is to recover the object on which the blood is found. This may mean removing floor tiles, wall paper, portions of walls and floors being cut out, and so forth, limited only by your imagination and determination. Be sure your agency is going to back you when it comes to cutting a hole in the middle of a hotel lobby carpet, or cutting a portion of a wall out of a hotel room, or peeling the wallpaper off the wall of a hotel room. These methods are sometimes warranted. These techniques are required more for bloodstain pattern analysis, however.

PRESUMPTIVE TESTING

There are several **presumptive tests** for blood. The main point to keep in mind here is that all of these are just that—presumptive—and simply mean the substance is possibly blood, but in no way is this definite, much less human or animal. There are various substances that cause a presumptive test to give a "false positive," and you should research the various causes for false-positive results for the specific test you run. What these test have in common is that they all react to blood. The more different presumptive tests you run, the stronger the implication that the questioned substance is blood, but a definitive test must be conducted in a laboratory to ascertain that the substance is, in fact, blood, that it is human blood, and then move toward a definitive test for the specific ABO type, and then further testing, up to and including DNA profiling. There is a blood test that can be used in the field today that is reportedly specific to humans. We discuss those as well.

Phenolphthalein

Phenolphthalein, also known as the *Kastle–Meyer test,* is one of the most commonly used presumptive tests. It is very simple, thereby making it perfect for field use. The procedure for this test in the kit form is as follows:

1. Use a cotton-tipped swab to gently swab the stain. If the stain is dry, slightly wet the swab with sterile water prior to swabbing.
2. Break the shaft of the swab off short enough to place in the provided tube. Replace the top.
3. Break the bottom ampule and allow the liquid to be absorbed by the swab.
4. Break the top ampule. A positive reaction is pink color within a few seconds, although it is usually instantaneous.

If you have someone mixing your phenolphthalein, you can still conduct your test by following the information and procedures described in this section.

You learned in your basic science courses that when testing, you have the unknown, which is tested with ***positive*** and ***negative controls***, and a substrate that should be tested in this manner as well. In the supplies described earlier, we mentioned sterile swabs in packs of two, which are used for these tests, and we can use phenolphthalein as an example. Our positive control is swabs that we have exposed to blood. The package of two sterile swabs provides us with the negative control and the unknown. The procedure is as follows:

1. Put on gloves.
2. Open the package of two swabs.
3. Take one of your positive control swabs.

4. Wet all three swabs with saline. Do not dip the swabs and do not touch the swabs with your dropper. This can result in cross-contamination.

5. Swab the unknown substance with a sterile swab. (This can be substituted with the filter paper if you are using capillary action to recover the sample. Drop the chemicals directly on the paper.)

6. Drop one or two drops of phenolphthalein on each swab again, being sure not to touch the swabs.

7. Place one or two drops of hydrogen peroxide on each swab.

Results

- The negative control should have no reaction.
- The positive control should change to a violet color within a second or two.
- The unknown substance immediately turns violet within a second or two if it is blood. If not, there should be no reaction.

The negative control assures you the swabs are not contaminated, and the positive control assures you that the chemicals are working. This procedure should be repeated for each test conducted.

TIP: Keep your chemicals in the cooler until you use them. As soon as you have finished, return them to the cooler again. If you do not, they begin to react to the air. It is for this reason that you cannot save the test for evidence. Even the negative control turns to positive in about 10 to 15 minutes. Be sure to document your test results, and video could even be taken of the procedure.

Benzidine

Benzidine is not used in the field and has fallen from favor in the laboratory because it is carcinogenic. This test produces a blue positive reaction.

O-Tolidine

O-Tolidine, like benzidine, produces a blue positive reaction. As with benzidine, this test has also been deemed hazardous because of its carcinogenic nature.

Leucomalachite Green

Leucomalachite green, also known as *McPhail's Reagent* and *Hemiden,* produces a green positive test result. It is available in kit form and is excellent for field testing. The procedure for this test when in the kit form is as follows:

1. Use a cotton-tipped swab and rub gently on the stain. If dry, you might have to slightly wet the swab with sterile water prior to step 1.

2. Break off the swab shaft to allow it to be placed in the tube provided.

3. Break the bottom ampule and allow the swab to absorb the liquid.
4. Break the top ampoule and if blood is present, there should be a rapid (within a few seconds) color change to a blue-green.

Remember, these tests are not specific, but presumptive in nature. Furthermore, they cannot indicate the substance being tested is human or animal in origin.

HUMAN-SPECIFIC FIELD BLOOD TESTS

There is a "human-specific" blood test known as Hexagon OBTI that can be conducted easily in the field. It is a test strip packaged with a solution. The package is opened and the kit removed. Gloves are necessary, of course. The procedure is as follows:

1. Unscrew the cap from the tube. There is a probe attached to the inside of the cap.
2. Collect the sample with the probe by rubbing or dipping it into the substance.
3. Replace the top, immersing the probe in the solution. The test can be completed later, but must be done within a week.
4. Shake the container to assure the proper mixing of the sample.
5. Remove the test unit from its packaging.
6. Break the protruding red shaft from the outside of the top of the container holding the sample.
7. Place two drops of the solution into the round well of the test unit. Negative results can be confirmed after 10 minutes. Wait for at least 5 minutes to read the test.

Results

- One blue band in the test unit window indicates the test was completed correctly and that the chemicals were functioning correctly.
- A second blue test band, even if weak, is a positive indication of human blood.
- If no blue lines show, the test is invalid and should be conducted again.

Another specific blood test is Hematrace and can also be done in the field. Simply follow the instructions for that product.

An important consideration when testing blood with these human-specific blood tests is that not all of your blood testing is for human blood. There will be cases in which the blood present is or is reported to be that of an animal. Know what you are really looking for when using these tests.

BLOOD-STAIN PATTERN REAGENTS

The following procedures are considered presumptive blood tests, but they are offered here and their true value is as **reconstructive agents** for detection of trace blood and specifically related to interpretation of patterns such as shoe prints, footprints, blood that has been cleaned up, and so on.

Luminol

Luminol is a presumptive test for blood, but experience has shown its value as a reconstructive agent for crime scenes. What we intend to convey by referring to luminol as a reconstructive agent is that it is valuable to provide patterns left in blood, even though cleaned after the incident. These patterns are specific enough to determine shoe patterns, possible shoe sizes, and determine various activities indicated or inferred as a result of luminol patterns. If there seems to be a lack of blood where you would expect to see it, luminol might be an option to attempt to locate it. It has the ability to provide you with images of blood stains that are very old and those that have been cleaned or even painted. It can also be photographed. This is wonderful evidence to provide for court, as it tends to have great influence with the jury.

Luminol is used in near or total darkness. Remember, it may affect your ability to conduct DNA profiling, although as mentioned earlier, recent literature reports that it does not significantly interfere with DNA analysis. If you contemplate using it, you must either wait for night to use it or have a way to cut off nearly all extraneous light. The reaction, a luminescence that glows a bluish color, lasts for about 20 seconds. The problem here is that you cannot do this without problems. If the surface is vertical, great care must be taken not to spray too much or the pattern distorts and runs down the wall. It is even possible to ruin the pattern on a horizontal surface. Multiple applications are necessary when photographing luminol. (Photography of luminol is covered in Chapter Five.)

Luminol Reagent

Luminol reagent consists of 25 g sodium carbonate and 0.5 g luminol (5-amino-2,3-dihydro-1,4-phthalazinedione). When you are ready to use the reagent, mix this with a solution of 3.5 g sodium perborate and 500 mL distilled water. You must mix this solution completely and use it within 1 hour. It is obvious from these instructions that you do not want to mix the reagent until you are ready to use it. It is interesting that the Lynn Peavey Company sells a luminol kit under the name NITE-SITE (item #5097/6020). The instructions state that it can be used within 2 to 3 hours after mixing. Although the author has not attempted to use this kit after 1 hour, it was found to be very easy to transport and use and provided excellent results.

As mentioned earlier, luminol excels as an agent for reconstruction of crime scenes where blood is present, although not readily visible. In scenes where the blood has been cleaned up to the point it can no longer be seen, luminol brings out the patterns left in blood (Figure 11–2). It not only provides the investigation with images of footprints and other indicators of movement, but can even show that the scene was cleaned. This reagent works well with old blood, and although the author has used it on fresh blood without any difficulty, it has been suggested that fresh blood be treated with a 1% solution of hydrochloric acid to lyze the blood cells.

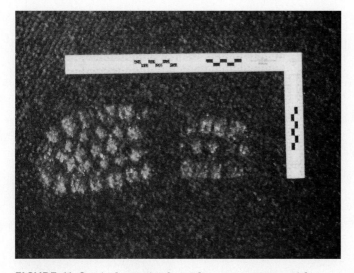

FIGURE 11–2 A shoe print brought out on carpet with luminol.

Another luminol formulation that appears to be just as good and reportedly definitely does not interfere with DNA profiling is a product known as BLUESTAR. This product is very simple to mix. It consists of two packages, each containing a single tablet. It is used as follows:

1. Place 125 mL of distilled water in a spray bottle capable of producing a fine mist.
2. Place one set of two tablets into the water. Allow 1 to 2 minutes for the tablets to dissolve. Stir gently. Do *not* shake the container. The container should be vented, as pressure may build if it is not allowed to vent.
3. In total or near-total darkness, spray a fine mist on the area to be tested.

Results

There should be a very bright and long-lasting blue **chemiluminescence** for a positive result (Figure 11–3).

Documentation

The results of this test may be photographed with a camera equipped with 400 ASA film or digital equivalent. A tripod and flash (external) should also be used. A remote shutter release or cable release should be used to trip the shutter. The procedure is as follows:

1. Place the camera on a tripod and focus the camera on the area where initial testing indicated the presence of blood.
2. Take a photograph of the area using standard photographic techniques or with the camera on automatic.
3. Set the flash on the lowest power possible.

   TIP: The author also places a frosted piece of thin plastic sheeting over the flash to further soften the effect.

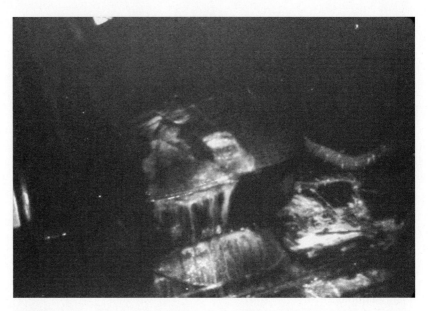

FIGURE 11–3   Blood stain patterns in a pickup truck documented with luminol.

4. Set the aperture at about *f*-8 and the shutter on bulb or time.
5. Take the photograph by tripping the shutter. The flash goes off, but your shutter remains open. Open your aperture fully and take an exposure of 3 minutes in total darkness.

Results

You should have one photograph as everything looks normally. The second photograph is taken from exactly the same perspective because the camera is mounted on a tripod. The difference is that you see the room as being rather dark, but you can easily see the items such as furniture in the room. At the same time, you have the positive on the actual photograph as you saw it when you were there. This avoids the use of questionable overlays. Bracketing might be well advised until you become proficient in the technique.

Fluorescein

Fluorescein is recommended for detection and documentation of trace blood for bloodstain pattern analysis. It works slightly different from luminol in that this process gives off a fluorescent pattern when exposed to blue or ultraviolet light. It uses a working solution and an oxidant. A fluorescein kit can be purchased from RC Forensic Inc., Bonita, CA, known as the Flora-Scene Kit. It is used as follows:

1. Add 5 mL distilled water to a small test tube with reagent. This is the working solution.
2. Let the zinc settle.

3. Mix this stock solution with distilled water at 1:100 dilution and placed in an aerosol bottle.
4. The oxidant, hydrogen peroxide, is mixed with distilled water to 1% to 3% and placed in another aerosol sprayer.
5. The working solution is sprayed on the suspected area.
6. The oxidant is sprayed on the area in question.
7. The results are illuminated with blue light, and an orange barrier filter is used by the observer and over the camera lens for photography purposes.
8. Photograph immediately with the still or video camera.

Results

Blue fluorescence is a positive finding.

RECOVERY OF EVIDENCE

When recovering bloody evidence, it should be dried prior to submittal. There is nothing wrong with recovering the items in plastic to transport to your facility, but once there, it must be removed and allowed to air dry. It should never be stored wet, as it will putrefy and lose all value as evidence. Bloody evidence can be placed in paper bags after drying, or better yet, in specially made paper evidence envelopes with a glassine window to allow it to be seen by the jury without removing it from the envelope in court. Paper allows the material to breathe and retain its value as evidence.

Clothing is often recovered from hospitals. Bloody clothing should be treated with care no matter where it is recovered from and should be spread out between papers such as butcher paper to preserve patterns. Hospitals are concerned with saving lives and are not very concerned with our evidence and cannot be faulted for this. With care, we can still salvage clothing that has been cut off and thrown on the floor or in the garbage.

▲ SUMMARY

It is not usual for a serologist to respond to most scenes and, as a result, most crime scene investigators are well versed enough to complete most tasks required. This has become an easier task with the commercial kits now available from the various supply houses. We are most concerned with safety when handling blood and other body fluids because of the concerns with AIDS and hepatitis. It is critical that shortcuts not be attempted.

■ REVIEW QUESTIONS

1. When storing bloody clothing, what are our most critical considerations?
2. Luminol is sometimes used as a presumptive blood test, but what other use is Luminol very valuable for?

3. With regard to pattern evidence, what is the procedure for recovering bloody clothing?

4. How do we document the results of Luminol examinations?

5. What are our concerns with regard to recovery of dried blood at a scene?

◆ REFERENCES AND SUGGESTED READING

RICHARD SAFERSTEIN, *Criminalistics: An Introduction to Forensic Science.* Pearson Prentice Hall, Saddle River, NJ, 2004.

PETER R.DE FOREST, R. E. GAENSSLEN, and HENRY C. LEE, *Forensic Science: An Introduction to Criminalistics.* McGraw-Hill, Inc., NY, 1983.

STUART H. JAMES and JON J. NORDBY, eds. *Forensic Science: An Introduction to Scientific and Investigative Techniques.* CRC Press, Boca Raton, FL, 2005.

HENRY C. LEE, TIMOTHY PALMBACH, and MARILYN T. MILLER, *Henry Lee's Crime Scene Handbook.* Academic Press, San Diego, CA, 2001.

WILLIAM G. ECKERT, MD and STUART H. JAMES, *Interpretation of Bloodstain Evidence at Crime Scenes.* Elsevier Science, NY, 1989.

BARRY A. J. FISHER, *Techniques of Crime Scene Investigation.* CRC Press, Boca Raton, FL, 2004.

Sexual Assault

Key Terms

Known Samples
Secretor
Fluoresce
Acid Phosphatase Test

INTRODUCTION/OBJECTIVES

Sexual assault is a category that demands extreme care when interviewing the victim. This is a traumatic incident not only physically, but emotionally as well. The manner in which you interview can have a direct impact on the satisfactory solution of the investigation. From a psychological standpoint, there are differing opinions as to the investigators being the same gender as the victim. For instance, if victim is female, the one school of thought says another female will be able to talk to her more openly and with more understanding and empathy. However, there is another school of thought that a female investigator is more doubtful of the complaint and sometimes feels that the victim in some way invited the assault by dress, activity, and/or location. We should not become involved personally in these or any other cases. We must be absolutely professional and unbiased while maintaining an air of compassion and understanding, as we do in child death investigation.

PHOTOGRAPHY

We obviously work with the standard crime scene photography as we would in any other case, but in addition, we must be very careful to document injuries, including bruises, which can be visible at the time of the investigation or later. It is a good idea to photograph any injuries over a period of 3 days to allow bruises to go through their normal transition, because they show different aspects as time passes.

A camera with color or black and white film and an 18A filter can be used to photograph bruises. Normal lighting provides quite a bit of infrared light for the photographs. Other techniques include the use of black and white film with a No. 25 red filter to bring out the bruising, and a newer technique is to use purple light with a yellow barrier filter over the camera lens. The photographs are shot at 200 ISO, 1/50th of a second. *Bracketing,* or taking photographs with settings both above and below what you feel is necessary, is recommended (see Chapter Five). An *alternate light source (ALS)* with its various filters can also be used to bring out bruises. Be sure to use the proper barrier filter on your camera lens, usually orange or yellow.

EVIDENCE AT THE SCENE

Although this scene is handled as any other overall, there are obviously certain classes of evidence we are very interested in, such as trace and serological evidence. Assume that the scene(s) are photographed, diagrammed, and processed for latent prints, as would other scenes coming to our attention. Therefore, we look next at the areas requiring special attention.

Pattern Evidence

Pattern evidence was chosen first for a specific reason. The suspect or victim, depending on whose property the offense occurred, would have entered and departed the scene. For this reason, we want to process the floor for footprints as well as palm prints, if the assault took place on the floor. As we work our way into the scene, we may detect prints by using oblique light from a flashlight or an ALS. Usually, the ALS is operated on "open" or white light. The main purpose is to provide three-dimensional attributes to the evidence to better visualize it.

RECOVERY OF PRINTS

The prints discovered in this initial search can be recovered using the following steps:

1. Locate the prints via visual inspection with and without ALS.
2. Photograph the prints both with and without a scale. The camera should be perpendicular to the print and mounted on a tripod to keep the camera steady.

   TIP: You may have to move the light around to see the print in the camera. If a flash unit is used, remove the flash unit and hold it at an oblique angle to the prints to visualize them. This may require a sync-chord or a slave unit (see Chapter Five) to trip the camera shutter.

3. A **static dust lifter** is an instrument that picks up prints in dust by using a high-voltage charge to cause the print to stick to a Mylar sheet that is placed over the print. The Mylar is then photographed to document the print. If the Mylar does not lift the print, or it is simply not available, a large print lifter (an enlarged version of a latent print lifter) can be used to lift the print. Should this not work, the print can be dusted as you would a latent fingerprint. It is then photographed again and lifted with an adhesive sheet of Mylar shoe print lifter. The key is to photograph all evidence first, as the prints are sometimes lost during the recovery process.

Fingerprints

We search and recover fingerprints from the scene as we would any other scene, but there are some specific areas we want to process, given the type of crime we are investigating. These areas include, but are not limited to,

- Bottom of toilet seat
- Flushing lever for toilet
- Door handles
- Anything handled by suspect or victim
- Glasses or cups that may have been used by the suspect or victim
- Condoms and condom wrappers (condoms are also important for recovery of **biological fluids**)
- Cigarette butts and ashtrays
- Partially eaten fruit, such as apples, that may have latent prints (food may also have bite patterns of extreme value to the case)
- Telephone

TRACE EVIDENCE

The successful investigation of sexual assaults often depends on various forms of **trace evidence**. This is one crime that is the perfect example of the theory of transfer. The average human loses about 75–80 hairs per day. This hair, from all over the body, falls off, and some may be pulled out. In a sexual assault, there is body-to-body contact, which means the victim's hair may be on the suspect and the suspect's hair may be on the victim (Locard's principle of exchange). Likewise, both may drop hair on the surfaces that they come into contact with. There is also the probability that they will pick up **fibers** (Figure 12–1) and other forms of trace evidence from contact with the environment within the crime scene. Hairs with follicles (Figure 12–2) may be subjected to DNA profiling, leading to the identity of the contributor of the hair. Because the recovery and submission of hair and fiber evidence is so important (Figure 12–3), recovery is recommended as follows (Figure 12–4):

1. First, perform a visual inspection. This can be with or without the aid of an alternate light source. Those hairs and fibers we see can then be

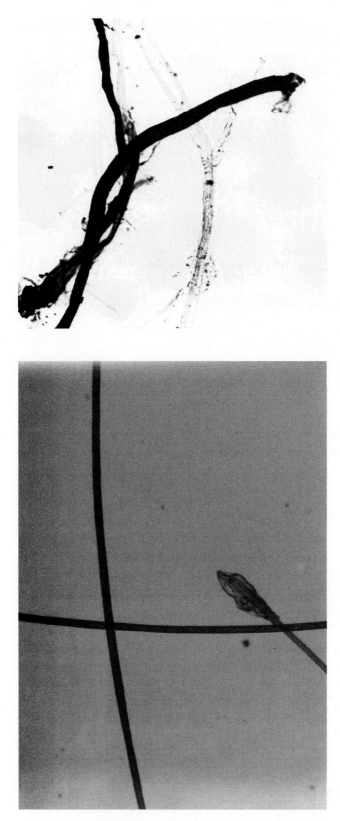

FIGURE 12–1
Photomicrograph of fibers.

FIGURE 12–2
Photomicrograph of hairs;
note the follicle at the right.

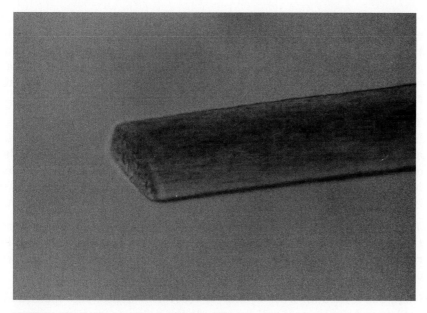

FIGURE 12-3   Example of cut hairs/fibers under a microscope.

recovered and placed in a paper envelope or folded piece of paper made into a ***druggist's bindle***.

TIP: Plastic containers are not recommended for this task because static electricity could cause the evidence to come out of the container as your fingers or forceps are removed. Furthermore, the evidence can breathe in paper, and therefore dry instead of putrefy. Be sure to document via photography and diagram from where the evidence was recovered.

FIGURE 12-4   Trace evidence kit with vacuum, filters, filter holders, tape, and Petri dishes.

2. Second, use tape to recover what is on top of the surface being processed. For example, what is on the top of carpet piling was deposited most recently. The tape used can be just about any, including fingerprint tape. There is a tape on the market today that dissolves when wetted with methanol. In the laboratory, this tape can be put in a laboratory funnel with filter paper; once the tape dissolves, you are left with the evidence.

   TIP: You can buy square, plastic disposable Petri dishes with covers from laboratory supply houses. Take the tape after having recovered the evidence and place it over the dish, and then place the cover on it to protect the evidence. The tape can then be peeled off in the laboratory to examine under a microscope. A square dish takes two strips of standard fingerprint tape. Again, you must diagram or chart from where you made each tape lift.

   TIP: You can use a lint roller for the taping process and do a small area at a time. Each time you remove the tape, be extremely careful that no evidence remains on the roller. Affix a single piece to the roller instead of using a roll of tape to lessen the chances of cross-contamination.

3. Next, use a vacuum with a ***filter*** to recover evidence. This method should not be used earlier as it will commingle the evidence from the various levels of the surface; for example, the top, midlevel, and webbing foundation of carpet. The most common filter is reusable and must be cleaned out after each section is completed. Filter paper is placed in the filter assembly, and after vacuuming a small section, the filter is folded and placed in a paper envelope. Each section is completed in this manner, with the filter assembly being cleaned between each sampling. This is the area of concern with this type of filter system. One must be extremely careful to clean the assembly completely and inspect it carefully to see that nothing remains that could cross-contaminate the following sample.

   TIP: An alternative to this system is one with disposable assemblies, with each separate filter housed in its own Petri dish. After each section is vacuumed, the filter assembly is removed and the cover replaced. The nozzle can then be discarded or cleaned very carefully. This system is more expensive, but there is little chance of cross-contamination of your evidence.

4. Finally we come to the point of recovering the entire piece of evidence, or cutting a section from the whole. This is then carefully slid into a paper bag and sealed.

STANDARD SAMPLES

Hair and fiber recovery are of little value unless there is some *standard* to compare them with. Simply put, if we recover hairs and fibers that we believe came from a blanket, carpet, animal, human, or any other source, we must have **known samples** from those sources. This means the recovery of hairs and fibers from whatever we believe is the source of those hairs and fibers. If the samples are hairs, we must have standards from those persons who might have contributed the evidence. Let's talk about recovery of standards.

Fibers

The recovery procedure is fairly straightforward. Gather samples from the believed source, preferably from an area that is less subject to contamination, such as a corner, under furniture, or another light- or no-traffic area. Gather several fibers (15–20), or possibly even cut out a small amount of carpet where it will not be noticed. These are packaged as any other evidence, but are labeled "Standards."

Hair

We take hair from the persons who might be the contributors of the evidence. We want to first comb the areas for evidence with the expectation that hairs from the other parties involved might be mixed with this subject's hair. Next, we must have the standards with which to compare the collected evidence. This is a representative sample from various areas of the body, including the head hair, pubic region, and any other part of the body with hair. The procedure is to pluck 10 to 15 hairs from each portion of the body. On the head, collect hair from the front, sides, and back of the head. These are labeled "Standards" and submitted for possible comparison. These hairs should have the follicles attached.

TIP: The hairs from the victim are usually recovered by staff at the hospital or sexual assault treatment center, if your jurisdiction has one. As for the suspect, the CSI is usually responsible for recovery of those hairs. This is a rather sensitive procedure, so you may wish to offer the suspect the option of plucking his own hair and then you recover and bag it. If the suspect declines, you recover the hair, but advise the suspect that the plucking might be painful.

BODY FLUIDS

Sexual assaults offer great potential for the recovery of body fluids, such as semen, and blood. These provide the investigative team with the basis for DNA profiling and, ultimately, identification of the contributors. We must understand the methods of recovering the evidence and, just as important, preserving it for laboratory analyses. We have the ability to use not only DNA profiling to identify either suspect or victim; about 75% of humans are **secretors**, meaning we can determine their blood type from body fluids as well.

Condoms and Semen

It is not uncommon to find condoms at scenes; should these contain fluid, they should be recovered as they were found. They should be kept cool and immediately transported to a laboratory. If this is not possible, the fluids can be absorbed with sterile cotton swatches and dried. This can then be kept cool and submitted when possible. If the semen is left in the condom in hot or humid conditions, there is a very good chance that it will degrade to the point of being useless.

If the fluids are dry, the entire object, such as underwear, a sheet, a towel, or whatever, can be recovered and dried, after which it should be transferred to a laboratory for analysis. When searching for semen on clothing or bedding, look for a yellowish stain with a starchy texture. Should you not be able to find the stains, either a **blue frequency light** with orange viewing filter or a **shortwave ultraviolet light** causes seminal fluid to **fluoresce** which means that when subjected to this light source, the substances become visible. Be aware that not all seminal fluid reacts in this manner. If semen is on a floor, it can be swabbed with a sterile cotton swab wetted with sterile water. The swab should then be dried and submitted to the lab.

TIP: Remember basic physiology and the laws of gravity. A suspect walking to the bathroom may have seminal fluid drop on the floor (Figure 12–5). This can be located with the shortwave ultraviolet light. Keeping this in mind, remember that when a victim goes to the hospital, he or she should take along extra clothing, at least underwear. Again, as a result of gravity, the underwear of the victim may well be a valuable resource for seminal fluid.

Semen Field Testing

When a stain is found and the question is "to recover or not to recover," our advice is to be safe and recover the evidence. You get only one chance. There is a field test that can be conducted and is available in kit form from various companies. Sirchie Fingerprint Laboratories, Inc., has a product, Cat. No. DCS100, **acid phosphatase test** reagent DISCHAPS, that is very simple to use, as follows:

1. Moisten a piece of test paper (provided) with distilled water.
2. Place paper on stain for 1 to 2 minutes to allow substance to wick into the paper.
3. Crush the two ampules in the test tube and shake for about 1 minute.
4. Remove the heavy paper "integrity cap" and hold the tube with the open end down. This results in the absorbent end of the "swab" becoming saturated with the solution.
5. Apply this reagent to the test paper from the stain. Do not apply it to the original stain.

Results

The test paper should turn purple within 3 seconds for a positive indication.

FIGURE 12–5   Using shortwave ultraviolet light to visualize semen on the floor.

Our advice is, if you think the stain might be semen, submit it. It is possible to get a negative test and still have semen present. Acid phosphatase (AP) is found in large amounts at puberty and remains high until about age 40, at which time there is a gradual decline.[1]

Clothes and Bedding

In sexual assaults, recover both clothing and bedding, if the crime occurred in a house or the suspect had a blanket or similar groundcloth in

---

[1]Stuart H. James and Jon J. Nordby, *Forensic Science: An Introduction to Scientific and Investigative Techniques.* Boca Raton, FL: CRC Press, 2005, p. 262.

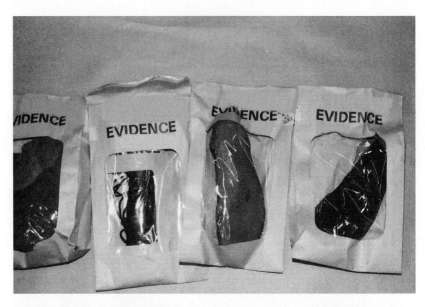

FIGURE 12–6   Proper method of packaging evidence, which may eliminate necessity of removing the evidence in court.

the car. It is critical that each piece of evidence be recovered in its own paper container (Figure 12–6). These should not be picked up where evidence might fall from it or blow away.

Clothing

1. Each piece of clothing should be placed in its own paper bag by sliding the object into the bag without picking it up. The object can be marked for evidence prior to bagging.
2. If the article of clothing is wet, it must be dried prior to packing it for evidence.
3. Take extreme care to keep clothing from the suspect and the victim from coming into contact with each other. They should be examined in different rooms.

Bedding

1. These items should be marked for evidence and then packaged in separate bags or containers.
2. They should be folded over to avoid any loss of evidence contained on them.
3. If stains are present and your agency includes it in their evidence protocol, you might want to circle those stains and place your initials near them. This helps avoid the evidence being missed during examination.
4. Loose hairs and fibers found on the surface of these items can be recovered as individual items and placed in separate evidence containers.
5. Again, these items must also be dried to avoid degradation of the evidence.

◢ SUMMARY

These cases are often made from the hair and fiber evidence collected as well as other forms of trace and transfer evidence. Always keep in mind Locard's Exchange principle, which states that we leave and take away evidence as we move about. Care should be taken to take full advantage of this form of evidence. Most of the evidence involves both the victim and suspect. Avoid cross-contamination at all costs, and store that evidence properly to prevent contamination.

◼ REVIEW QUESTIONS

1. What is Locard's Exchange principle?
2. About how many hairs does a human lose in 1 day's time?
3. What is a *secretor?*
4. Is it possible to conduct DNA analyses on hairs?
5. If the proceeding question is true, then what criteria, if any, must be present to do so?
6. Why do we want the suspect's and victim's clothing?

◆ REFERENCES AND SUGGESTED READING

BARRY A. J. FISHER, *Forensic Science: An Introduction to Scientific and Investigative Techniques.* Boca Raton, FL: CRC Press, 2005.

HENRY LEE, TIMOTHY PALMBACH, and MARILYN T. MILLER, *Henry Lee's Crime Scene Handbook.* Academic Press, San Diego, CA: 2001.

BARRY A. J. FISHER, *Techniques of Crime Scene Investigation.* Boca Raton, FL: CRC Press, 2004.

Elder, Child, and Spouse Abuse and Neglect

Key Terms

Decubitus Ulcer
Bedsore
Blanching
Positional Asphyxia
Ambient Temperature
Livor Mortis
Apnea Monitor

INTRODUCTION/OBJECTIVES

It is unfortunate that this type of abuse is somewhat commonplace to-day. It might be that it was simply not reported before and was some-thing kept secret by the family, a sort of "Don't air the family's dirty laundry in public" attitude. For whatever reason, we find this form of crime being reported more often. Learn to detect the physical evidence necessary to prosecute these crimes, because they are crimes in which cooperation is often extremely difficult to obtain. As a matter of fact, even victims may become hostile to law enforcement when asked to provide evidence. Even more concerning is the fact that many of these cases come to the attention of law enforcement only after there has been a death.

Investigations involving the neglect and abuse of our elders have become fairly common. This abuse may result from incidents within a "home care" or other residential setting, and, in some instances, even the victim's own home. The neglect can be either intentional or simply inattention to the needs of the victim. This type of case, like that of child abuse and neglect, may be altered either intentionally or as the result of life-saving efforts. Crime scene investigation should be mandatory in these cases.

The case might come to the attention of authorities after the victim has received emergency care from an ambulance unit or in a hospital. It may come to light as the result of a death investigation that had nothing to do with abuse, but after examining the body, sores and other evidence are detected. If the victim is away from the primary scene, then it is imperative that the investigators gain access to the scene before it is destroyed. Often, no one is at home, as they are at the hospital. Arrangements can be made to meet the family at the home after the hospital visit is completed.

ELDER ABUSE AND NEGLECT

Investigators should be careful to determine that injuries are the result of neglect or abuse because some injuries that may indicate foul play are in fact the result of normal circumstances.

CASE STUDY

A female was found in her kitchen, deceased. This elderly female appeared to have died as the result of natural causes. However, on being examined at the morgue, it was noticed that she had what appeared to be a ligature mark on the front of her neck that did not slant upward. This could be indicative of a homicidal ligature, but after visiting the scene it was noted that there was an aluminum walker near where the body was found. It was noted that the diameter of the walker tubing was the same as the pattern on the victim's neck. After further investigation, it was determined that as she collapsed, she had fallen with her neck over the overturned walker. The first persons at the scene had moved her and pushed the walker away so they could examine her.

EVIDENCE

When arriving at a scene that was not initially reported as abuse or neglect, investigate with an open mind. There are certain clues that, when put together, might indicate something out of the ordinary. Each should be documented with photography. Some of these clues are

- Little or no food in the residence
- The residence is dirty and messy (remember, however, that some elderly persons may not be the best housekeepers)
- Little evidence to indicate persons attempting to care for the victim
- **Decubitus ulcers** (bedsores) beyond what one would expect with proper care (Figure 13–1)
- **Bedsores** that are bleeding and draining (Figure 13–2)

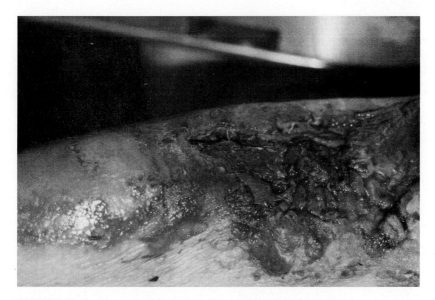

FIGURE 13–1 Sore on elderly decedent infested with maggots. (Photo courtesy of the Honolulu Medical Examiner.)

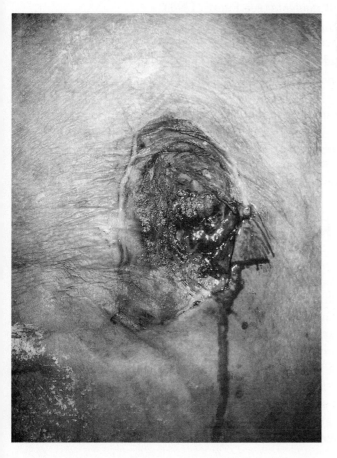

FIGURE 13–2 Draining bedsore of elderly decedent. (Photo courtesy of the Honolulu Medical Examiner.)

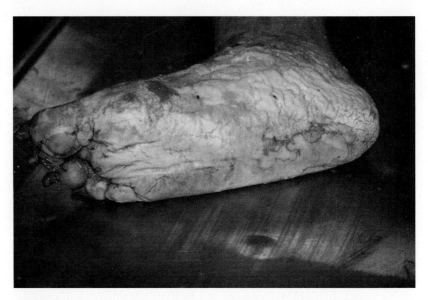

FIGURE 13–3 Foot of elderly decedent. Note the long toenails and infected foot.
(Photo courtesy of the Honolulu Medical Examiner.)

- Bedsores infested with maggots (see Figure 13–1)
- Bedclothes and clothing dirty, and possibly containing urine and fecal matter that appears to have been that way for some time (eg, dried fecal matter)
- Hair matted, dirty, and messy to extremes
- Long, untrimmed toenails and possibly fingernails (Figure 13–3)
- Nothing to entertain the victim (this may not seem important, but from a psychological standpoint, it is a factor)
- If this is a home-type of care facility, is there a caretaker living in the residence? Some state laws require a caretaker live at the facility. There are some "care homes" in which one of the resident patients is in charge of the home and little (if any) care is provided.

CHILD ABUSE AND NEGLECT

Child abuse and neglect are very detailed investigations that require as much, if not more, attention than many adult death cases. There is a lot of follow-up investigation that may be required of the CSI or the detective or both. Much of the investigation is the same in abuse cases not involving death as in those involving death, but after those initial steps, the death investigations become very detailed.

All CSIs involved in these investigations must remember that information provided at the death scene may not be as it was at the time of the incident. Sometimes the scene is altered as a part of life-saving efforts or because of fear of investigation by the caregivers. Also, some evidence may not be easy to detect, so care must be emphasized.

The Scene

On arrival, the scene is documented in the standard manner with regard to the scene photographs and drawings. Time is important here, however, because after initial photography of the body, one must examine the body before it changes with regard to **blanching**. Some points unique to infant and child deaths are

- Blanching of the face that might indicate the infant was sleeping in the *prone* (face down) position. Infants should be in the *supine* (face up) position when sleeping and can suffer from **positional asphyxia** because of the inability to move their head when face down.
- Does the evidence indicate possible "*over lay*," where an adult's leg, torso, or arm is on an infant sleeping with the adult? Look for blanching and other evidence that must be photographed immediately.
- Is bedding in crib or bed too soft (Figure 13–4)? The author investigated a case in which the mother put comforters under the infant to make the bed more comfortable. The infant was prone and suffocated.
- When examining the bedding, take the usual photographs of the crib or bed. Take photographs with a measuring device to indicate the thickness of the mattress. Also photograph other items, such as blankets, comforters, and pillows, to show everything in its entirety. Any items believed to be involved should be recovered for laboratory examination.
- Does the bedding show impressions where the child might have been positioned? If so, take detailed photographs.
- If the child was caught in a bed rail or between the railing and the mattress, that area should be photographed, even though the child has been removed.

   TIP: When investigating these cases, if the child has been removed, you can use a doll of the same average size to replicate the infant and demonstrate

FIGURE 13–4   The bedding in an infant death.
(Photo courtesy of the Honolulu Medical Examiner.)

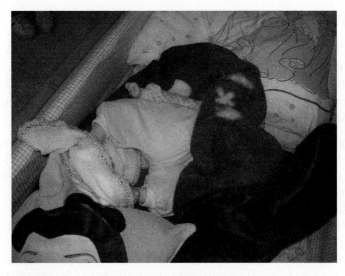

FIGURE 13–5 The same bedding as in Figure 13–4, but using a lifelike doll placed in the bed in a reconstruction showing how the infant was found.
(Photo courtesy of the Honolulu Medical Examiner.)

its positioning in the photographs (Figure 13–5). Some medical examiner's investigators carry such dolls to help with the investigation. Remember to photograph both with and without the doll.

- Very detailed photographs of the child, alive or deceased, should be taken showing bruising or other signs of injury, both accidental and deliberate.

TIP: Bruises may be photographed using standard photography, but *infrared photography* and photography using an 18-A filter may show bruises that are not visible to the naked eye. Another advantage to the 18-A filter is that it does not record "*mongoloid spots*" that are common on the upper buttocks of children of Asian ancestry (Figure 13–6). These are often mistaken for bruises, but they are not. This filter also shows bruises that may be masked by these spots.

TIP: Another suggestion with bruising is to photograph the bruises over a period of time or even over several days. Bruises change, and you might see more extensive bruises in later photographs than in photographs taken immediately. A good rule of thumb is 3 days.

- Were there toys in the bed or crib? Could any of these been the cause of or contributed to death? Photograph and recover any and all suspected items.
- Is there a baby bottle in the sleeping area? If so, photograph it, and after it is properly documented, photograph it upright to indicate the level of any contents.
- Is there any sign of mucus or evidence that the child might have vomited? Photograph and recover the item.
- The condition of the house should be documented to indicate the quality of care and surroundings.

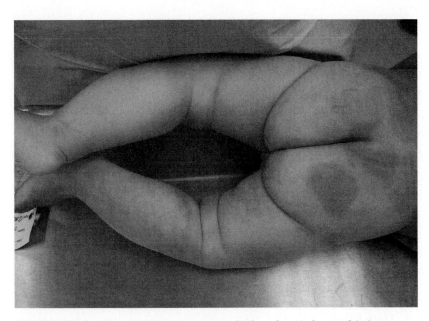

FIGURE 13–6 Mongoloid spots commonly found on infants of Asian ancestry. They are not bruises and are not a sign of abuse. (Photo courtesy of the Honolulu Medical Examiner.)

- **Ambient temperature** should be taken of the death scene as well as that of the body.
- Are there signs of **livor mortis** (***postmortem lividity***) present? Photograph to indicate if the body is in the same position or has been moved.
- Is ***rigor mortis*** present? Sometimes photography can show this by the position of fingers and other parts of the body.
- If clothing was removed from the child and left at the scene, this should be photographed, documented, and recovered.
- Was the clothing sufficient for the temperature of house? Was the clothing either insufficient or overdone?
- Was there a heater or air conditioner in operation? Photograph, if appropriate.
- Is the infant's diaper soiled (Figure 13–7A)? Are there signs of severe diaper rash (Figure 13–7B)? Document and, if necessary, recover the diaper.
- Is there a ***nebulyzer***, an air pump that atomizes medication for asthma patients? Photograph it if one is there. Was it in use? Was one prescribed?
- Is there an **apnea monitor** (a monitor that sets off an alarm if the infant stops breathing)? Was one prescribed? Was it in use?
- Is there any sign of medication? Photograph and recover it. Document the following:

  1. Name of medication
  2. Strength of medication
  3. Dosage of medication
  4. Prescribing doctor and contact information
  5. Date prescribed

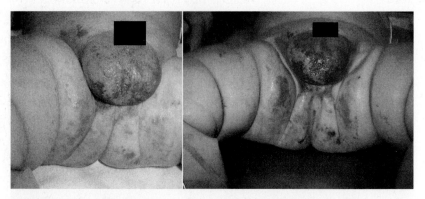

FIGURE 13-7   Severe diaper rash on an infant. Note that how the photo is taken is very important; they look like two different children. (Photo courtesy of the Honolulu Medical Examiner.)

6. Pharmacy that filled the prescription
7. Name of the patient on container
8. Date filled
9. Amount of medication issued
10. Amount of medication left

As you can see from this list, many questions can be answered. Is the medication for this victim, or for another person? Was the medication being taken as intended? Was the medication fresh? Could this medication have reacted with another medication being used? You can go on with the advantages of such information, and, of course, recover the medication to test the contents, if necessary.

- Are folk or herbal remedies being used? If so, these should be documented in the standard manner, and it might be advisable to recover the medication for testing in the laboratory. It is not uncommon for such remedies to be used, and when used in conjunction with modern medicines, some folk or herbal remedies may be extremely detrimental.
- Are there signs that the occupants drink and/or smoke in the residence? Does the victim show any signs of congestion?
- In suspected abuse cases, it is important to check other children to see if they also have injuries. The detective facilitates this, and photographs of any injuries to those victims should be taken as well.

CHILD INJURIES

Some of the injuries you might find in child abuse cases vary somewhat because of young age, because the body may not have developed enough to avoid the trauma. These might include, but are definitely not limited to,

- Bruising of the brain from being shaken
- Twisting-type fractures of bones
- Pinch marks

- Bite marks
- Burns to various or all parts of the body from cigarettes or similar items
- Scalding from immersion in hot water on feet, hands, or buttocks
- Welts or linear injuries from belts, switches, and other items

SPOUSE AND FAMILY ABUSE

Spousal abuse is much like the other forms of abuse, except possibly less reported than the others because other, nonfamily members may notice and report physical abuse of elders and children. Psychological abuse is much more difficult to see and document, at least from our viewpoint.

EVIDENCE OF ABUSE

Evidence is found more in the form of bruising and, sometimes, broken bones. Bruising can be documented by standard photography for what is visible, but we can also use infrared and ultraviolet photography to document these injuries. Broken bones, of course, would be documented by x-ray.

Photography

Standard photography is used initially and should be done with color film. The injuries should be recorded for a period of about 3 days, as the injuries change during that time, with different phases visible during that period.

Photography of bruising can be conducted using ultraviolet and infrared photography and is covered in detail in Chapter Five. Remember that if you are using infrared film, there are some restrictions because of the sensitivity of the film, and you must follow the directions explicitly for decent results. Also, ultraviolet light can be hazardous to the subject of the photography, and you must take appropriate precautions.

Patterns

Bruises can be brought out for about 1 year under optimal conditions, but like everything else, this is not written in stone. While you are conducting all phases of photography of abuse, look carefully for patterns. What you might see could indicate the method used to inflict the injuries and could also indicate specific portions of the body that are attacked. Remember, many of the abusers do not want anyone to know what they are doing and may limit their physical abuse to parts of the body that are normally covered by clothing. They may hit or pinch the buttocks or the under or back side of the arm, and so forth. This pattern is important from the standpoint of modus operandi (MO). We tend to be creatures of habit, and that goes for abuse as well.

DEATH OF VICTIM

There are instances in which the victim dies, and this is not rare among child-abuse victims. In those cases a complete postmortem examination is required, and you may be involved in this portion of the investigation as well. Dissection of injuries can indicate possible cause, such as a "mosquito bite" that turns out to be a pinch mark. Furthermore, postmortem examinations can turn up past healed and partially healed injuries, such as broken bones that were never reported or treated. These are extremely valuable as evidence of behavioral patterns on the part of the offender.

◣ SUMMARY

Abuse is a phenomenon that occurs across all age groups. Infants to the elderly are victims of both intentional abuse and abuse by neglect. You must be aware of the possibility when investigating all injury cases. Some children are said to be "accident prone," but are, in fact, victims of abuse. Keep an open mind and be impartial in your investigation. Put that extra effort into your documentation process, not just to solve the case, but hopefully to save a life or remove an innocent victim from that environment.

◼ REVIEW QUESTIONS

1. When investigating elder abuse, who might we want to look at as the perpetrators?
2. What are some of the signs of neglect with elders?
3. What are some types of injuries you might find in abuse cases?
4. What are some injuries that might be specific to children?
5. What do we mean by *abuse by neglect?*
6. What are some of the indicators of elder neglect?

◆ REFERENCES AND SUGGESTED READING

BARRY A. J. FISHER, *Techniques of Crime Scene Investigation.* Boca Raton, FL: CRC Press, 2004.

KANTHI DE ALWIS, *Departmental Procedures.* Chief Medical Examiner, Department of the Medical Examiner, City and County of Honolulu, HI. 2004.

Death Investigations

In this section, understand that not all death investigations are the same, and that the differences can vary greatly. As a result of these differences, there are many forms of evidence that, although important to one death investigation, may have nothing at all to do with others. Understand these differences and then know how each advances your investigation the most. Also, understand how to go about getting the necessary information to investigate your particular case effectively.

There are considerations in death investigations that, although not directly related to solving your case, are critical in that not understanding them can result in considerable difficulty and embarrassment to you, your agency, and other agencies as well. These are considerations related to cultural differences regarding death and religion, and even individual considerations concerning how you talk about the death to how you handle the body.

Furthermore, you must always be fully aware that these are emotionally traumatic events to the families, and how you talk to them might make the difference between a smooth, uneventful investigation and one of animosity and even personal threat. You must constantly be alert to your surroundings and your actions.

Death Investigation: General Considerations

Key Terms

Manner of Death
Cause of Death
Postmortem Interval (PMI)
Postmortem Lividity
Tardieu Spots
Rigor Mortis
Cadaveric Spasm

INTRODUCTION/OBJECTIVES

All death investigations have certain aspects in common, but there are enough differences to warrant looking at each individually. Note that every section contains a section on safety, which we cannot stress enough. It is not just a case of your getting injured or sick, but by not taking the necessary precautions, you can cause your family, friends, and associates to become ill as well. Do not take shortcuts when it comes to safety issues.

We look at death investigation, beginning with subject matter that can be applicable to many different types of deaths, and then proceed to specific types of deaths in the latter part of this chapter.

MULTIAGENCY INVESTIGATIONS

There are many types of investigations that involve various agencies working together. This is very common in death cases, and even more common in serial murder cases. Be aware of the fact that there are various protocols and courtesies that must be addressed when working with these agencies. We do not wish to spend a great amount of time on this subject, but some points to consider include the following:

- All members of the task force must be included in everything. One of the fastest ways to alienate a member is to leave that agency out. The knowledge of one should be the knowledge of all, unless there is some compelling reason to keep some specific portion secret. Avoid this when possible.

- Follow protocol when possible. For example, some requests are supposed to be addressed to the chief of police or the Special Agent in Charge (SAC). Remember, most law enforcement agencies are administered in the same manner as military structures.

- Look at the capabilities of each specific agency. There are instances in which one particular agency should be the "lead" agency for advantageous reasons, such as stiffer penalties under federal jurisdiction or "deeper pockets" with regard to budget. Serial murder and clandestine drug laboratory investigations are very costly, and if the federal agencies take the lead, your jurisdiction might just save a lot of money.

- Keep in mind that "We are all on the same team and striving for the same results." Leave your "attitudes" at home.

CULTURAL DIFFERENCES

When working with death cases there is not only more than one agency involved that you must coordinate with, there are also jurisdictional, procedural, and even cultural awareness considerations as well. This is even more of a concern in our extremely multicultural society today. For example, in most Asian families, shoes are not worn in the house. It is rude to fail to remove your footwear when entering. However, there is also the possibility of walking in blood and other body fluids as well as stepping on something that might result in cuts or other injuries. Investigators in some jurisdictions carry hospital/laboratory booties that can be placed over the shoes to allow you to keep your shoes on and at the same time not walk in the house with dirty shoes. Little things such as this go a long way to keep everyone happy and, as a result, cooperative. What you do, or do not do, not only reflects on you and your agency, but on all the others involved as well. By the same token, "stick to your guns" and do what you are required to do to accomplish your assignment.

The Royal Canadian Mounted Police (RCMP) published a booklet regarding cultural awareness. They have protocols regarding "biker" groups, "aboriginal" groups, and so on. These efforts may make the difference between a successful and a failed investigation.

Although we strive to be impartial and as businesslike as possible, there are some instances in which we must adjust our techniques to satisfy local needs. You might be in an area where removing the body feet-first or placing the body in the vehicle head-first makes the difference in a successful investigation with no complaints versus a difficult investigation. Try to become aware of considerations, such as customs, or just simply to ease the stress of a death. If you must take a dead baby from the parents, the manner in which you do it makes a world of difference. If you must examine the body, ask the parents to step outside while you do so. Probing the body in their presence might be seen by the parents as hurting their child, even though it can no longer be felt.

Be aware and alert that death cases are potentially explosive. It is not rare to be threatened by family members who are adamant there will be no *autopsy*. Similarly, take care who is allowed to view the body. First of all, consider contamination of the scene; second, be alert to grieving family members becoming very upset on seeing the body. There is also the consideration that the family may in some way be a part of the criminal activity.

Unless duties are very specific, it is a good idea both as a matter of protocol and as a matter of being considerate to check with other investigators prior to making any major changes in procedure.

GOALS OF INVESTIGATION

The goals of the investigation of death are to determine the **manner of death** and the **cause of death**. We must determine whom, if anyone, is responsible for the death. The detective, of course, is also interested in the "why" of the death.

Manner of Death

The manner of death is seen as *natural, accidental, suicide,* or *homicide*. Another possible finding is *"undetermined,"* in which we may have a very good idea as to the manner of death, but simply do not have sufficient evidence to make a definitive classification. It is better to use "undetermined" if there is a possibility that there is another explanation for the death.

Cause of Death

The *cause of death* is the actual mechanism of death. What caused the subject's death? For example, a person can die from *asphyxiation*, and if it were the result of a trench caving in on the victim, the most likely manner of death would be accidental. If the victim was asphyxiated as the result of a pillow being placed over the face, the manner of death would be homicide. If the person hanged him- or herself, cause of death would be asphyxiation and manner of death suicide. If the victim asphyxiated as the result of choking on vomit, the manner of death could be seen as natural.

Time of Death (Postmortem Interval)

The time at which a person died may be witnessed and documented in a hospital or by a relative at home. If, however, the victim was found dead, then the time of death would be estimated based on one or more of a series of indicators. Note that *time of death* for death certificate purposes may differ. When a person is found deceased, the ambulance, county physician, or medical examiner's investigator may make the time of death as that time confirmation of death was made. These indicators are not definitive in nature, and the most accurate is not often even considered. They are

1. *Livor mortis, also known as* **postmortem lividity**, is observed as a reddish-purple to purple color, usually along the portion of the body closest to the surface on which it is found. This is simply the pooling of blood because of gravity. If it is also found on the upper surface of the body, it is an indication that the body has been moved. The purple area has some blanched or white areas where the body came into contact with the surface. It is usually found anywhere from 30 minutes to 2 hours after death, and is said to be "*fixed*" around 8–12 hours. The investigator should look at this as an investigative lead and nothing else. There are many variables involved in livor mortis setting in such as body weight, ambient temperature, and so on.

2. **Tardieu spots**. Tardieu spots are found where portions of the body (such as an arm hanging over the side of a bed) fill with blood as a result of the pressure of gravity, thereby causing *petechiae,* from the rupture of small capillary blood vessels. They resemble various-size blood spots on the skin.

3. *Rigor mortis*. Rigor mortis is the stiffening of the body because of early decomposition of the body. It usually begins setting in at about 2 to 4 hours after death, and is fully set by 12 hours. Again, this is simply an investigative aid. It can be thrown off by a number of factors. Infants may go into rigor shortly after death. Sometimes an infant is transported to the hospital and on arrival it is very difficult to perform endotracheal intubation on the infant because rigor has begun to set in the jaw. In one case, an adult male with emotional problems and on medication was throwing objects around his room. He picked up a large television and died while attempting to throw the object. The author arrived at the scene a short time later only to find the victim in rigor. This is sometimes referred to a **cadaveric spasm**. When the rigor is "broken," as in the flexing of the hands during the fingerprint process, the rigor does not return.

4. *Forensic entomology*. Forensic entomology determines the **postmortem interval (PMI)** by examining the various insects and successive generations of insects on a body. This can be accomplished based on the knowledge that certain insects begin their egg-laying at about the time of death to about 10 minutes after death, with various other insects visiting the remains at successive times; as a result, the presence or absence of a specific insect can be an indicator of time of death. This means the entomologist works backward from the time of discovery (assuming samples are recovered at that time) to the time of initial deposit of eggs. This technique is very accurate when compared with all the other methods.

▲ SUMMARY

The cause of death is closely related to manner of death, but we must not forget that the cause of death is sometimes rather broad and can be related to various manners of death determinations for a single cause, as shown in the asphyxia example described in this chapter. These are major goals of crime scene investigators, but the reason is something the detective is responsible for determining.

The "traditional" determining factors for time of death are described and shown to be not as specific as many believed, and forensic entomology has made the postmortem interval a more accurate and attainable goal.

▮ REVIEW QUESTIONS

1. Explain the basis for entomology in determining PMI.
2. Give some examples of cause of death.
3. Give some examples of manner of death.
4. Provide examples where the classification of "undetermined" would be a plausible manner of death determination.
5. Explain what is meant by *postmortem lividity*.
6. Explain what is meant by *rigor mortis*.

◆ REFERENCES AND SUGGESTED READING

WILLIAM D. HAGLUND and MARCELLA H. SORG, eds., *Forensic Taphonomy: The Postmortem Fate of Human Remains.* Boca Raton: CRC Press, 1997.

WERNER U. SPITZ, MD and RUSSELL S. FISHER, MD, eds., *Medicolegal Investigation of Death.* Springfield, IL: Charles C. Thomas, 1980.

Multi-Agency Investigative Task Force (MAIT) Manual. U.S. Department of Justice, Federal Bureau of Investigation.

Forensic Anthropology and Archaeology

Key Terms

Forensic Anthropology
Forensic Archaeology
Forensic Odontology
Forensic Entomology

INTRODUCTION/OBJECTIVES

Forensic anthropology and **forensic archaeology** are often considered interchangeable in the forensic field. They work together and often overlap, so if you require field services you can take the specialist available to you. Our objective in this chapter is to make you aware of what is available and how to locate and best use the experts available. There is no possibility of your gaining any significant knowledge from a general text. This is a field you must study under the direction of an expert. You can, however, learn to determine what might be important, as well as how and what to do or not do until you can get professional help.

LOCATING EXPERTS

Assistance is often as close as your local university. In some locations, like Hawaii, there is help from the university level, as well as anthropologists, archaeologists, and **forensic odontologists** available from the U.S. Army Central Identification Laboratory (CIL), all of whom are true experts in their disciplines.

The question on the reader's mind is just how these people can aid our investigations. We cover some of their work, but, of course, as in everything else in this book, we cannot cover everything in depth. First, we must know what these specialists do. The **forensic anthropologist** studies bones from the legal standpoint. Skeletal material is often all we have to work with, and the interpretation of these bones must be left up to the experts. **Forensic archaeologists** study humans, looking at all aspects, not just the skeletal material, but also what is with humans: their tools, food, clothing, dwellings, and even their garbage. The **forensic odontologist** looks at dentitions, or teeth, often to make identification of persons based on the comparison of dental records, x-rays, and charts of possible victims. Although they work mostly with human teeth, they sometimes work with other animals, such as dogs, when related to death.

The forensic anthropologist can assist you with answering some basic but critical questions, such as[1]

- Age at time of death
- Height of individual
- Race of individual
- Sex of remains
- Identification via x-ray, medical history, and forensic odontology

There are some other questions that they can answer that overlap that of the forensic pathologist, such as

- *Cause of death,* such as illness, injury, or the actual mechanism of death.
- *Manner of death,* such as homicide, suicide, natural, or accidental.
- Interpretation of traumatic injuries.

The forensic anthropologist can also assist with other interpretations, such as lifestyle, type of physical labor performed, pipe smoking, medical interventions, illness, and so on.

SUGGESTED PROCEDURES

If you are working on a criminal case involving skeletal remains, you are advised to seek the assistance of one of these experts. You should include them as soon as the beginning of field operations. If you cannot find a forensic expert, an option is to go to a university with an anthropologist on staff and inquire as to what assistance they can provide or if they can refer you to someone. Universities are a wonderful source of information and assistance. Take full advantage of these resources. Treat them well, and they will treat you well.

---

[1]STEVEN N. BYERS, *Introduction to Forensic Anthropology.* Boston: Allyn & Bacon, 2002.

Ancient Remains

If you are not on a criminal case but are simply responding to skeletal remains found at a location, then you have no idea as to what you are responding to with reference to final classification of the case. Be aware of local protocols. As an example, in the State of Hawai'i, we have many ancient remains; as a result, we must look at the scene and determine if the remains are ancient or, as is most likely, historic. The general rule is the police and medical examiner cannot touch any ancient bones, but instead contact the State Archaeologist, who responds to the scene and takes charge of the remains. They are usually reburied at the same site. This is most likely true in your jurisdiction as well, which, like ours, is governed by various local and federal laws concerning repatriation of all ancient remains and artifacts.

We determine which remains are most likely ancient by answering some basic questions, such as

- Do the bones have the appearance of being old (dark tan, etc.)?
- Are there any signs of clothing?
- Are there any signs of modern objects, such as a watch, jewelry, and so on?
- Are there any bullet holes or other traumatic injury suggestive of murder (Figure 15–1)?
- Is there any dental work?
- Are the teeth worn down?
- Are there any artifacts suggesting the remains are ancient?
- Are you in an archaeologically rich area?
- Does the "burial" or find meet with past ancient finds?

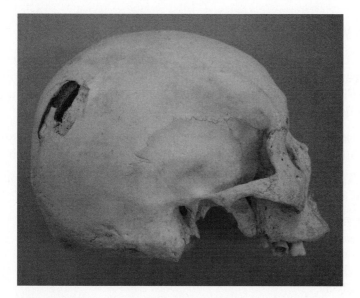

FIGURE 15–1   Skull showing postmortem damage.

Another critical question, but not as simple as one might believe, is, are the bones human or animal? Small animals, especially those with the head missing, might appear to be the bones of a human infant. If you are in the slightest doubt, call for an expert.

Modern Remains

If your find is found to be other than ancient remains, you are involved in a case with which you have probable jurisdiction. This is when you should request for the services of the forensic anthropologist, archaeologist, and possibly **forensic entomologist** (covered in Chapter Seventeen) prior to doing anything else at the scene.

TIP: If the remains are determined to be fairly fresh skeletal artifacts, proceed very carefully around them. The skin is very often sloughed off the body during the decomposition process, often aided by maggot activity. A portion, or even the entire "glove" of the skin on the hands, may be in the near vicinity of the bones. They may appear to be crumpled, dried-out leaves. These can be rehydrated and printed. Take care to recover any dried skin for examination.

TIP: If possible, do not begin your "dig" without the forensic experts because they can often advise you as to the age of the burial, and may even be able to determine if the scene has been dug more than once, in certain instances. Your attempt at recovering the remains might cause difficulty because they will not be seen in context to their burial. You might destroy evidence that the expert can recognize that and you will surely miss without extensive training. Proper recovery is a slow and tedious process, but rightly so.

Recovery of Remains

Although it is not advised that remains be recovered without one of these experts present, there may very well be instances when this might be imperative (Figure 15–2). In that case, it is recommended the remains be recovered following these steps:

1. All stages of the recovery process must be photographed in detail.
2. A detailed drawing must be made of the site, with exact location, if possible.

   TIP: This can be established with the aid of a geographic positioning system (GPS), which is not expensive and is very accurate.

3. The remains *must not be cleaned.*
4. The remains must be placed in a protective container with appropriate padding to avoid any further damage.
5. Everything recovered with the remains must be included with the remains for analysis.

FIGURE 15-2 Skeletal remains that provided significant entomologic evidence.

6. Soil samples must be collected to include all apparent changes in soils or their consistency.
7. Care must be taken to recover entomologic samples (covered in Chapter Seventeen).

SUMMARY

Forensic anthropology is a discipline requiring years of study and research under the direction of an expert. You can learn the basics of forensic anthropology in a few courses that should suffice in keeping you from ruining the evidence and to get some ideas of what you have. Although this knowledge will help you direct your investigation, it is not meant to be a substitute for professional help.

REVIEW QUESTIONS

1. Identify and explain a few ways in which a forensic anthropologist might assist you in an investigation.
2. When bones are recovered at a scene, what steps should be taken by the police agency prior to being turned over to an expert for examination?
3. When we recover remains, what procedures should be followed concerning other items that were included with the remains?
4. If the remains we find appear to be ancient, what procedures should be followed?

5. What are some of the indicators that bones are not ancient?
6. Is it possible to determine if a "grave" has been dug more than once?

▓▶ REFERENCES AND SUGGESTED READING

STEVEN N. BYERS, *Introduction to Forensic Anthropology.* Boston: Allyn & Bacon, 2002.

WILLIAM M. BASS, *Human Osteology: A Laboratory and Field Manual.* Columbia, MO: Missouri Archaeological Society, Inc., 1995.

Forensic Odontology

Key Terms

Dentition
Bite Marks
Oblique Lighting
Superimposition

INTRODUCTION/OBJECTIVES

Forensic odontology was originally included with Chapter Fifteen, but after some thought, it was decided this topic should stand alone because forensic odontology is used with live persons almost as much as with deceased persons. Our goal in this chapter is to have you understand the value of forensic odontology in the investigation of both live and deceased persons, and the various methods used that advance your investigation.

BITES

Odontology is the study of human **dentition**, or teeth (Figure 16–1). It also involves the study of injuries to humans as the direct result of both human and animal bites, and not only with a human as the recipient of the bite; it can involve other objects as well.

There are cases involving animals that may come to your attention. Animals have been used to attack persons intentionally and, of course, we read fairly often in the news about animals getting loose and attacking persons. These cases involve animals such as dogs, but other than that, the handling of the case is handled in much the same way as any other case involving a person.

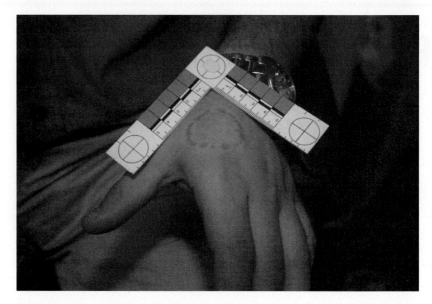

FIGURE 16–1 A bite mark. This should be photographed the following day to show the bruising that follows.

BITE MARKS

Impressions on Live Persons

There are various categories of **bite marks**, or the impressions or punctures resulting from the pressure of the bite. We most often think of this as a person biting another person. If this was your impression, then you are partially correct. A person may be bitten in fight, where a victim may bite a suspect or a suspect may bite a victim. There is a variation of this in which the bite mark can be seen as a form of defense wound. An example of this would be the victim of a sexual assault biting the assailant (Figure 16–2).

Another instance in which bite marks can be used as evidence includes when the recipient was not another person. It is not that uncommon for an individual to eat food at a crime scene and leave portions of that food behind. This may be in the form of cheese, chocolate, or other relatively dense food that may contain the teeth marks of whoever bit into it (Figure 16–3). This is valuable evidence, as it may be the one item that puts the suspect at the scene.

Impressions in Food and Other Items

The evidence we recover in the form of food, Styrofoam cups, and other portable items should be taken immediately to a laboratory. If this is not possible, some processing is in order. Always remember that bite-mark evidence of any kind is subject to time constraints. We discuss the documentation procedures briefly here, but they are described in more detail in Chapters Five and Eight. It might be advisable to refer to these chapters if you are in doubt.

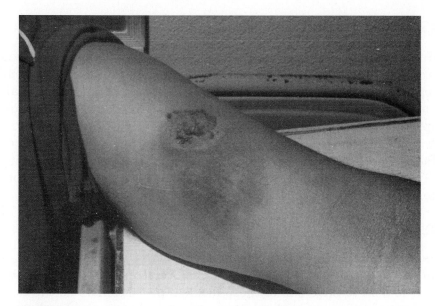

FIGURE 16–2 A bite mark left by a deceased victim. Note the bruising. Detailed photography is required to facilitate comparison.

PHOTOGRAPHY

Take close-up and macro photographs with and without a scale, preferably an ABFO #2 scale. **Oblique lighting** is best because it causes three-dimensional patterns to be optimized. It is best to have your camera mounted on a good tripod because fine detail is critical in these photographs. Remember when using a tripod that it is also advisable to use a cable or other form of shutter release to avoid "camera shake," even on a tripod. For more detailed instructions concerning the photography, please refer to Chapter Five.

FIGURE 16–3 A piece of candy that was bitten in half and contains some very nice tooth impressions.

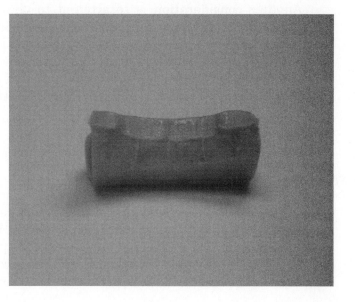

CASTING IMPRESSIONS AND PATTERNS

Again, as with photography, should you require detailed instructions for casting, refer to Chapter Eight concerning pattern evidence. Remember, our casting material is a simple two-part mixture that is very straightforward to mix. Following the instructions on the container or those in Chapter Eight, mix it very well and then spread it on the pattern you wish to cast. Allow it to dry about 10 minutes, and then test the outer surface to ascertain it is dry enough to handle. Remove the cast and store it pattern side up in a container that does not put pressure on the pattern.

Live Persons

If the pattern requiring casting is on a live person, consult an expert, such as an odontologist or a medical doctor, before attempting to cast the pattern. It is best to have one of these medical professionals do the casting. Should you decide to cast the pattern, you may have some legal concerns if the person being cast has an infection or anything else they might associate with you casting the pattern.

MISSING PERSONS

If you have a potential victim who is missing, get a head start on possible future examinations. It is a good idea to attempt to obtain or at least determine the location of any dental x-rays and charts of that person. This way, should remains be found, you might be able to make an identification or elimination more expediently.

Another consideration is to attempt to obtain photographs of the missing person that show the person smiling with teeth showing. This may be valuable for **superimposition**, a process in which an x-ray or an image of skeletal remains can be used to superimpose or overlay on a photograph of the victim to see if there is a match of the tooth patterns. Although this does not result in a positive identification, it can speed things up through inclusion or elimination.

OBTAINING DENTAL RECORDS

Possibly the most difficult task regarding dental records is locating them. Family may be able to assist you in this matter, but should that fail, it might come down to investigators (not CSI personnel) hitting the telephones or pavement to find them. Once the records have been located, the process is not difficult. Most jurisdictions have regulations or laws that direct medical facilities to assist law enforcement in the identification of deceased persons if they possess the records that may aid in the endeavor.

Contact the dental office and identify yourself and the need for the records properly. From experience, these professionals usually assist you by either giving you the original records or, more likely, providing you with copies of the records or loaning you the records to complete your task. Be sure to return these records as soon as you finish your work. If, however, you have a habit of not returning things, you will soon find less and less cooperation.

◤ SUMMARY

Dental evidence is very useful when investigating assault cases of various types, but may be critical when considering the identification of decomposed and skeletal remains. Odontology is a very common specialty among medical examiner's facilities. Should you have difficulty in locating an odontologist contact your nearest medical examiner's facility, although they will most likely be involved in your investigation at this point.

◤ REVIEW QUESTIONS

1. What is odontology?
2. In a few words, describe the process for casting bite marks.
3. Again, in a few words, what is the photographic process for bite marks?
4. Why do we want to have photographs of the missing person that show the teeth?
5. Why are we concerned with casting bite marks on live persons?

◆ REFERENCES AND SUGGESTED READING

STEVEN N. BYERS, *Introduction to Forensic Anthropology*. Boston: Allyn & Bacon, 2002.

WILLIAM M. BASS, *Human Osteology: A Laboratory and Field Manual*. Columbia, MO: Missouri Archaeological Society, Inc., 1995.

Forensic Entomology

Key Terms

Maggot Mass
Pupae
Pupate

INTRODUCTION/OBJECTIVES

The forensic entomologist is an extremely important part of the crime scene investigation team. When a person has been dead for some time, the forensic entomologist can be the most accurate source of **postmortem interval (PMI)**. *Postmortem lividity,* or **livor mortis** *and* **rigor mortis,** are subject to many variables, such as **ambient temperature** (the temperature of the surroundings) and body weight. When the body begins to decompose, however, these methods are no longer accurate. This is not true with the entomologist, who may be able to provide you with the PMI even when the body has reached the skeletal stage. The catch is that you must bring the entomologist to the scene as soon as possible; in the event that it is not possible, it is up to you to properly recover the required evidence and make the correct documentation. The old saying about "He who helps himself, receives help" is true here. If you provide the entomologist with the proper information, he or she can help you. Our goal in this chapter is to help you gain the knowledge needed to recover samples properly for the entomologist should he or she be unable to come to the scene, as well as learn how to ship the samples to your entomologist and have them arrive in a condition that can be analyzed.

Note that the forensic entomologist is not limited to helping you with death cases but can provide assistance in cases involving live persons as well. This is very true in cases of elder and child abuse in which the victim is so neglected that maggots have invaded bedsores.

FIGURE 17–1 Flies on a pig being used for study of postmortem interval (PMI).

PHOTOGRAPHY OF BODY AND SCENE

If the entomologist is not coming to the scene, take photos of the body with particular interest to fly eggs, maggots, **maggot masses**, other crawling and flying insects, and any trails leaving the body. Also photograph the surrounding area, vegetation, soil conditions, and so on.

FLY EGGS

At any time from immediately at death to about 20 minutes afterward, flies begin to lay eggs on the body (Figure 17–1). These eggs are clumped together and almost look like a cross between crumbled cheeses and scrambled eggs. The location of the eggs is very important. Although they are usually placed in normal body openings such as eyes, nose, mouth, anus, and vagina (Figure 17–2), check the body for eggs or maggots in other, more unusual locations, such as stab wounds, bullet wounds, and bedsores. When you see eggs or maggots in an area with no normal opening, it is wise to suspect a possible wound. Note these and be sure to photograph them.

MAGGOTS

Maggots are the larvae of various insects; although you should collect samples of all insects at the scene, the first insects present are usually immature flies. Again, document where these are on the body. Note any difference in them, such as some being smooth whereas others are not. They are usually different species of fly larvae.

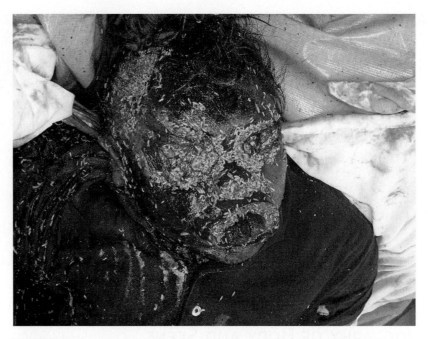

FIGURE 17–2   Maggot infestation on a decomposing body. This evidence is sometimes the best available to determine PMI.
(Photo courtesy of the Honolulu Medical Examiner.)

Maggot Mass

Maggots form masses around the body openings and are in a constant state of motion, going in to feed and coming back out to cool off (Figures 17–3, 17–4). Anything that decomposes increases its temperature significantly, and maggots must maintain proper temperature; hence the constant movement from "feeding ground" to the cooler areas on the outer edges of the mass.

Pupae

Maggots leave the body and go to a cool, covered place to **pupate**. At this point, they are known as **pupae**. Document these trails. The maggots develop a hard casing (puparium) that they exit after developing into an adult fly. These cases should be documented and recovered, both with pupae inside and empty.

Measurements at the Scene

Take the *ambient temperature,* if at all possible. It is a good idea to carry a thermometer. You may also want to shoot the core temperature of the body via the ear. This is not intrusive, nor is it going to be problematic to the medical examiner or anyone else.

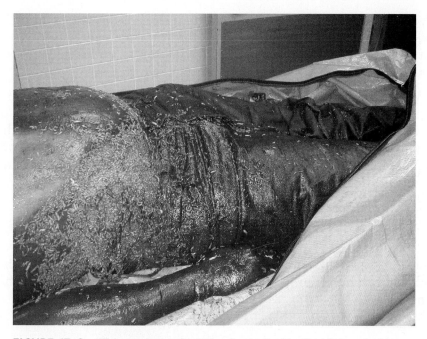

FIGURE 17–3 This maggot infestation is atypical in that it is not at a normal body opening, an indicator that there may have been a wound on the side of the stomach, where the maggots are thickest.
(Photo courtesy of the Honolulu Medical Examiner.)

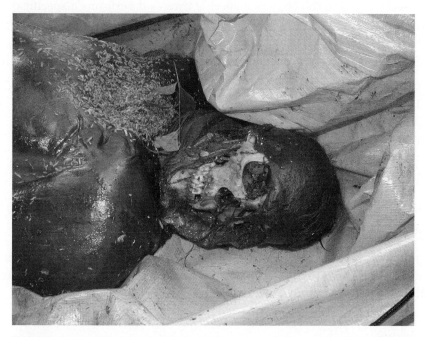

FIGURE 17–4 Decedent showing different rates of decomposition and maggot infestation.
(Photo courtesy of the Honolulu Medical Examiner.)

TIP: Carry an infrared electronic thermometer of the type sold at Radio Shack. Although not accurate enough for scientific use, it provides temperature readings within reasonable limits and at a reasonable price. Of course, if you can afford something better, go for it.

With very little trouble, you can find a weather report for the area where the body was found, possibly from the local weather bureau or an airport, among other sources. Note the precipitation, humidity, high and low temperature, elevation, and any other factors you might deem of possible value. Remember, you can never provide too much information, but you can certainly provide too little.

SPECIMEN RECOVERY

This is a critical task, and the better you accomplish this, the more the entomologist can help you. This means you must recover any or all of the following:

- Eggs
- Maggots
- Pupae
- Flies
- Pupal cases
- Other insects (e.g., spiders, bees, wasps, centipedes, beetles). Each of these insects comes to the body at a specific time and performs a specific duty; as a result, the presence or absence of a specific insect may be critical to the determination of the PMI.

Recover samples of each type of insect from various areas, including

- On the body
- Inside the body
- Around the body (to about 6 meters away)
- Under the body
- In the soil under the body
- Flying over and around the body

Necessary Equipment

There is a minimal amount of equipment required for recovery. It can be stored in the office until needed. It is possible to make do with other material, but as much as possible, adhere to this simple list:

- Surgical/examination gloves
- Forceps
- Glass vials (Vacutainers for blood are excellent)
- Trowel

- Insect net (If you cannot find one, a bird net from a pet supply house will suffice; however, it is a poor substitute for the real thing.)
- Killing jar (These can be purchased from a biological supply house or from a university, who might even give you one. They are only about $2.00.)
- Ethyl acetate (for killing live insects)
- Small artist's brush (A cosmetic/make-up brush can also be used.)
- Paper and plastic bags
- Ice cream (or similar) cartons
- Vermiculite or sand
- Ethyl alcohol (70%–80%) or isopropyl alcohol (cut 1 : 1 with water)
- Can of dog food or small piece of liver (If liver, pick up from the store as needed.)
- Cottonballs
- Sugar cubes

Recovery of Adult Insects

1. Flying insects are caught with the net.

   TIP: Instruct everyone to leave the body for about 10 minutes to allow the insects time to return. Then quietly go to the body and wave the net over the body in a figure-eight motion, ending by flipping the net over itself. This traps the insects in the net.

2. The insects are then killed using a killing jar (Figure 17–5). A few drops of *ethyl acetate* are dropped onto the ceramic disc affixed to the inside of the screw-top lid. The insects will go to the apex of the net when it is held up like a tent. Remove the top of the jar, put it inside the net going to the apex,

FIGURE 17–5 Tools of the trade: a net for catching insects and a killing jar.

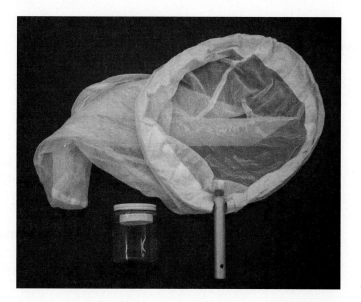

thereby trapping insects between net and jar. Place the lid on the jar over the net for a minute or so.

3. The insects can then be placed in glass tubes with a preservative (70% ethyl alcohol or 70% isopropyl alcohol cut 1:1 with water).

Recovery of Immature Insects

Immature insects (larvae, usually maggots) are recovered and placed in two suitable containers. A representative sample of all those found should be collected.

1. The maggots from the first container are then placed in KAA (1 part glacial acetic acid, 1 part refined kerosene, and 30 parts 95% ethyl alcohol). The maggots are left in this solution for 5–10 minutes. This breaks down the waterproof coating on the maggots. If this is not done, the maggots will rot. Remove the maggots and place them in a container of 70% ethyl alcohol for storage.

   TIP: If you do not have KAA, then you can simply use hot water, 76°C or 170°F. (You can obtain this in the field by going through a fast-food drive-through and ordering hot tea. Simply discard the unused tea bag and place the maggots in the Styrofoam Cup with the lid firmly attached.) Place the maggots in the water and leave them for a few minutes. They will sink to the bottom. This indicates the coating has been breached and the maggots can now be transferred to 70% ethyl alcohol, as you did the adults.

2. The maggots from the second container should be placed in a rearing chamber or an ice cream container with holes punched in the lid for air. The container should have some vermiculite (or moist soil if vermiculite is not available) in the bottom.

3. Place a small piece of beef liver or some canned dog food for the maggots to eat. The maggots must be delivered to the entomologist as soon as possible.

SHIPPING SPECIMENS

The materials should be shipped to the entomologist with consideration of the following points:

- Wrap all vials individually.

  TIP: If you are using Vacutainers, after placing the samples in the vial and adding the preservative, replace the top and then take a hypodermic needle and remove some air from the Vacutainers. This replaces the vacuum in the vial. This is important, because containers not treated in this manner may pop open during shipment as the airplane gains altitude.

- Place on a container with Styrofoam peanuts (or similar padding) all around.
- Place the containers of live specimens where they can best get air circulation. Never place on plastic or wrap the box in plastic because the live specimens will not survive the trip.

- Do not send live specimens via U.S. Mail.
- Containers should be labeled with background information such as date collected, time collected, portion of body from which collected, inside or outside the scene, and contact information for the persons collecting the samples. Other information as described earlier in this chapter should also be included.

▲ SUMMARY

Insects are very important to the determination of postmortem interval. Entomology is often more reliable than any of the more traditional methods, because insects invade a corpse at given times and under specific circumstances. This can be followed for multiple generations of the insects. It is also extremely important to get the expert to the scene as soon as possible; if not possible, then personnel should be trained in the proper techniques of recovering samples that can aid in the investigation. If the evidence is recovered properly, then the evidence supporting the case will be recovered.

■ REVIEW QUESTIONS

1. After placing our specimens in the test tubes, why should some of the air in the tubes be removed?
2. How should live specimens be recovered?
3. What should be fed to the maggots after recovery?
4. What do we place the maggots in after we have killed them?
5. From what areas do we take samples at the crime scene?

◆ REFERENCES AND SUGGESTED READING

E. PAUL CATTS and NEAL H. HASKELL, eds., *Entomology and Death: A Procedural Guide.* Clemson, SC: Joyce's Print Shop, Inc., 1990.

JASON H. BYRD and JAMES L. CASTNER, eds., *Forensic Entomology.* Boca Raton, FL : CRC Press, 2001.

WAYNE P. LORD and M. LEE GOFF, Chapter 43: Forensic Entomology: Application of Entomological Methods to the Investigation of Death. In *The Handbook of Forensic Pathology,* RICHARD C. FROEDE, ed. Northfield, IL: College of American Pathologists, 2003.

Injury and Wound Patterns

Key Terms _____

Abrasion Ring
Asphyxiation
Laceration
Ligature
Shored Wound
Stellate Wound

INTRODUCTION/OBJECTIVES

Wounds can be very valuable in that they can tell you a lot about what activities occurred at a given scene. We discuss some of the more common wounds and injuries as well as some other phenomena that may seem to be wounds but are not. This is meant to be an overview to familiarize the reader with what you might see and how it can guide and assist you in your investigation. We caution you that although these injuries are indicative of their origin, you will from time to time come across atypical injuries.

Wounds exist as the direct result of some action, and the wounds we examine here are indicative of those actions. Be aware that although nothing is written in stone, the information contained in this section may well assist you in coming to the correct conclusions.

SPECIFIC WOUNDS

Abrasion Rings

Abrasion rings are round or elliptical bands around the entry wound or defect that is raw in appearance because the projectile abraded or rubbed against the skin as it entered the body. The shape depends on the angle at which the projectile entered.

Binding Marks

Binding marks are actually a form of rope burn in that they are the result of a binding device such as a rope, telephone line, or clothing. They sometimes leave a friction burn that may break the skin, but may also leave welts and bruising to the bound area. They may be as simple as the mark left by clothing, such as elastic waistbands. Binding may be assaultive in nature, but can also be the result of autoerotic sadomasochistic activity, such as when persons involved in these sexual activities bind themselves, or have someone else bind them. These are desired activities and not the result of attack. Be on the lookout in sexual **asphyxiation** cases for "safety" devices to release the participant or allow escape. Deaths are often the result of the failure of these safety devices. Often, the ligature has a towel, or some other padding used to prevent bruising, that has fallen out. Some persons get pleasure from lack of oxygen, and intentionally cause air to be impeded by a ligature, pillow, blankets, or other air-restricting device around their neck, over their head, or covering their nose and mouth. The intent is to have the device release prior to passing out, but if they do, the safety is supposed to prevent death. Unfortunately, these safety devices sometimes fail, and the participant dies of asphyxiation as a result. You might look for a video camera, because some film these activities so that they can visually relive them at a later time. You might indeed have a video of the person's death.

Bruising

Bruising is something we all recognize but sometimes fail to understand. Bruises may be indicative of age, lifestyle, or, if observed properly, might have patterns such as hand marks. As we get older, bruises become more commonplace. Likewise, alcoholics tend to have bruises all over their bodies, especially around the legs and arms. Consider the scene as a whole before coming to a conclusion as to the cause of bruises.

Defense Wounds

Defense wounds are injuries, often *incised* (longer on the surface than deep) or *stab* *wounds* (deeper than surface length), caused by the victim putting up their hands to protect themselves. Wounds may be apparent on the front and back of hands and forearms. It is often believed that the victim will have stab wounds to the secondary hand from blocking (Figure 18–1) and incised wounds to the primary hand as a result of grabbing the blade or weapon (Figure 18–2). Although this is a common finding, it is

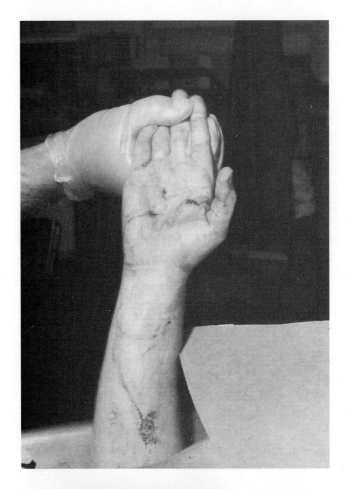

FIGURE 18-1 Defense wounds; stabbing on nonpredominant hand.

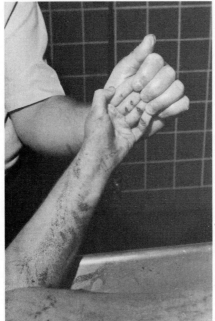

FIGURE 18-2 Defense wounds; incised wounds on predominant hand.

FIGURE 18–3 Child abuse; burn marks. (Photo courtesy of the Honolulu Medical Examiner.)

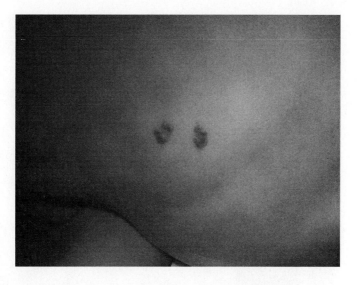

meant only as a guide and nothing else. Another misconception is that defense wounds result only from warding off an attack. This is not necessarily true.

Electrocution Contact Points

Electrocution contact points are those points of contact where the electric charge enters and/or exits the body. They are burns, sometimes resembling cigarette burns (Figure 18–3) or nail-puncture marks. The entry wounds might be on the hand, where the victim picked up or grabbed onto a "hot" object, but you commonly find an exit point, sometimes the feet and shoes.

Entry Wounds (Gunshot)

Entry wounds, especially gunshot entry wounds, have several different characteristics. They are usually puncture wounds that may be smooth, jagged, star-shaped (Figure 18–4), have an abrasion ring, or be shored. If the firearm was close enough, there might be tattooing or stippling (Figure 18–5A), very valuable evidence when considering distance determinations.

Exit Wounds (Gunshot)

One should be very careful about expressing opinions regarding entry and exit wounds unless well versed in them. They are often not that easy to distinguish, and the opinions expressed might reflect negatively on you at a later time. Exit wounds associated with bone are commonly found with

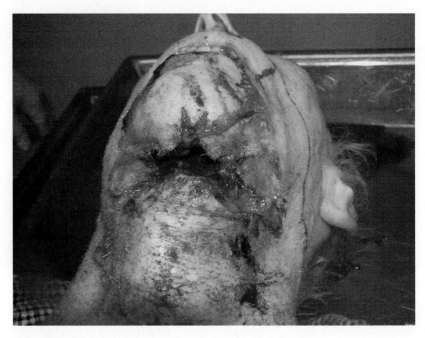

FIGURE 18–4   Stellate wound.
(Photo courtesy of the Honolulu Medical Examiner.)

the entry wound smaller than the exit wound. The exit wound also exhibits the beveling that makes it crater-like (Figure 18–5B).

Incised Wounds

Incised wounds are generally clean, being cut with a sharp instrument. They are generally longer on the surface than they are deep.

Lacerations

Contrary to common belief, **lacerations** are jagged cuts, typically longer on the surface than they are deep, and are the result of impact force tear-

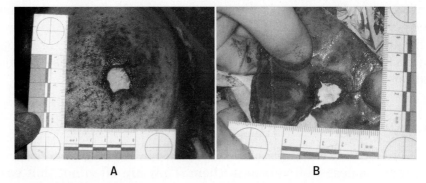

A	B

FIGURE 18–5   (A) Entry wound; (B) exit wound, note the beveling on the interior of the skull.
(Photo courtesy of the Honolulu Medical Examiner.)

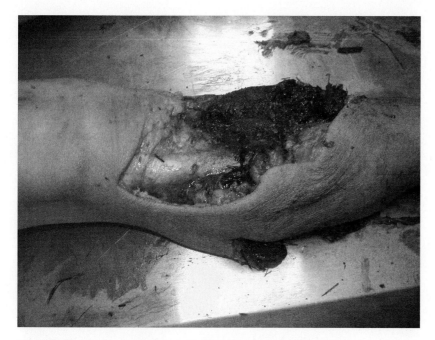

FIGURE 18–6 Lacerated wound, motor vehicle fatality.
(Photo courtesy of the Honolulu Medical Examiner.)

ing apart the surface (Figure 18–6). It is not a clean wound, but is irregular along the edges of the wound. Many persons confuse incised wounds with lacerated wounds. They are the result of different mechanisms.

Rope Burns

Rope burns are the result of a ligature of some sort rubbing across the skin. This can be from hanging, but can also be on the hands from a rope pulling through the hands rapidly when held to the skin surface. Again, do not jump to the conclusion that this is the result of some intentional assault.

Ligature Marks

Ligature marks (Figure 18–7) are, in many ways, the result of rope burns. When a person is bound, compression results in swelling, bruising, and possibly even breaking of the skin. This may be accidental or intentional. There is a widely held belief that in death by asphyxiation, ligature use is different in suicide and homicide. The reference concerns the ligature going up behind the neck in a suicidal hanging and going straight back in a homicide. Again, this is a guide and nothing more. There are suicidal cases in which the ligature went straight back. A lot has to do with the manner of "hanging," because many suicides are either not fully suspended or not suspended at all. It is also possible to have ligature marks as the result of autoerotic activity.

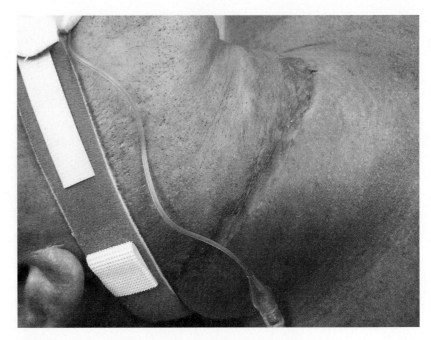

FIGURE 18–7   Ligature mark, braided polypropylene rope.
(Photo courtesy of the Honolulu Medical Examiner.)

Shored Wounds

Shored wounds are defects caused by a bullet striking a surface at almost a parallel angle. It results in a rather long, very shallow wound with tear marks, the apex of which points in the direction of projectile travel.

Stab Wounds

Stab wounds are the result of a knife or similar instrument being plunged into a body (Figure 18–8). It is typically deeper than it is long on the surface.

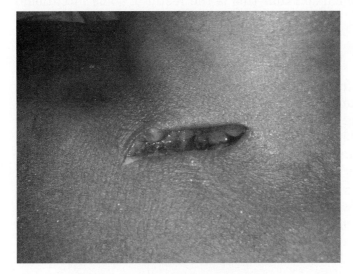

FIGURE 18–8   Stab wound.
(Photo courtesy of the Honolulu Medical Examiner.)

The depth of the wound is not necessarily indicative of the length of the blade. If the blade is not inserted all the way to the hilt, you have a shallower wound than the length of the blade; if it is pushed very hard, pushing in the skin surface, you have a wound deeper than the length of the blade.

Stellate Wounds

Stellate wounds are typically gunshot wounds at close range, usually over bone (e.g., the skull) as a result of gasses tearing the surface of the skin (see Figure 18–4). As a result of gas pressure and natural lines of tension in the skin, the wounds are star-shaped. It is also possible to get a similar wound from the impact of a blunt instrument on the head.

 ## SUMMARY

Wounds can be useful tools in determining what transpired at a scene, but we must be careful in describing them to avoid inaccuracies and possible damage to our credibility as a witness in the proceedings. Possibly the most important piece of advice to offer in this section is to remember: "Never say never and never say always."

 ## REVIEW QUESTIONS

1. What is a possible implication of a victim having incised wounds on one hand and stab wounds on the other hand?
2. If a person was shot at very close range, what would we expect to see at the entry wound?
3. What might a "stellate" wound imply?
4. What is an "abrasion ring," and what is it the result of?
5. Describe how one would acquire a ligature mark.
6. Describe a technique used by persons participating in autoerotic activities to prevent ligature marks.

REFERENCES AND SUGGESTED READING

HENRY C. LEE, TIMOTHY PALMBACH, and MARILYN T. MILLER, *Henry Lee's Crime Scene Handbook*. San Diego: Academic Press, 2001.

VINCENT J. M. DIMAIO and PATRICK E. BESANT-MATTHEWS, *Investigation of Asphyxial Deaths*. Unknown date and publisher; booklet furnished in Death Investigation Seminar.

VICENT J. DIMAIO and CHARLES S. PETTY, *Investigation of Handgun Wounds*. Unknown date and publisher, Booklet provided in Death Investigation Seminar.

STUART H. JAMES and JON J. NORDBY, eds., *Forensic Science: An Introduction to Scientific and Investigative Techniques*. Boca Raton, FL: CRC Press, 2005.

BARRY A. J. FISHER, *Techniques of Crime Scene Investigation*. Boca Raton, FL: CRC Press, 2004.

Bloodstain Pattern Analysis

Key Terms

Exsanguination
Passive Patterns
Projected Patterns
Transfer Patterns
Castoff
Area of Convergence
Area of Origin
Satellite Spatter
Swipe Patterns

INTRODUCTION/OBJECTIVES

Bloodstain pattern analysis has been around for some time. For example, it was mentioned in the investigation of the Sam Sheppard murder case, which occurred in the mid-1950s. There have been many publications addressing various aspects of bloodstain patterns, including works by Dr. Herbert MacDonell, Laber, Dr. Henry Lee, and Dr. William Eckert, some of which are required reading to this day. In the study of bloodstain pattern analysis, the material contributed by these pioneers in this field is invaluable. This chapter is in no way meant to be an exhaustive or self-standing course, but simply an introductive overview of the field. You obviously will not be able to do any examinations with the material in this text. You should be aware of photographic procedures and the need to preserve the scene for a bloodstain pattern expert.

BLOOD FACTS

Our bodies contain between 4 and 6 liters of blood, and the loss of about 40% (1.6–2.4 liters) of that amount results in death.[1] The loss of any amount of blood results in bloodstain patterns that can be documented and studied. When interpreted properly, bloodstain patterns enable reconstruction of complex scenes. It is possible to replicate much of what occurred through both reenactment and computer graphics. Bloodstain pattern analysis is a valuable tool, and it should never be taken lightly. There is a much better understanding of this form of evidence, and it is requested and, for that matter, expected more often. It has become well known to the point that there are two forensic organizations addressing blood evidence: the International Association of Bloodstain Pattern Analysts and the International Association for Identification.

SAFETY

For those of us working with blood, safety is a major concern. Today there are serious concerns with both hepatitis and the AIDS virus. Many, if not most, forensic scientists working with blood receive immunization for hepatitis; unfortunately, it does not cover all forms and offers no protection against AIDS. For this reason alone, it is imperative that gloves be worn, as well as safety goggles and a mask if working with dried blood.

Care should be taken to clean all equipment with products such as Vironox-9 or Sideswipes. If you do not have anything designed for this purpose, it is generally agreed that a 10% solution of Clorox is sufficient. Equipment that can be autoclaved should be, and your crime scene rubbish should be disposed of following those regulations or laws in your jurisdiction. Incineration is definitely a viable option.

ADVANTAGES OF ANALYSIS

Bloodstain pattern analysis can provide us with the answers to many questions, including the following:

- What is the origin of the blood? A three-dimensional projection can provide us with the distances from an object, such as a wall, as well as the elevation above the floor.
- The information provided can in turn provide us with possible positions of the victim, such as prone, sitting, kneeling, standing, or walking.

---

[1]Instructor, Bloodstain Pattern Analysis Tutorial, International Association of Bloodstain Patterns Analysts. http://www.bloodspatter.com/BPATutorial.htm (3.21.2005).

- The movements of both suspect and victim.
- The type of weapon. This could be as general as a "blunt object" to as specific as a "hammer."
- Was the pattern the result of a gunshot, such as high-velocity back spatter or forward spatter?
- Was the blood expectorated (coughed-up)?
- Was the blood arterial spurting or gushing?

There are many other answers that can be provided through bloodstain pattern analysis. These may be case-specific, and to use any of these with any certainty of accuracy, you are advised to take the basic and advanced courses offered by various organizations.

PROCEDURE

It is critical to have someone who is competent in bloodstain pattern analysis conduct your actual analysis. We discuss the procedure here to provide you with a basic understanding of bloodstain pattern analysis and with the tools to recognize various stain patterns. This is important, considering you must continue with your investigation while possibly waiting for results from an expert. With some basic skills and understanding, you will be capable of furthering your investigation.

PHOTOGRAPHY

Prior to doing anything else concerning bloodstains, you will need to properly document them for the examiner if the examiner cannot come to the scene. You can follow these basic steps for the photography:

1. Overall photographs of the scene, with the bloodstain patterns included.
2. The overall photos of a single wall should be taken both with and without scales.

   TIP: Use a large measuring tape running at right angles, such as one vertical on the wall and another horizontal, to provide ready reference. There are large tapes, some made of paper and disposable, made specifically for this task.

3. The photographs of individual pattern areas should be taken with the camera on a tripod and set at 90° from the plane of the stain patterns. This is critical.
4. The pattern area, such as a single wall, should then be broken into quadrants that can be covered in enough detail to have scales for some individual drops that can be measured by the examiner. An ABFO #2 scale designed specifically for this task should be used. Remember, if the scale cannot be read, then the drop cannot be analyzed. This is a good time to mention that each of these photographs must have some reference to relate them to the overall views or they are just little bits of useless information.

DIAGRAMS

Make a detailed drawing of the scene. Not of every drop, but detailed enough to place specific patterns, such as handprints, in a specific location. Follow the directions in Chapter Six for drawings and diagrams for details on how to accomplish these.

INDIVIDUAL PATTERNS

To have any understanding of bloodstains, we must understand that those patterns were the result of any of three different sources of bloodshed: passive, projected, or transfer. **Passive patterns**, occur when blood exceeds its surface tension and falls freely from its source to impact. **Projected patterns**, are the result of blood leaving its source as the result of some force, such as blood pressure projecting from a severed blood vessel or blood projected by coughing, impact by some instrument (e.g., a hammer), or being blown from the body by a projectile (e.g., a bullet) striking the body, possibly causing high-velocity back spatter and forward spatter. Finally, **transfer patterns** are created by something becoming contaminated with existing blood and then brushing or touching another object. This is a very simplistic overview, and there are several subcategories of each of these.

When blood comes in contact with a surface, the pattern shape is the result of the surface texture, volume and velocity of blood, and other factors. (For the sake of this discussion, we assume that the average drop of blood is about 0.05 ml; if not projected, it remains attached to a surface until surface tension is exceeded, at which time it falls freely.) For example, should a free-falling drop of blood strike a piece of glass or an otherwise smooth surface at 90 degrees it will leave a perfect circle (Figure 19–1).

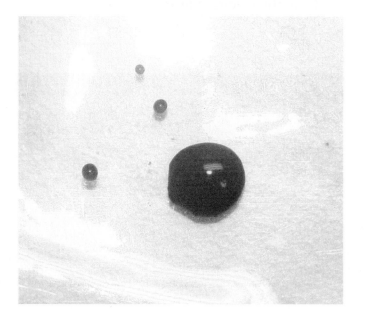

FIGURE 19–1   A drop of blood on a smooth surface.

FIGURE 19–2 A drop of blood on a nonsmooth surface; note the scalloped edges.

However, should that same drop of blood strike a rough surface, a scalloped pattern is created around the periphery of the pattern (Figure 19–2). If that same drop of blood were to strike the surface at an angle, an elliptical pattern (teardrop) with *the tail pointing in the direction of travel* would result (Figure 19–3). The angle at which it was projected can be determined by measuring the length and width of the blood drop and then applying the following formula:

$$\text{Angle of Impact} = \text{arc sin } W/L$$

FIGURE 19–3 Bloodstain pattern caused by blood striking the surface at an angle; note the tail pointing in the direction of travel.

FIGURE 19–4 Satellite spatter on the side of a tub.

Should the source of blood be stationary, such as in the case of a person slumped on a desk after having shot him- or herself then successive drops will fall onto one another, and the result is a pool with satellite spatter coming from the pool (Figure 19–4).

TERMINOLOGY

We use the suggested terminology of the International Association of Bloodstain Pattern Analysts (IABPA) to promote standardization within the field.[2] This suggested list is being revised by the FBI's Scientific Working Group for Bloodstains (SWGSTAIN) and should be published about the same time as this book.

- *Angle of Impact.* The angle of impact is the acute angle formed between the direction of a blood drop and the plane of the surface it strikes.

---

[2]Suggested IABPA Terminology List, November 7, 1996; International Association of Bloodstain Pattern Analysts.

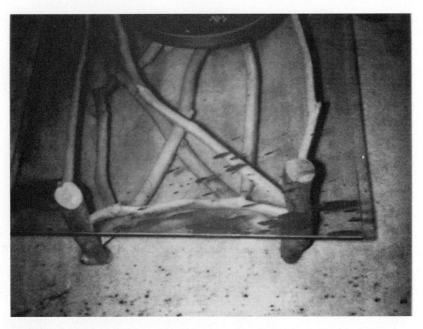

FIGURE 19-5 Arterial spurt showing movement from left to right.

- *Arterial Spurting (or Gushing) Pattern.* An arterial spurting or gushing pattern (Figure 19–5) is the bloodstain pattern resulting from blood exiting the body under pressure from a breached artery.
- *Back spatter.* Back spatter (Figure 19–6) is blood directed back toward the source of energy or force that caused the spatter.

FIGURE 19-6 High-velocity back spatter from a gunshot wound.

FIGURE 19–7   Cast-off blood (accidental death).

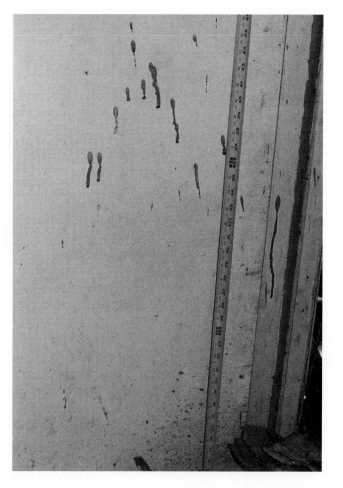

- *Bloodstains.* Bloodstains are the result of liquid blood that has come into contact with a surface.
- *Bubble Rings.* Blood rings are rings of blood that are the result of blood containing air bubbles that have dried and retained the circular pattern of a ring.
- **Cast-Off** *Patterns.* Cast-off patterns (Figure 19–7) are stains created as the result of blood being thrown from an object in motion.
- *Directionality.* Directionality is established by the pattern's geometric shape assumed after coming into contact with a surface.
- *Directionality Angles.* Directionality angles are the angles between the long axis of a bloodstain and a predetermined line on the plane of the target surface that represents 0°.
- *Direction of Flight.* Direction of flight is the trajectory of a blood drop that can be established by its angle of impact and directionality angle.
- *Drawback Effect.* Drawback effect (Figure 19–8) is the blood in the barrel of a firearm that has been drawn backward into the muzzle.
- *Drip Patterns.* Drip patterns are bloodstain patterns resulting from blood dripping into blood.

FIGURE 19–8   Blood on a pistol as a result of back spatter, and the drawback effect.

- *Expectorated Blood.* Expectorated blood (Figure 19–9) is blood blown out of the nose, mouth, or a wound as a result of air pressure and/or air flow as the propelling force.
- *Flight Path.* The flight path is the path of the blood drop from the point of origin to the target of impact.
- *Flow Patterns.* Flow patterns are the paths taken by blood as the result of gravity or movement.
- *Forward Spatter.* Forward spatter is the result of blood traveling in the same direction as the source of energy causing the spatter.
- *High-Velocity Impact Spatter.* High-velocity impact spatter (HVIS) is a bloodstain pattern caused by high-velocity force to the blood source, such as a gunshot or high-speed machinery.

FIGURE 19–9   Expectorated blood (bottom left foreground).

FIGURE 19–10 Impact spatter.

- *Impact Patterns.* Impact patterns (Figure 19–10) are bloodstain patterns created when blood receives a blow or force resulting in the random dispersion of smaller drops of blood.
- *Impact Sites.* Impact sites are the points where force encounters a source of blood.
- *Low-Velocity Impact Spatter.* Low-velocity impact spatter (LVIS) is a bloodstain pattern resulting from a minor impact or force to a blood source.
- *Medium-Velocity Impact Spatter.* Medium-velocity impact spatter (MVIS) is a bloodstain pattern that is caused by a medium velocity impact or force to a blood source. A beating typically causes this type of spatter.
- *Misting.* Misting is blood that has been reduced to a fine spray as a result of the energy or force applied to it.
- *Parent Drops.* Parent drops are any drops of blood from which a wave, cast-off, or satellite spatter originates.
- *Passive Drops (Bleeding).* Passive drops consist of blood drops created or formed by the force of gravity acting alone.
- *Perimeter Stains.* Perimeter stains are bloodstains that consist only of the outer periphery, the central area having been removed by wiping or flaking after liquid blood has partially or completely dried.

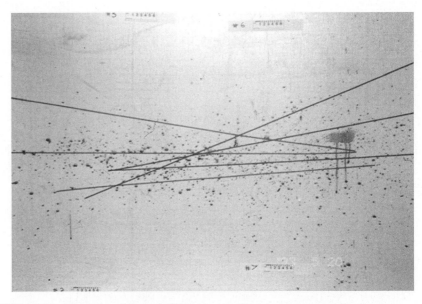

FIGURE 19–11   The colored lines indicate areas of convergence on two patterns.

- **Area of Convergence**. An area of convergence (Figure 19–11) is that common area, on a two-dimensional surface, over which the directionality of several blood drops can be traced.
- **Area of Origin**. An area of origin (Figure 19–12) is that common area in three-dimensional space to which the trajectories of several blood drops can be retraced.
- *Projected Blood Patterns*. Projected blood patterns are bloodstain patterns that are produced by blood released under pressure as opposed to impact, such as arterial spurting.

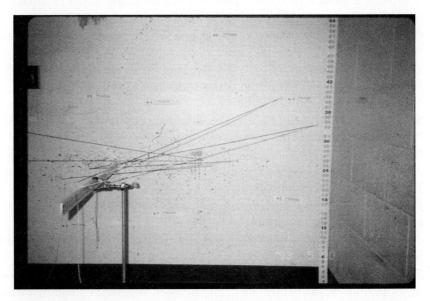

FIGURE 19–12   Yellow scale on a laboratory stand indicating area of origin.

FIGURE 19–13   Swipe pattern made by hair.

- *Ricochet.* Ricochet is the deflection of blood after impact with a target surface, resulting in the staining of another target surface.
- **Satellite Spatter**. Satellite spatter consists of small droplets of blood that are distributed around a drop or pool of blood as a result of blood landing on a target surface.
- *Spatter.* Spatter consists of blood that has been dispersed as a result of force applied to a source of blood. Patterns produced are often characteristic of the nature of the forces that created them.
- *Spines.* Spines are the pointed or elongated stains that radiate away from the central area of a bloodstain.
- *Swipe Patterns.* Swipe patterns (Figure 19–13) are the transfer of blood from a moving source onto an unstained surface. Direction of travel may be determined by the feathered edge.
- *Target.* Target is the surface on which blood has been deposited.
- *Transfer/Contact Patterns.* Transfer/contact patterns (Figure 19–14) are bloodstain patterns created when a wet, bloody surface comes in contact with a second surface. A recognizable image of all or a portion of the original surface may be observed in the pattern.
- *Voids.* Voids (Figure 19–15) are the absence of stains in an otherwise continuous bloodstain pattern.
- *Wave Cast-Off.* Wave cast-off is a small drop of blood that originates from a parent drop of blood because of the wavelike action of the liquid in conjunction with striking a surface.
- *Wipe Patterns.* Wipe patterns are bloodstain patterns created when an object moves through an existing stain, removing and/or altering its appearance.

FIGURE 19–14 Transfer pattern on the victim's left thigh made by a red pillow between the victim and the bed.

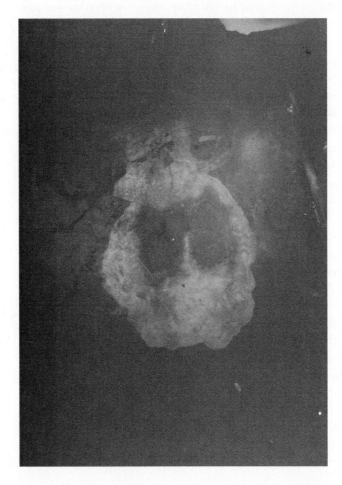

FIGURE 19–15 Although the yellow pattern is a urine stain fluorescing under short-wave ultraviolet light, the center pattern exhibits a void made from the victim's hips. The victim's head would be at the top of the photo.

CASE STUDY

A man was found dead in an abandoned latrine in a military training area. The man exhibited typical defense wounds on his hands and fore-arms. His neck had a gaping incised wound that resulted in the severing of his artery. As a result of this injury, the man died from **exsanguination**. A detailed investigation of the scene indicated the death was not the result of an attack, but the result of an accident.

The man had been standing on an old sawhorse. There was a light fixture on the floor, as well as wire that was not faded. The conduits above the sawhorse were empty, indicating that the man had been pulling the wires from them. That is why the wire was not faded—it had just been pulled from the conduit. On a ledge to one side of the sawhorse was a new pair of pliers and a screwdriver. Outside the scene were coils of wire, and there were others in the bed of the victim's pickup truck.

On the floor area of the latrine were many pieces of broken porcelain from broken urinals and toilets. These were covered with bloodstain patterns. On a wall were two patterns indicating arterial spurting just a few inches off the floor. The sawhorse was broken.

An analysis of the pattern evidence along with the other physical evidence resulted in a determination that the manner of death was accidental. This was based on the following additional information:

The broken sawhorse was kicked over and had a fresh break. Bloodstain patterns on the porcelain in the center of the room beneath the light fixture indicated that the blood fell straight down. This was indicated further by the victim's clothing, which exhibited bloodstain patterns running down the front of his body.

His wounds were consistent with falling and putting out his arms to break his fall, a typical defensive move when one falls. His palms were cut by the broken porcelain, and a wound on his arm was not only incised, but also showed indications of having been pushed back as a result of continued movement in the direction of the fall.

The arterial spurting was at a level and direction consistent with his being prone after the fall. Further patterns indicated he was standing, possibly holding his lacerated neck as he attempted to leave the latrine. The blood ran down the front of the victim. Handprints indicated where he exited the latrine and then crawled toward his truck, but died prior to reaching it.

▲ SUMMARY

Bloodstain pattern analysis is a very valuable tool in those cases where blood has been shed. Our documentation of these scenes must be accurate. We must evaluate these scenes by attempting to anticipate what questions will be asked and provide that material necessary to address those questions. Detailed photographs, taken perpendicular to the plane on which the stains are found, must be taken. There should be photographs depicting the overall patterns as well as close-up photographs of the various patterns to be analyzed. These must be with and without scales. Analyses of the various patterns must be done by a person who is trained and experienced in these interpretations. Remember, you may be asked to replicate some of your theory in court.

■ REVIEW QUESTIONS

1. What is the average volume of a drop of blood?
2. What fact concerning a drop of blood tells us its direction of travel?
3. What is the *area of convergence?*
4. What is the significance of an elliptical bloodstain pattern?
5. What is the approximate amount of blood loss that would be considered fatal?
6. How does surface pattern affect bloodstain patterns?

◆ REFERENCES AND SUGGESTED READING

STUART H. JAMES, WILLIAM G. ECKERT, and FORIDA ECKERT (eds.), *Interpretation of Bloodstain Evidence at Crime Scenes,* 2nd Ed. Boca Raton, FL: CRS Press, 1998.

TERRY L. LABER, *Blood Spatter Classification.* (n.p., n.d.).

TERRY L. LABER, "Diameter of a Bloodstain as a Function of Origin, Distance Fallen, and Volume of Drop." *Quinnipiac Health Law Journal,* 1996.

TERRY L. LABER and BARTON P. EPSTEIN, *Bloodstain Pattern Analysis.* Minneapolis: Callin Publishing, 1983.

HERBERT L. MACDONELL, *Flight Characteristics and Stain Patterns of Human Blood.* Washington DC: National Institute of Law Enforcement and Criminal Justice, 1974.

HERBERT L. MACDONELL, *Bloodstain Pattern Interpretation.* Corning, NY: Laboratory of Forensic Science, 1993.

HERBERT LEON MACDONELL and LORRAINE FISKE BIALOUSZ, *Laboratory Manual on the Geometric Interpretation of Human Bloodstain Evidence.* Corning, NY: Laboratory of Forensic Science, 1963.

Natural, Accidental, and Undetermined Deaths

Key Terms _____

Medical Misadventure
Autoerotic Death
Ligature
Petechial Hemorrhages
Industrial Fatalities
Motor Vehicle Accident (MVA)

INTRODUCTION/OBJECTIVES

Because of the legal requirements for reporting death and the need for investigations in deaths that exhibit suspicious or questionable elements, we must be able to recognize the difference between all types of death. Just as importantly, we must realize that we will not always be able to establish cause and/or manner of death and, therefore, classify the case as "undetermined." This classification can be changed later, should there be justification for such a change.

NATURAL DEATHS

We are called quite often to investigate deaths that are the result of natural causes. This is because these deaths fall under particular criteria, such as the persons not being under the care of a doctor, having died within 24 hours of being admitted to a hospital, or having died with signs of trauma. These vary little from jurisdiction to jurisdiction, but they require a determination be made as to the actual cause and contributing causes of the death. These cases are normally decided by the Medical Examiner, but in most cases are actually decided by the medical examiner's investigator (MEI). They conduct their own investigation including the following:

- Past medical history
- Hospital records of this incident, and those possibly related from prior history
- Medications being used
- Is the patient under a doctor's care?
- Is the patient compliant? When was the last visit?
- What is the victim's age?
- Is the victim's death consistent with the decedent's health condition?
- Is there anything suspicious?
- Are there any injuries on the patient?
- Is there a *subdural* or *subaracnoid hemorrhage?*
- Are there any signs of what is known as "**medical misadventure**," or death as the result of mistakes in the health-care process?

ALCOHOL-RELATED DEATHS

Alcohol-related deaths (Figure 20–1) can be troubling because they can be confused with deaths resulting from assault. We discussed this previously to some extent in earlier portions of the book. They do have many similarities in that they are both deaths that often involve struggle and an extremely chaotic scene. The difference, however, is that in the case of assault, the violence is between two or more persons, whereas the alcoholic death is the result of struggle with the victim by the victim.

One case of alcoholic death seemed to be the result of a great deal of struggling, such as with another person, but it soon became evident

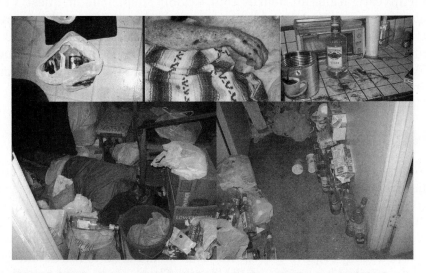

FIGURE 20–1 Scene of an alcoholic death. Note the bruises and the bottles in an unkempt house.

there was no one else involved. There was furniture turned over and the scene was a terrible mess, with items all over the floor and blood everywhere. On examination of the body, however, there did not appear to be any large wounds, but many small abrasion-type wounds to the arms and backs of the hands. Some of these were fresh, whereas others appeared to be much older.

There was a horrible odor in the apartment and the blood was very dark in color; close observation indicated much of the blood was mixed with fecal matter. The decedent was nude from the waist down and there was a lot of blood in the toilet and on the bathroom floor and walls.

Alcoholics in later stages of alcoholism sometimes hemorrhage and bleed from the rectum, and this blood is mixed with fecal matter. There are several things you can look for to make a determination as to the type of case. In alcohol-related deaths, there are usually large alcohol bottles in various stages of being consumed. There may be several empty bottles in the rubbish container, and the house is usually poorly cleaned and maintained. A check of the cupboard usually provides little in the way of real food, but maybe candy and/or cookies or other snack food. There may be a lot of unopened mail and many other signs of not taking care of oneself.

CASE STUDY

An individual was found in his house sitting on a sofa in the den. He had a head injury and had died following the injury. At the front of the house there was a stoop, where the person entering had to take three steps down to the entry to the living room and dining room. At the base of these stairs was blood, and a little further in were two large circular patterns of blood. The blood trail then led to the den, where the decedent was found.

The house was very messy, with coffee grounds and large, empty vodka bottles on the kitchen counter. On checking the kitchen garbage, the author found more empty vodka bottles. The scene was looking more like an alcoholic death.

The two circular patterns on the carpet looked as if someone had been sitting on the floor and moving around in circles. There was blood on the floor and on the mail that was, for the most part, on only one side. It appeared the mail had been used as a compress to stem the flow of blood. The remaining question was, where did the head injury come from?

After examining the area around the stairs, a cabinet was observed that was rather heavy. It was obvious that the cabinet had been moved slightly away from the entrance. It appears the victim had gotten the mail and fell forward on the stairs, striking his head on the cabinet, and thereby shifting its location slightly.

Other indicators that the victim might be an alcoholic were typical bruises on the arms and legs and the lack of regular food in the house. The door was also locked from the inside.

ACCIDENTAL DEATHS

Autoerotic Death

Autoerotic death is a form of accidental death associated with sexual activity and is found predominantly in men. A unique characteristic in this type of death is that the victim is often found dressed in female underwear, and there is often pornography and women's intimate clothing spread about on the bed. The victim masturbates while looking at these *fetish* items and often uses a ligature device to cut off air flow to the body. They often also tie themselves up, and sometimes do this under several blankets or with something strapped over the face. It appears the lack of oxygen and the heat elevates their sexual gratification.

When a person dies while practicing autoerotism, it is usually of *asphyxiation* by ligature or suffocation. What typically occurs is the noose around the neck tightens and the person passes out and dies. Usually the **ligature** (a rope, belt, or anything else to make a noose) is loose, and should the person pass out, the weight of their body causes the head to fall out of the noose. Occasionally, the safety device fails and their head is trapped after they pass out. As a result, they die of asphyxia from oxygen starvation.

In the case of a pillow or similar object being strapped over the face, the victim sometimes loses consciousness and suffocates because of lack of oxygen. As you can see, in both scenarios the victims died of accidental asphyxiation.

Autoerotic death is often looked on as suicide by those who are not familiar with autoerotism. This is sometimes the result of the death scene being altered by the family to avoid embarrassment. Sometimes the victim is found cut down and dressed as one would expect, with the paraphernalia associated with such deaths missing. It is, in fact, an accidental death. Go with your experience and investigative ability. If the clothes are not on properly, or there are other things about the scene that seem not to add up, suspect a possible altered scene.

Autoerotic death is the result of asphyxia caused from ligature or suffocation from having a facial covering too tight. It is commonly found among Caucasian males in their teens and twenties, but it is not limited to this group. It is sometimes found with older males and females. The theory here is that the victim gets an erotic high resulting in climax from oxygen depravation. Some possible indications of autoerotic death are

- A noose that is just loosely looped over the head
- Some sort of "safety" device to allow the head to fall out of the noose should the victim lose consciousness
- Pornographic pictures spread out to view
- Women's underwear spread out
- Sometimes a video camera on a tripod with which to film themselves. (Check the video. Sometimes they have videotaped their own death.)

- Very commonly, a towel between the neck and noose. This prevents a ligature mark so others will not guess at their activities.
- Sometimes they are tied up and under many blankets, possibly with a pillow strapped over their face to cut off air and provide heat. The key here is that on examining the bonds, you find that they are actually easy to escape.
- The victim is nude, partially nude, or possibly wearing female underclothing.
- There may be a vibrator or massager present.

There are commercially available safety devices, such as nooses, that release when pressure pulling on them reaches typically around 15 pounds. This way, if the victim should pass out, as soon as body weight is placed on the ligature it releases, and the victim simply falls down and begins breathing again. The homemade safety devices often fail because of design flaws or because the vigorous activity causes the safety to slide down toward the neck, therefore preventing the head from falling out of the noose. This is discussed to some extent in Chapter Eighteen.

Drowning

Drowning is usually the result of an accident or related to an existing natural cause, such as a heart attack. The cause of death is asphyxiation by drowning, and the manner is usually accidental.

When a person has been removed from the water after a short period of time, there may not be many signs other than **petechial hemorrhages** in the eyes and inside the mouth. There may also be a froth coming from the mouth and/or nose, sometimes pinkish because of blood.

A person who has been in the water for some time might have abrasions to the backs of the hands, knees, tops of the feet, and the forehead. This is not the result of assault, but is from the body being partially buoyant and these heavier extremities rubbing on the bottom of the body of water.

Further exposure to the water can cause skin slippage, loss of color, and certain parts of the body being eaten by crabs and fish. These are usually found at the lips, eyelids, and other soft areas within reach of the scavengers.

The body decomposes and forms gases that float the body. After a period of time, the body settles back to the bottom and remains there.

If injuries are found on the body, they may be from boat propellers, sharks, or other forms of sea life.

CASE STUDY

A male drowned in the ocean and was found floating a day or so later. The body was beginning to decompose, and although there were no signs of foul play, the victim had some very unusual round wounds on his body (Figure 20–2). After consulting with the university, it was learned that these were the bite marks of the cookie cutter shark, a small but very aggressive shark

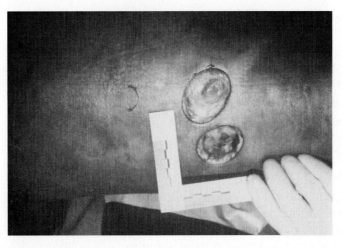

FIGURE 20-2 Bites from a cookie cutter shark.

that lives in very deep ocean waters but comes to the surface sometimes at night to feed. They have been known to attack whales and even nuclear submarines.

Electrocution

Electrocutions are almost inevitably accidental or industrial deaths. This is not to say that electrocution is never suicide or homicide. Such cases do exist, although they may date back to the 1930s.

Electrocutions can be hazardous, as one might guess. It is extremely important to determine that the electricity is no longer active. The body should never be touched until this has been determined.

As with any properly investigated case, photography is extremely important to document what occurred. It is also important to determine what the victim was attempting to do at the time of the incident, as well as any training or experience the victim may have had in the field of electricity or electronics.

Typically, we want to look at the entry and exit points on the body (Figures 20–3A, 20–3B, and 20–3C). Electricity travels in a line from entry to a grounding point, often the feet. The exit points often resemble burns, and they are, in fact, thermal burns that almost look like cigarette

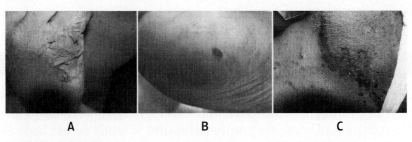

A   B   C

FIGURE 20-3 Electrical burns. (A) Entry point. (B) Exit point from the foot. (C) Electrical burn resembling a ligature mark.

burns. When looking at the bottoms of the shoes, there might be multiple holes in the soles of the shoes as well as the socks and the soles of the feet. The exit or grounding point is not always on the feet, however. It can be the opposite hand or any other part of the body that came in contact with something sufficient to ground the body.

Industrial Fatalities

Industrial fatalities occur at work. This is not necessarily a construction site, but could be an elevator repair, a garage repairing cars, or any number of scenarios (Figure 20–4). A major concern in the investigation of these cases is safety. You are often required to wear closed shoes and hardhats to enter these scenes. Always check with persons in charge to determine safety and safety requirements to operate in that area. Follow those rules.

Crime scene investigators do not know everything, so when you are not sure what is important as evidence, feel free to check with those at the scene who are knowledgeable in the methods used for that particular job specialty. Do not put yourself or others in harm's way.

- Determine and photograph the presence or lack of safety equipment at the scene.
- Was there a failure of any of the equipment (Figures 20–5A, 20–5B, and 20–5C)? If so, photograph the failed portions in detail, and they should be recovered as evidence.

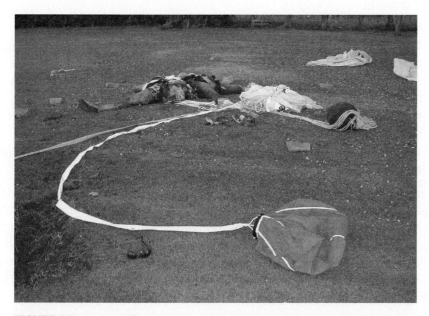

FIGURE 20–4 Parachute fatality. Note the impact point in the left foreground and the pilot chute in the right foreground. The main chute tangled and reserve chute in parachute bag. (Photo courtesy of the Honolulu Medical Examiner's Office.)

| A | B | C |

FIGURE 20–5   (A) Industrial fatality. (B) A man trimming trees experienced safety-belt failure. (C) Broken snap. (Photo courtesy of the Honolulu Medical Examiner.)

- Was it used improperly?
- Was it altered?
- Recover the equipment for independent evaluation.

Home Accidents

Many people are killed each year in accidents at home, such as from electrocution, falling from a ladder or the roof, or being crushed by a car jacked up improperly. These must be investigated, just as all other deaths falling under the jurisdiction of the medical examiner's office. The investigation can move along the same basic lines as that of an industrial accident. These include

- Was the person trained to use the equipment?
- Were they using the equipment improperly, such as using electric equipment on a wet or damp floor?
- Did they interfere with built-in safety devices on the equipment, such as removing a safety shield on an electric saw?
- Was the equipment grounded with a three-prong plug?
- Was the decedent wearing the proper clothing?
- Was the decedent disregarding common safety rules, such as cutting off the electricity prior to working on the wiring?

You must exercise extra caution in these cases because there may still be danger as a result of the activity that could cause you to become a victim as well. For example, during one investigation of a suicide a mortar round was found near the body. The projectile, which was found on a bookshelf, was reportedly a war trophy belonging to the decedent and was not deactivated. In such a case, military EOD or the local bomb squad should be called to properly recover and dispose of the device.

Motor Vehicle Collisions

Motor vehicle collisions, or "accidents" as they are often called, are very common and sometimes fatal in nature (Figures 20–6 and 20–7). We discuss

FIGURE 20–6 Motor vehicle collision. (Photo courtesy of the Honolulu Medical Examiner.)

these to some extent, but do not spend a great deal of time on them because larger agencies have Vehicular Homicide Details who are specialists in this area. This type of investigation can get very technical and for a person who is not a specialist, this might be over their head.

A **motor vehicle accident (MVA)** is the result of one or more motor vehicles coming into contact with another vehicle, an object, or a person. The causes of these incidents are sometimes complicated and difficult to

FIGURE 20–7 Motor vehicle collision resulting in multiple fatalities. (Photo courtesy of the Honolulu Medical Examiner.)

determine. They may result from equipment failure; natural causes, such as snow or ice; operator error, such as falling asleep or being intoxicated; or even attempted murder because the operator attempted to kill the other person involved in the case.

Necessary Equipment

- A measuring device, such as a tape measure. This should be steel because cloth measures can be challenged as the result of stretch factors. It should be about 100 feet.
- A camera. Single-lens reflex (SLR) format is a good choice, and a good external flash is needed for night, but also advisable during the day in order to eliminate shadows.
- Sketching supplies.
- Clipboard
- Safety vest for moving about in traffic

Procedure

- Take photos of the vehicle and all occupants, even though they may be only slightly hurt. Take photographs of all injuries. If at all possible, do this over a period of days, because the bruises change over time, as discussed Chapter Thirteen. The bruises may show patterns, such as the shoulder-belt strap, that can place occupants in a particular position in the vehicle. Steering wheel patterns are in this category as well.
- Take photographs of alcohol containers in and around the vehicle. Make notations as to how many containers, the brands, and indicate the amount left in the container.
- Pay close attention to the speedometer, as it may indicate the speed of the vehicle at the time of crash. Photograph this, if there is such an indication.
- Check the decedents' watches to see if any of them are stopped at a particular time, as this may be the time of the accident.
- The ***point of impact*** is usually detectable because there is dirt from under the fenders and bumpers that is dislodged from the impact. Likewise, there may be other related debris, such as broken headlights, lenses, and so forth.
- If the accident was at night, there may be questions concerning the headlights being on or off. This may be documented by checking and photographing the headlight switch in the vehicle.
- The lights themselves may answer the question as to their being on or off. If the light is broken, the filament is stretched from its original tight coil and should show oxidation colored from brown, gray, to black if the light was on at the time that it broke. If, however, the filament is still a tight coil and not oxidized, the light was not on when it broke. These should be documented with photography, using a macro lens, and the lights should be submitted into evidence.
- Check the ignition switch to see if there is a key in the ignition. Sometimes these cars are unreported auto thefts.
- If operational, check the brakes and brake lights, and document the results.

- Check and document the last safety inspection for the vehicle.
- Check and photograph the tires and tread in fatality cases.
- Anything unusual about the vehicle should be documented, such as parking stickers and other obvious identifying characteristics on the car. These may not seem important, but may be later critical if someone saw the vehicle and recognized it as having been at some location as a particular time.

Diagram the accident scene showing all debris, skid marks, impact points, and other significant pieces of evidence.

Undetermined Deaths

"Undetermined" is a classification of death that you most likely would never expect to see, but there are instances where a determination cannot be made or there are other compelling reasons to withhold a decision. *Undetermined* is a classification that is possibly best described by using the following examples.

CASE STUDY

An individual is found on the ground outside a tall building and appears to have jumped. There is no sign of forced entry, and the door may or may not be locked. There is no note, and the neighbors have heard nothing out of the ordinary. There are mixed reports about possible depression. The family is extremely insistent that their son would never commit suicide: "He had everything going for himself." There are no reports of previous attempts or any major health concerns.

CASE STUDY

Two persons are found hanging side by side in a vacation rental cottage. They are almost holding hands and are facing each other. There is no note, nor is there any sign of struggle. They had had problems with their relationship in the past, and family and friends related that the female had been threatened with physical force by the male in the past and had a court restraining order for some time. There was a major upcoming event in the life of the female that had a very positive implication on her future. Family and friends felt she was murdered.

The rental was made by the female, and the staff of the facility related that the couple seemed to be very affectionate with each other and indicated absolutely no problems. In fact, the two persons acted as if they were a "honeymoon couple." Was this a double suicide or a murder–suicide?

▲ SUMMARY

Death investigation covers a wide range of deaths, and, while we think of murder as being what we investigate, the vast majority of death investigations are other than murder. The majority of cases that come to our attention are in fact not even under our jurisdiction but simply need to be declined because of statutory requirements.

Most of these cases are not difficult to categorize and are very simple to investigate. There are those that have potential for becoming problematic. These are suicide and undetermined. Suicide can be a problem because so many family and friends do not want to accept the fact that their relative took his or her own life. Other reasons could be insurance related. The other problematic classification are those we classify as "Undetermined." If we cannot determine the manner of death we sometimes use this classification because it allows us to easily post a proper classification at a later date should it be determined.

■ REVIEW QUESTIONS

1. Explain in a few words what we mean by *undetermined* for manner of death.
2. Name one safety precaution when investigating an electrocution death.
3. Why would a natural death be reported to the medical examiner?
4. Why is an autoerotic death considered an accidental death?
5. Why are measurements so critical in deaths resulting from falls from height?
6. Briefly describe some factors in an alcoholic death.
7. Why should you not untie the ligature in a hanging case?

◆ REFERENCES AND SUGGESTED READING

HENRY C. LEE, TIMOTHY PALMBACH, and MARILYN T. MILLER, *Henry Lee's Crime Scene Handbook*. San Diego: Academic Press, 2001.

Techniques of Crime Scene Investigation. BARRY A. J. FISHER, Boca Raton, FL: CRC Press, 2004.

Suicide

Key Terms

Suicide Note
Hesitation marks
The Final Exit
Depression

INTRODUCTION/OBJECTIVES

Suicides are often confused with homicide, and this is partially the result of family and friends who do not want to believe the decedent would take his or her life. Many persons committing suicide do not leave **suicide notes**. Although this is very common, it is also very common for people to believe all suicides leave a note. Many family members are insistent that the victim would never have done this without leaving a note. If, however, they were able to look at the situation without their emotions hindering their thought processes, they would realize there were many signs the person was at least contemplating suicide. There is also the feeling among some that suicide has a stigma of some sort and implies that there is *mental illness* in the family, or that the family was in some way responsible for the death. This feeling of guilt and sometimes the question of insurance result in a lot of difficulty for the investigator, who must keep an unbiased and professional attitude toward the investigation. The family, however, is often less than helpful and may even be antagonistic because of the factors described previously. You must recognize these events and learn to collect evidence that distinguishes suicide from a crime such as murder or manslaughter. You must also understand how to communicate with family and friends who may be less than cooperative.

The Decedent

The investigators must keep in mind that persons who commit suicide might be very inventive. Some persons show real consideration for those who will find them, and try to make the event as stress-free as possible. For many, however, there is no real planning, and the death was the result of a "spur of the moment" decision. Following are some examples to illustrate to extremes of suicide.

CASE STUDIES

Case One: One suicide was documented in which the person committed suicide with a homemade guillotine. It was constructed in a room in the house where he lived with other people who knew nothing of his intentions. Other suicides take extraordinary steps to keep the scene clean and not cause unnecessary stress to others.

Case Two: One victim who shot himself called the police prior to committing suicide and stated he would be in the kitchen. He would leave the door unlocked to avoid having the police break in. He also stated the gun registration and his identification would be in the living room taped to the television set so the wind would not blow them away with the door open. He placed a bedsheet under the kitchen table and shot himself at that location. This was a very analytical man who was a math teacher and played chess.

Case Three: A newly married woman found her husband has been with a prostitute and suddenly ran and jumped over the balcony railing, falling many floors to the street.

Case Four: A male called the medical examiner's office to report a death. It was learned the male caller was at the apartment of a friend who was sitting on the porch with a plastic bag over his head and a hose going into the bag from a tank on the floor. After determining the victim was still alive, the police and an ambulance were called to respond to the scene. The male was saved. One year later a call was received from the police at the same location. On arrival at the scene, it was observed that the victim was on the kitchen floor with a plastic bag over his head and a tank of helium next to him. A hose ran from the tank to the bag. On the counter was a plate with two crackers on it and next to that a book entitled **The Final Exit**. The suicide scene was a classic "final exit" scenario. This individual left very detailed notes to the police and friends. He also signed each paragraph in the book that was related to the method he used for his suicide. This was the action of a very determined man who had given much thought to his intended actions. ***The Final Exit*** is a must for any crime scene investigator and is recommended for any forensic library. There are many suicides where the plan was taken from this book. It is important to be aware of it, because some of these could be misunderstood for homicides.

If a person is determined to commit suicide, they will succeed. There might even be evidence of other attempts, the most common of which are **hesitation marks** on the wrists that may be healed or in various stages of healing from previous attempts.

When looking for suicide notes, do not limit yourself to the traditional suicide note. Today, notes may be found in the computer. There have been indications contained in a diary, and other writings found written in magazines and books. Are there references to **depression** or hopelessness in the writings?

INTENTIONAL FALL FROM HEIGHT

Persons who choose to jump from high places (Figures 21–1A, 21–1B) are relatively common and require some specific attention be given certain concerns. These include

- Was furniture pulled up to the railing?
- Were handprints found on the railing?

FIGURE 21–1 Suicide by jumping from height. (A) The floor she jumped from. (B) The impact point. (Photo courtesy of the Honolulu Medical Examiner.)

- Were the palms facing in or out? This can indicate the location of the victim as having been inside the balcony or on the outside of the railing.
- Were footprints found on the furniture and railing?
- How high was the railing?
- How far did the victim fall?
- How far from the building did the victim impact the ground? In other words, did the victim fall, or was the victim thrown from the balcony?
- Was the front door locked from the inside?

> **TIP:** With "jumpers," always check the wristwatch or other time-keeping device to see if it stopped. This might well provide the **time of death**. The fact that the body does not have a watch may be misleading. Does the wrist have tan lines indicating the person usually wore a watch? If so, look around, because often the watch band breaks on impact.

Hangings

Hangings involve a **ligature**, such as a rope, electric wire, dog leash, or other ropelike device be placed around the neck in such a manner as to cut off the air and/or blood to the brain, thereby resulting in the death of the victim. Another common misconception is that all suicidal hangings are in the "traditional" style of being fully suspended off the ground. This is, in fact, not true. There are many suicides in which the victim is not suspended at all (Figures 21–2, 21–3). This is also the source of a guide that is commonly misleading. It is often believed that a *ligature mark* traveling straight to the back of the neck is homicidal in nature, and that a ligature mark traveling up behind the ears is suicidal in nature. Although there is some truth in this from the standpoint of the ligature going up behind the ears, many suicides have a ligature mark traveling straight back to the back of the neck. The explanation is easy: Many hanging suicides do not involve actual hanging, but simply leaning forward, often resulting in a level line from the front to the back of neck. Whatever the circumstances, do not remove the ligature from the victim if it has been determined the victim is dead. The rope or other material should be left on the decedent, and the loop should be cut where it is attached to the object from which the victim is suspended. Tape the two cut pieces back together and submit the entire item to the medical examiner with the body. Knots can be very valuable from the standpoint of occupation or knowledge.

To provide the reader with an idea of some of the variations, following is a partial list of methods:

- The victim stands up, attaches the ligature to the door hinge, and simply bends the knees.
- The victim attaches the ligature to a coat-hanger pole in a closet and kneels down.
- The victim ties the ligature to the bathroom doorknob and sits down.

FIGURE 21–2 Suicide by hanging. Note that the victim is not fully suspended. (Photo courtesy of the Honolulu Medical Examiner.)

FIGURE 21–3 Hanging by sitting. Note the "hangman's noose" used by the victim. (Photo courtesy of the Honolulu Medical Examiner.)

- The victim attaches an electric cord from an iron to a closet coat-hanger pole and lays prone on the floor. He smoked a cigarette as he died.
- The victim tied an electric cord onto a tree branch and stood on chair, which was kicked out after the ligature was attached to the neck.

What did each of these have in common? None of them were suspended off the ground and none of them left a suicide note.

OVERDOSE

Suicide committed by an overdose of medication is not that uncommon and is popular for several reasons. First, there has been quite a bit of literature available in the past several years concerning how to commit suicide. Second, medication seems to thought of as a fairly painless way to die, as well as not being too gross. Third, medication is fairly easy to come by, making it an accessible method to use. There is a downside to using medications for suicidal purposes: It is, unfortunately, much easier for others to say the victim was unknowingly overdosed by another person, or that suicide was not intentional but was an accidental overmedication.

Evidence

Persons using medication to overdose tend to be those who spend time thinking about it. This might equate to more of a possibility of their leaving a suicide note. Look for notes in these cases. Specific items of evidence are

- Medication bottles
  - For whom was it prescribed?
  - Prescribed by what doctor?
  - To treat what illness?
  - When was it prescribed?
  - What pharmacy filled the prescription?
  - What is the name of the medication?
  - What strength was the medication?
  - How many doses were originally in the container?
  - How many doses are left?
  - Is the amount consistent with the instructions? (Remember, this must be done for all the medications you find.)
- Over-the-counter medication
- Any unfilled prescriptions found
- Any notes or scribbling concerning depression, suicide, etc.
- Determine if the victim was under the care of a psychologist or psychiatrist.
- Signs of excessive alcohol use
- Check the body for hesitation wounds that would indicate other suicide attempts possibly of a different variety.

CARBON MONOXIDE POISONING

Another method of committing suicide is to do so with carbon monoxide (CO) poisoning. There are two common methods used with this type of death. One is to simply turn on the car motor within an enclosed garage with the car windows down. The person dies after some time. Often the death is discovered and the ignition is still on, but the car is out of gasoline. The second is to place a garden hose in the exhaust pipe of the vehicle, stuffing the surrounding gaps with a towel or similar cloth to force the fumes through the hose. The victim then sits in the car with the motor turned on and the windows rolled up. These suicides may be found in a garage or even on the side of the road. Carbon monoxide poisoning leaves a "rosy" look to the victim, although not always. This coloration does show on the tissue samples during postmortem examination.

GUNSHOT

Gunshot suicides are usually males, but occasionally females use this method as well. The choice seems to be handgun more than any other firearm, but both rifles and shotguns are sometimes used.

SUICIDE NOTES

There may or may not be suicide notes, possibly because this is often a spur of the moment action, and a note is just not written. A note tends to imply planning. The person might not even have thought about it, or was too depressed to write one. There are usually signs that all was not well with the individual, if one knows what to look for. Some possible signs are

- Prior emotional problems
- Prior suicidal attempts or ideations
- Family problems
- Alone, possibly no friends or family, or alone on holidays
- Reckless activities, such as binge drinking or drug use
- Personal problems
- Illness
- Religious concerns. Some of these also include self-mutilation, such as to the genitals, as a result of having "evil" or "sinful" thoughts.

▲ SUMMARY

Suicide is accomplished by one of many different methods, or even a combination of methods such as hanging, shooting, poisoning, overdose of medication, cutting of wrists, and others that are dependant upon many factors. Be careful to keep an open mind and do not let family wants or desires influence your duty to an impartial investigation.

REVIEW QUESTIONS

1. What is a ligature?
2. How do we submit the ligature?
3. What are some reasons for lack of a suicide note?
4. Are victims of suicide always fully suspended?
5. What are some other methods of committing suicide?
6. Are suicides always planned?
7. What is *The Final Exit*?
8. What are some reasons family members might not be honest with you?

REFERENCES AND SUGGESTED READING

DEREK HUMPHRY, *The Final Exit*. New York: Dell Publishing, 2002.

VERNON J. GEBERTH, *Practical Homicide Investigation: Tactics, Procedures, and Forensic Techniques,* 4th ed. New York: Elsevier Science Publishing Co. Inc., 2006.

CHARLES R. SWANSON, NEIL C. CHAMELIN, and LEONARD TERRITO, *Criminal Investigation.* New York: McGraw-Hill, 2003.

Homicide

Key Terms

Homicide
Manslaughter
Primary Crime Scene
Secondary Crime Scene
Individualization
Class Characteristic
Theory of Transfer

INTRODUCTION/OBJECTIVES

Homicide is the killing of a human being. We tend to look at the term *homicide* as synonymous with murder. This is not accurate, because there are various different classifications of the killing of another, from **manslaughter**, which is not intentional even though often without regard to the danger the act imposes, to justifiable homicide, such as the judicial killing of another (Figure 22–1). We leave this up to the courts, however, and concentrate on the investigation of these deaths, keeping in mind that the taking of any life is a very serious act from which there is no turning back. The success of homicide investigations depends on teamwork, more than anything else. You must recognize these crimes and be able to collect the physical evidence to establish the elements of the crime.

SCENE

There may be one scene to a killing or there may be several. We tend to look at homicides as having a primary scene and one or

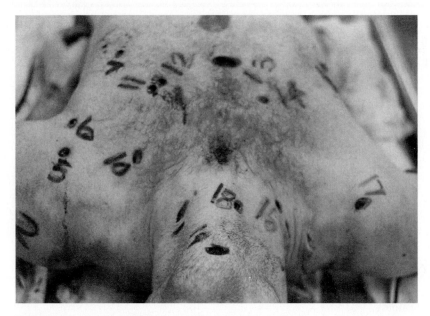

FIGURE 22–1   Justifiable homicide. Note the multiple gunshot wounds. (Photo courtesy of the Honolulu Medical Examiner.)

more secondary scenes.[1] Simply put, the **primary crime scene** would be where the act took place and the **secondary crime scenes** would be where other related acts took place. Having multiple scenes is common in many types of investigations.

CASE STUDY

A high school student was waiting at a bus stop near her school to catch the bus home. The suspect in this case picked the victim up at this bus stop and took her to another location, where he attempted to sexually assault her. She fought back vigorously and was killed during the struggle.

The victim was able to bite the suspect during the struggle and kicked out the front window of his car. She, in turn, was stabbed repeatedly and exhibited defense wounds, including stab wounds to one palm and incised wounds to the other hand. She caused major damage to the suspect's car in the struggle.

The suspect drove the victim to another location, where he dumped her body. The body was found, and so began the investigation of the case

---

[1]Henry C. Lee, Timothy Palmbach, and Marilyn T. Miller, *Henry Lee's Crime Scene Handbook.* San Diego: Academic Press, 2001, pp. 2–3.

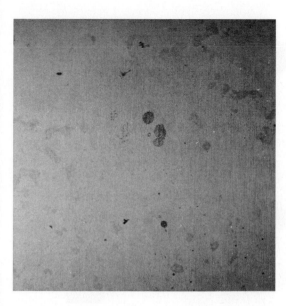

FIGURE 22–2 Drops of blood on a garage floor. Note the tread pattern in blood. This can include or exclude, but cannot individualize.

as a homicide. This dump site was initially processed as the only known scene in the case.

Police patrolling a beach park found the suspect cleaning his car. The front windshield of the car was broken and the suspect had a bite mark on his arm that he stated was the result of his being attacked by several males at another park. The suspect later took his car to a repair shop to have the window replaced. While the car was at the repair shop it was determined he was a likely suspect in the homicide. His car was examined at the repair shop, where processing began. The car was then transported to the police garage, where it was subjected to very intense examination.

While the car was at the police garage, an elderly man related he had seen a male and a female fighting in a similar car in the carport of a house in the same neighborhood as the abduction and dumping of the body. This scene was in turn searched, and in a garbage bag on the carport was found a very small piece of plastic and a piece of metal tubing. Also found at this location were some traces of **blood spatter** and larger drops on the floor that had tire-tread impressions in them (Figure 22–2) as well as small pieces of glass resembling window glass.

This newly found evidence refocused the examination of the suspect's car to look for the source of the evidence found at the scene of the attack.

Blood was found at the scene of the attack as well as from the suspect's vehicle. These were both type O positive blood, which was shared by both the suspect and victim. This was prior to the use of DNA, but it was determined the blood in both cases was female blood. Likewise, there were hairs recovered from the scene that were of the same type as that of the victim.

FIGURE 22–3 Broken windshield wiper bushing. The top piece was found at a murder scene, and the bottom piece was still attached to the suspect's car. This bushing put the suspect's car at the murder scene.

Photographs and molds of the victim's teeth were recovered and compared with the bite wound on the suspect; although there were many similarities, it was deemed the wound had healed too much to make a definitive determination.

After looking at the evidence, it was determined that

- The bite mark on the suspect's arm was very similar to that of the victim's dentitions. The odontologist stated that the bite mark on the suspect's arm had healed to the point that a definitive determination could not be made.
- The blood in the car was O positive, as was the suspect's and victim's blood. It was determined that the blood in the car was female blood, however. (This was prior to DNA profiling.) This is a **class characteristic**.
- The broken piece of plastic from the scene of the assault (in the garbage bag) was matched to the fractured portion of the bushing to one of the windshield wipers on the suspect's car (Figure 22–3). This was an identification to the exclusion of all others, also known as **individualization**.
- The metal tubing was that of a windshield gasket assembly of the same type of car. This is a class characteristic.
- The hair from the car was similar to that of the victim (Figure 22–4). This is another class characteristic.
- Glass from the scene of the attack was identified as being from that make and year of car based on emission mass spectrophotometry, and matched with data furnished by the car's manufacturer.

FIGURE 22–4　Interior of the car door. Note the single blonde hair and the single drop of blood.

- No glass from the park where the alleged attack on the suspect took place matched the suspect's car, but glass from the assault scene was the same type.
- The tire-tread pattern in the blood at the assault scene was similar to that on the suspect's vehicle. This is a class characteristic that included the suspect's car as a possible donor of the impression.
- The hair located in the car was similar to the victim's; she was therefore, included as a possible donor of the hair.

When considering this case, we are reminded of the Locard's Theory of Transfer, where the suspect left evidence behind and took evidence away with him. Also, much of the evidence in this case was pattern in nature, and when taken in totality and combined with the other evidence available, it resulted in the successful conclusion of this investigation. It is an example of many different types of evidence as well as many types of analyses. This case was also an example of what forensic science and criminal investigation can accomplish when there is teamwork. We all depend on each person fulfilling their individual assignments and then cooperating with all persons involved.

Priorities

When a homicide call is received, it is important to determine if the scene is inside or outside, as well as what kind of weapon was used. It is hoped that you already know the weather conditions, but if you do not, then that is also a major consideration.

As stated earlier, cases are investigated by following some basic rules that are generally the same in the beginning. They include the fact that we usually photograph the scene, diagram the scene, and then begin the other tasks involved in the investigation and documentation. However, when the scene is outside and the weather is not good, then photographs may have to be taken rather rapidly and then the evidence recovered and replaced by markers. This is to avoid damage to evidence by the rain. We must be flexible when handling scenes. The photographs indicate the actual point where each piece of evidence was recovered, and the diagram is based on the markers that replaced the items of evidence.

PRIMER RESIDUE

Primer residue consists of antimony, barium, and lead. These elements are found in the discharge of the vast majority of cartridge discharges. There are several tests but each of these has one basic limiting factor: They are less effective after about 4 hours, and for that reason most laboratories will not accept **gunshot residue** (GSR) kits after a period of 4 hours. There are three major GSR kits used today (Figure 22–5).

- *Scanning electron microscopy (SEM)*. With the SEM, it is possible to visualize actual particles and other trace evidence that can confirm a firearm was used. This is the most specific of the tests we are considering. The kit can be made in the laboratory, but most agencies use commercially available kits available from major supply houses. The kits typically have three samplers, one being a control, another for the left hand, and the remaining one for the right hand. Some may have samplers for both the inside and outside of the hand. The residue is typically on the web portion of the inside and outside of the hands, and it is a simple matter to take the samples. The kits provide a pair of gloves, which should be worn by the person taking the sample. Remove a sampler and dab it on the area indicated, then simply replace it in the kit. This is done with each sampler, with the exception of the control, which should just be left in the kit. The kit is sealed, labeled, and turned in to the laboratory or sent to a laboratory contracted to do the work.

    TIP: Do not have a police officer or anyone handling firearms conduct this procedure. By the simple fact that they carry a firearm, police officers are prone to cross-contamination. These procedures must be done as fairly and honestly as possible. It is not recommended that any firearms examiner ever conduct these tests, nor should they operate the SEM. The procedure should be done on the victims, suspects, and anyone who may be faintly linked to the firearm. Taking the samples does not mean they must be processed. They may be stored and the victim and suspect kits

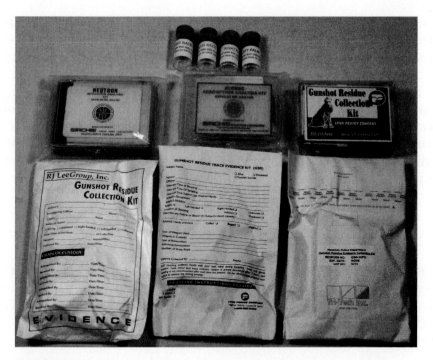

FIGURE 22–5 Various GSR kits. Included are (top left) the neutron activation analysis (NAA), (top center) the atomic absorption analysis (AAA) kit, and the remaining kits for scanning electron microscopy (SEM).

processed. Should others be questioned, then they may be processed as needed.

- The second kit is the ***neutron activation analysis (NAA)***, which comes in a kit obtained from a supply house. They have several swabs, each in a separate container. They have a solution of nitric acid that the swab is wetted with and then simply placed back in the container after having been rubbed on the area indicated on each container. The control is wetted with the solution and then placed back into its individual container. Again, the precautions mentioned earlier pertain to this test as well. The test is nonspecific, and tests for barium, lead, and antimony.

- The third kit is the ***atomic absorption analysis (AAA)*** kit, and, other than the color of the container, it is exactly the same as the NAA kit. The sampling is also done in exactly the same manner. It also tests for the same elements.

The GSR kits should be conducted on everyone involved. There is nothing to say the kits must be processed, but if you have not bothered with them in the beginning, you will have nothing to work with later should it become necessary. The purpose of the kits is not only to determine the suspect, but to eliminate others as well. When a case goes to court, the defense will likely ask if kits were used with all persons. If your answer is negative, then you can expect there will be suggestions that someone else was responsible, "But since the police didn't bother to take the samples, we will never know, will we?" You owe a complete investigation to the victim as well as the suspect. It is your duty. It is just as important to clear an innocent person as it is to convict a guilty one.

It is a good idea to gather exemplars from everyone with regard to any evidence that aids in the successful and complete conclusion of an investigation. This is for inclusion as well as exclusion. This goes for fingerprints, GSR, and even shoe print patterns. We have had investigations in which there were shoe prints that we were never able to associate with any individual. That really should not happen.

CONFUSION AT THE SCENE

It is fairly common for inexperienced investigators to misinterpret the evidence at crime scenes, thereby classifying cases as homicide when they are not, and, likewise, cases that are homicide as something else. Training and experience are critical, and it is to your advantage to have a crime scene analyst or reconstructionist on your staff.

MEDIA

Homicisdes are notorious for attracting the media and curious people. It is a good rule to rope off the scene a lot farther out than you think in the beginning. The purpose is not to keep the media from doing their jobs, but to protect the scene. Remember, it is always easier to make a scene smaller than to extend the boundaries. Furthermore, if the perimeter is too small, any evidence outside the limits you have set may have been destroyed, contaminated, or taken away by someone who wants a souvenir.

The media has a job to do, as do we. Let them do their job as long as it does not interfere with your duties. It is your scene, and should be under your control. You have the final word. All news agencies should be allowed the same access and limited by the same restrictions. Do not show bias—it will get you in trouble.

TRAINING

Scenes such as homicides can be good training grounds. Therefore, once the scene is secure and everything documented, there is no reason why new investigators cannot be taken for a walk-through of the scene. Their presence must be documented and their activity controlled. They will be better prepared to take over as the senior investigators rotate out. Training definitely has a place in actual investigations. Likewise, persons training as crime scene technicians and other legitimate staff positions should be included. The rule of thumb here is that you should do nothing to lose control of the scene or endanger the evidence or the investigation.

RELATED CASES

It is critical that investigators communicate with one another to determine at the first possible opportunity that they may have a series starting. **Serial murderers** often strike several times prior to anyone realizing it is a series, or at least admitting to the belief. It is critical to ask for assistance at the earliest possible time. Remember that although a series may go on for some time, historically speaking, the name of the suspect usually comes up early in the investigation. It is important to keep looking over all of the evidence for signs pointing to this fact. It is also good to get fresh investigators to summarize evidence from time to time. This is one of the elements of the so-called cold case units. Summary of the investigation by others often leads to new evidence or new focus in the investigation.

▲ SUMMARY

Homicide is the killing of another with intent, whereas manslaughter is the killing of another without intent. There is a thin line between the two, and that difference should not bear any influence on your handling of the case.

Homicide is an example of a type of case almost always requiring the participation of many investigators as well as forensic scientists. It is a case where the victim cannot speak for him or herself, but the evidence will speak for them. The scene has a lot to say if you understand the language. You must keep an open mind and never forget that the success of your investigation is TEAMWORK.

■ REVIEW QUESTIONS

1. What is the difference between *murder* and *manslaughter*?
2. If one term were to illustrate a good homicide investigation, what would that term be?
3. In a few words, what is a *class characteristic*?
4. In a few words, with regard to evidence, what is *identification*?
5. What are the three elements found in primer residue?
6. What is meant by SEM?

◼▶ REFERENCES AND SUGGESTED READING

Stuart H. James and Jon J. Nordby, eds., *Forensic Science: An Introduction to Scientific and Investigative Techniques*. Boca Raton, FL: CRC Press, 2005.

Henry C. Lee, Timothy Palmbach, and Marilyn T. Miller, *Henry Lee's Crime Scene Handbook*. San Diego: Academic Press, 2001.

Barry A. J. Fisher, *Techniques of Crime Scene Investigation*. Boca Raton, FL: CRC Press, 2004.

Appendix A

Equipment Sources

AFIX Tracker
www.afix.net
Phone: (877) 438-2349

Armor Forensics
www.armorholdings.com/productsdiv/
armorforensics.asp
Phone: (800) 852-0300
Fax: (800) 588-0399

Arrowhead Forensic Products
www.crime-scene.com
Phone: (913) 894–8388
Fax: (913) 342-2128

BLUESTAR Forensic
www.bluestar-forensic.com
Roc Import Group
P.O. Box 246
Monte Carlo
98005 Monaco

Evident Crime Scene Products
www.evidentcrimescene.com
Phone: (800) 576-7606
Fax: (888) 384-3368

Fast SCAN
www.polhemus.com
40 Hercules Drive
P.O. Box 560
Colchester VT
Phone: (800) 357-4777

FITZCO
www.fitzcoinc.com
4300 Shoreline Drive
Spring Park MN 55384
Phone: (800) 367-8760
(952) 471-1185

identix
www.identix.com
5600 Rowland Road,
Minnetonka MN 55343
Phone: (954) 932-0888
Fax: (952) 932-7181

Kinderprint Company, Inc.
www.kinderprint.com
Phone: (800) 227-6020
Fax: (800) 327-2363

Lightning Powder Company, Inc.
www.redwop.com
Phone: (800) 852-0300
Fax: (800) 588-0399

Lynn Peavey Company
www.lynnpeaveycorp.com
Phone: (800) 255-6499
Fax: (913) 495-6787

MapScenes Systems
www.mapscenes.com
Phone: (800) 668-3312

Payton Scientific Inc.
www.paytonscientific.com
964 Kenmore Avenue
Buffalo NY 14216
Telephone: (716) 876-1813
Fax: (716) 876-8957

Sirchie Finger Print Laboratories
www.sirchie.com
100 Hunter Place
Youngsville NC 27596
Phone: (800) 356-7311
Fax: (800) 899-8181

Spex Forensics
www.spexforensics.com
Phone: (913) 764-0117 (800) 657–8739
Fax: (913) 764-4021 (800) 438–8739

UltraLite ALS
Cao Group Inc.
www.caogroup.com
www.ultralite-als.com
8683 South 700 Wests
Sandy, UT 84070
Phone: (801) 256-9282
Phone: (877) 877-9778

Wheel Ware
www.wheelwaresoftware.com

Appendix B
Organizations

American Academy of Forensic Psychology (AAFP)
www.abfp.com/academy.asp

American Academy of Forensic Sciences (AAFS)
www.aafs.org

American Board of Criminalists (ABC)

American Board of Forensic Anthropology (ABFA)
www.csuchico.edu/anth/ABFA/

American Board of Forensic Document Examiners (ABFDE)

American Board of Forensic Odontology (ABFO)

American Board of Forensic Pathology (ABFP)

American Board of Forensic Psychology (ABFP)
www.abfp.

American Board of Forensic Toxicology (ABFT)

American Board of Medical Legal Death Investigators (ABMDI)

American Board of Pathology

American Society of Crime Lab Directors (ASCLD)

American Society of Forensic Odontology (ASFO)

American Society of Questioned Document Examiners (ASQDE)

Association of Forensic DNA Analysts and Administrators (AFDAA)

California Association of Criminalists (CAC)

California Criminalistics Institute (CCI)

Canadian Society of Forensic Science (CSFS)

Council of Forensic Science Education (COFSE)

FBI National Academy Associates

International Association of Bloodstain Pattern Analysts (IABPA)
www.iabpa.org.

International Association for Identification (IAI)
www.iai.org

National Association of Medical Examiners (N.A.M.E.)
www.thename.org

Association of firearm and Toolmark Examiners
www.afte.org

Appendix C
Charts and Forms

CONTENTS

CRIME SCENE WORKSHEET

DATE OF INCIDENT: _____   DATE OF ASSIGNMENT: _____

LOCATION OF INCIDENT: _____

LOCATION OF ASSIGNMENT: _____

SENT: _____   ARRIVE: _____   BACK: _____   REPORT NO.: _____

NOTIFIED BY: _____   INVESTIGATOR: _____

ARRIVAL

Day: _____   Officers at Scene: _____
Night: _____   Others at Scene: _____
Indoor or Outdoor Scene (Circle)   Lighting Type: _____
Weather: _____   Briefed By: _____
Visability: _____   Assisted By: _____

PHOTOGRAPHY

Date/Time: _____   Camera Type: _____   Film: _____

Lighting Used: Lens Used: _____   ASA/ISO: _____
Flood _____   Lens Speed: _____   Color / BW / Neg
Strobe _____   Aperture Opening: _____   Slide _____
Natural _____   Lens Filter(s): _____   Video _____
Laser _____   Light Filter(s): _____
Xenon _____
U.V. _____
Other _____

DIAGRAM/SKETCH

Date/Time: _____   Scene: _____   Scale: _____

Type:
Overhead   Diagram #1 _____
Elevation   Diagram #2 _____
Exploded   Diagram #3 _____
Combination   Diagram #4 _____
Cutaway   Diagram #5 _____

CRIME SCENE WORKSHEET

LATENT PRINTS

Date/Time: _____   Location #1: _____   Pos / Neg

Location #2: _____   Pos / Neg

Location #3: _____   Pos / Neg

Location #4: _____   Pos / Neg

Location #5: _____   Pos / Neg

Methods Used:
A. Latent Powder
B. Cyanoacrylate
C. Dye Stain   Type: _____
D. ALS   Type: _____
E. Other _____

BLOOD/BODY FLUIDS

Phenolphthalein: Pos / Neg   Notes: _____

Luminol: Pos / Neg   Notes: _____

Semen: _____

Laser: _____   U.V. Light: _____

Xenon: _____   Other ALS: _____

Sample Recovery: Wet: _____

Dry: _____

HAIR/FIBER EVIDENCE

Date/Time: _____

Hair: Source _____   Type _____   Control _____

Source _____   Type _____   Control _____

Source _____   Type _____   Control _____

Source _____   Type _____   Control _____

Source _____   Type _____   Control _____

Fiber: Source _____   Type _____   Control _____

Source _____   Type _____   Control _____

Source _____   Type _____   Control _____

Source _____   Type _____   Control _____

Source _____   Type _____   Control _____

Other Procedures: _____

CRIME SCENE WORKSHEET

FIREARMS/TOOLMARKS

Date/Time: _____   Location: _____

Firearm Type(s): _____

Tool Type(s): _____

Procedures:
TMDT: _____   Pos / Neg (circle)   Location: _____
SEM: _____   NAA: _____   AA: _____
Other: _____

EVIDENCE

Date/Time: _____   Location #1: _____
    Location #2: _____
    Location #3: _____
    Location #4: _____
    Location #5: _____

Synopsis of what recovered: _____
_____
_____
_____
_____
_____
_____
_____

PHOTOGRAPHS

#1 _____
#2 _____
#3 _____
#4 _____
#5 _____
#6 _____
#7 _____
#8 _____
#9 _____
#10 _____

MALE ANATOMIC CHART

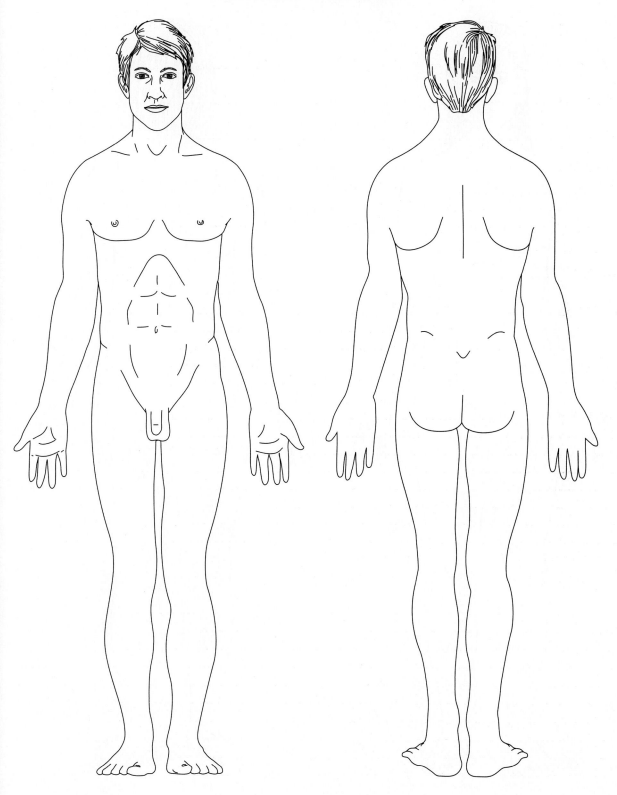

FEMALE ANATOMIC CHART

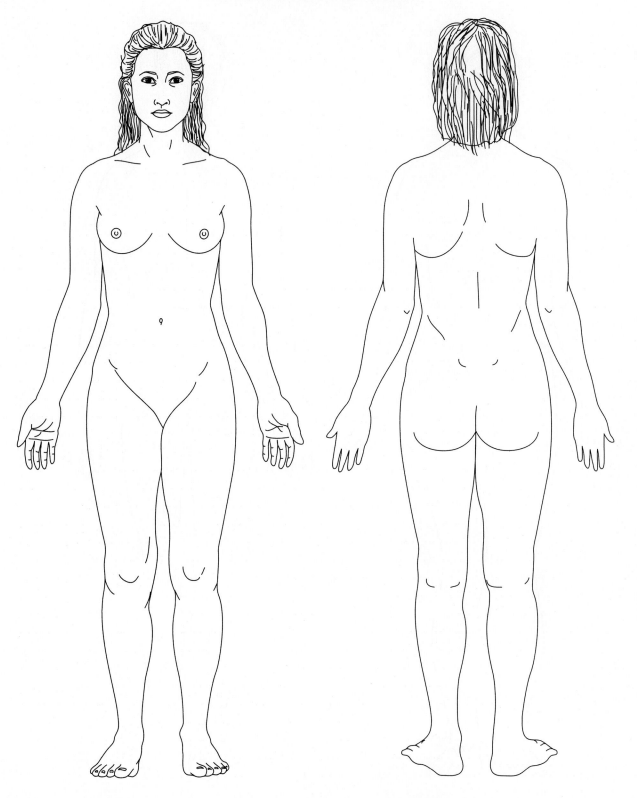

PHOTO LOG

Name:			Report No.:		Date:	
Camera:		Model:			Serial Number:	
Lens:		Type:			Speed:	Filters:
Flash:			Model:			Filters:
Film:			ASA/DIN/ISO:			Type:

Frame:	Speed:	f-stop:	Subject:	Light:	ALS:
1.					
2.					
3.					
4.					
5.					
6.					
7.					
8.					
9.					
10.					
11.					
12.					
13.					
14.					
15.					
16.					
17.					
18.					
19.					
20.					
21.					
22.					
23.					
24.					
25.					
26.					
27.					
28.					
29.					
30.					

MEDICATION WORKSHEET

Decedent's Name _____   Case No. _____

Investigator _____   Date of Death _____

Med Name, Potency, Dosage, & Frequency	Pharmacy, Phone, Rx No.	Prescribing Physician	Qty.	# Left	Prescribed To	Where Found & Remarks

Report No. _____
District No. _____

MODUS OPERANDI REPORT

CLASSIFICATION _____

Victim _____

Residence _____

_____ Phone _____

Where committed _____

_____

Date committed _____ Day of Week _____

Time committed _____

Person attacked _____

_____

Property attacked _____

_____

How committed _____

_____

Means of attack (Instrument) _____

_____

_____

Object of attack _____

_____

Trademark _____

_____

_____

_____

_____

Investigators _____

Suspect No. 1 _____

Address _____

Ethnicity _____

Hair _____ Eyes _____

Height _____ Weight _____

Age _____ Build _____

Marks _____

_____

Dressed _____

_____

_____

Suspect No. 2 _____

Address _____

Ethnicity _____

Hair _____ Eyes _____

Height _____ Weight _____

Age _____ Build _____

Marks _____

_____

Dressed _____

_____

_____

Vehicle used _____

LIST OF PROPERTY STOLEN AND DETAILED REPORT OF INVESTIGATORS:

Signed, Officer _____ Badge _____ Date _____ Time _____

Approved _____ Rank _____ Date _____ Time _____

EVIDENCE REPORT

Classification			Report Number	Status: __Open __Closed		Disposition
Complainant				Location of Offense		Date of Incident
Item #	Status	Type	Serial or Engravings	Description		Quantity

Circumstances of Recovery

CHAIN OF CUSTODY

Item	From	To	Date and Time
Disposed by: Date/Time		Final Disposition	
Writer		ID Number	Date/Time

DEATH INVESTIGATION WORKSHEET

DATE: _____   CASE NO.: _____
                                CLASSIFICATION: _____

Notified by: _____   Date/Time: _____
Affiliation: _____
Name of Decedent: _____   Age/DOB: _____
Address: _____
Race: _____   Marital Status: _____
Arrived by: _____   Date/Time: _____
Cause of Death: _____
Place of Death: _____
Place of Injury: _____   Date/Time: _____
Primary Care Physician: _____
Address: _____
Telephone: _____
Death Certificate: Yes / No   Cause of Death: _____

Identified by: _____   Relationship: _____
Address: _____
Telephone: _____
Date/Time Identified: _____   Witness: _____

Arrival at Scene   Date/Time: _____
Observations at Scene: _____
_____
_____
_____
_____

Police Investigator (s): _____
Police Report No.: _____   Classification: _____

Request Removal: _____   Date/Time: _____
Body Removed: _____   Date/Time: _____
Removed By: _____

Arrival at Morgue   Date/Time: _____
Photos: Yes / No   Prints: Right thumb / 10 Print / Hands (circle)
Height: _____   Weight: _____

DEATH INVESTIGATION WORKSHEET

<u>Examination at Morgue</u>

Injuries: _____

_____

_____

Rigor/Lividity/Blanching: _____

Tattoos: _____

_____

_____

Other Observations: _____

_____

Property: Yes / No   Description: _____

_____

Scars: _____

_____

Incisions: _____

_____

Medical History: _____

_____

_____

_____

Synopsis: _____

_____

_____

_____

_____

_____

_____

_____

_____

_____

<u>Recovery</u>

Blood: Yes / No   Urine: Yes / No

Ambulance Report: Yes / No   Admission Records: Yes / No

DEATH INVESTIGATION WORKSHEET

<u>Witness Statements</u>

Name: _____

Address: _____

Telephone: _____

Statement: _____

_____

_____

_____

_____

_____

_____

_____

_____

<u>Law Enforcement Information</u>

Name: _____   Badge No.: _____

Statement: _____

_____

_____

_____

_____

_____

_____

_____

LATENT PRINT PROCESSES CHART

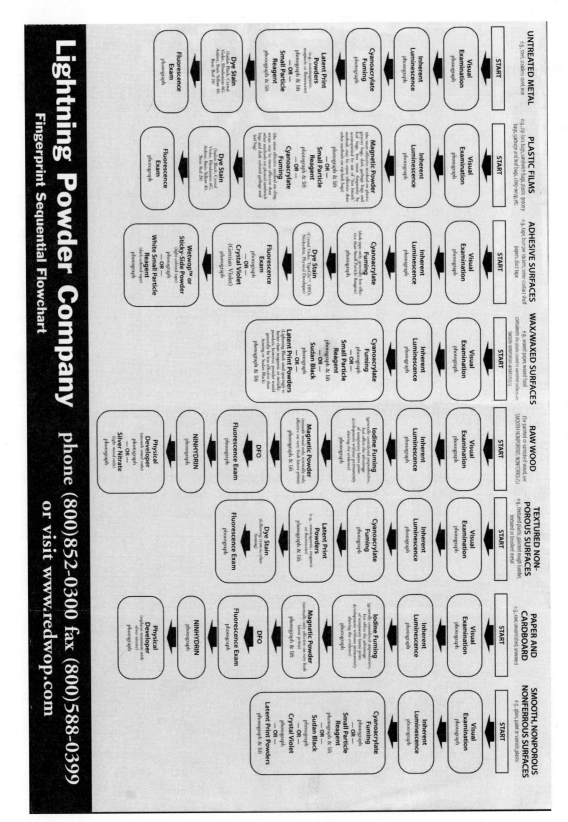

Lightning Powder Company

Fingerprint Sequential Flowchart

phone (800)852-0300 fax (800)588-0399 or visit www.redwop.com

Glossary

4 × 5 format camera: A large-format camera (usually referring to the Kodak Speed Graphic or Kodak Crown Graphic cameras or variants) used for fingerprint photography. The name comes from the fact they use a 4- × 5-in. sheet of film.

ABFO#2 scale: American Board of Forensic Odontologists' scale; a right-angled photo scale with measurements, a gray scale, and focusing targets.

Abrasion ring: A red ring around the periphery of some bullet entry wounds caused by abrasion.

Accidental death: A death that is not suspicious, but not natural (eg, drowning).

Acid phosphatase test: An enzyme found in seminal secretions; detected with field kits and laboratory analysis.

Aerial photograph: Photographs taken from an aircraft. Usually referring to film, but can be digital imaging and infrared imagery as well.

Alligatoring: A deep charring resembling alligator skin that indicates a long burning time.

Alternate light source (ALS): Often referring to a laser or xenon light, but can be any light that is not normal.

Ambient light: Natural light.

Ambient temperature: The temperature of the surrounding area, such as that near a body.

Anatomic chart: A chart of the human body that usually shows the various body parts.

Angle of impact: The acute angle formed between the direction of a blood drop and the plane of the surface that it strikes.

Aperture (*f*-stop): The opening of the diaphragm or iris on a camera lens that controls the amount of light that strikes the film surface.

Apnea monitor: An instrument that monitors the breathing of an infant; normally used to alert someone of the infant's cessation of breathing.

Arterial spurting: Bloodstain pattern resulting from blood exiting the body under pressure from a breached artery.

Asphyxiation: Death because of a lack of air. May be the result of strangulation (manual), drowning, or other causes.

Assault: The overt movement to attack another. It is often used as a generic term for assault and battery.

Atomic Absorption Analysis (AAA): A technique that tests for primer residue—barium, lead, and antimony—which is found in most modern cartridge primers.

Autoerotic death: Accidental death by asphyxiation as a result of strangulation from a ligature used during masturbation.

Automated Fingerprint Identification System (AFIS): A single-print system that searches both inked (known) and latent (unknown) prints, as well as combinations thereof. It is a filing system as well as search engine.

Automatic operation: Camera that operates by program.

Autopsy: The postmortem examination of a human body with the purpose of determining the cause and manner of death.

Backspatter: Blood that is directed back toward the source of energy or force that caused the spatter.

Barrel: The tube through which a projectile is launched from a firearm.

Barrier filter: A filter that blocks certain light frequencies, such as ultraviolet.

Baseline method: A method of crime scene sketching where a straight line is set up (baseline) and all evidence is measured from the baseline to the object at a right angle.

Battery: The injury inflicted as a result of an assault; hence the term *assault and battery.*

Bedsore: A decubitus (bedsore) ulcer from not being turned and cleaned.

Bichromatic powder: A fingerprint powder that has additives, such as orange, to make the black powder look gray on black objects.

Binding marks: Marks left from a binding (ligature), usually referring to the wrists and ankles.

Biohazard bag: A bag that is usually red in color with a biohazard symbol on its surface and is used to dispose of contaminated material, such as items with blood and other body fluids.

Biological fluids: Usually referring to blood, semen, urine, saliva, and other body secretions.

Bite mark: An impression on an object, such as a body or food, that may produce pattern evidence with which to identify its contributor.

Blanching: A pale area on a body where livor mortis is not apparent because of pressure.

Blasting cap: A copper cylinder containing a highly sensitive explosive (PETN) used to initiate the discharge of explosives, such as dynamite.

Blood spatter: Patterns resulting from force acting on blood, thereby projecting it.

Blood: The liquid and its suspended elements that are circulated through the body via the heart, arteries, veins, and capillaries.

Bloodstain: A pattern stain that is produced when blood comes into contact with a surface.

Blue-frequency light: A light in the blue frequency range used as an alternate light source (ALS) to search for body fluids and latent fingerprints.

Bolt face signature: The face of the bolt (the flat surface that comes in contact with the base of the cartridge) has grinding marks from its manufacture; those marks are imparted onto the base of a primer, located in the center of a cartridge case.

Bolt: A metal device that holds a firearm cartridge in the chamber during firing.

Booby trap: An improvised explosive device set off clandestinely.

Booster: An explosive charge (such as TNT) used to boost a very high explosive, such as ANFO, to critical level.

Bore: The hollow core of the barrel of a firearm that contains the "rifling," or a system of lands and grooves, the purpose of which is to impart a spin on the projectile, resulting in a more accurate shot.

Bracketing: The procedure of taking a photograph and then taking another photo with an exposure both above and below the original.

Breech-face signature: The imprint on the primer of a cartridge left by the impact of the bolt or breech face.

Briefing: A conference at a crime scene where the crime scene investigator(s) are briefed on the case.

Bruising: A discoloration of the skin resulting from trauma to that surface.

Bubble ring: Blood that once contained an air bubble has dried and retained the circular pattern of a ring.

Burglary: The entry of another's dwelling or a business (during the closed hours) with the intent to commit a theft or felony therein.

Bypass filter: A photographic filter that allows certain light frequencies to pass through to put an image on film.

Cable release: A remote camera-shutter release that allows the shutter to be tripped while away from the camera.

Cadaveric spasm: Refers to the unintentional cramping of muscles that results in a decedent moving (eg, cramping hand muscles that result in the decedent gripping a gun).

Cartridges: A projectile system referring to cartridge casing, primer, projectile and propellant for the ammunition.

Cast: The mirror-like reproduction of an impression pattern by using a liquid medium that dries hard or pliable.

Castoff: Bloodstains resulting from an object bearing blood being moved in such a way that the surface tension of the blood is exceeded and it strikes another object.

Cause of death: The actual mechanism of death, such as asphyxia or stroke.

Certification: Referring to the professional level of an employee as contrasted with accreditation of the facility.

Chain of custody: A detailed list of the signatures, dates, and times that evidence changed custody.

Chamber marks: Marks left on the outside of a cartridge resulting from its being rammed into the chamber of a firearm.

Chemiluminescence: Luminescence as a result of a chemical reaction.

Civilian staff: Staff who are not sworn (gun-carrying) operatives of an organization.

Class characteristics: Some point of identification that puts a piece of evidence into a broad grouping (class).

Computer-aided drawing (CAD): A computer program that lets the user produce a drawing or image of a particular object.

Concentric fracture: The portion of a mechanical fracture that is circular.

Conversion filter: A photographic filter that changes the frequency of light.

Court drawings: Usually larger "finished" drawing for courtroom purposes.

Crime scene: Where a crime or some element of that crime occurred. It can be the primary crime scene or a secondary crime scene(s).

Crime scene diagram: A detailed scale drawing of the scene.

Crime scene drawing: A drawing of less detail than a diagram.

Crime scene investigator (CSI): A generic term for a crime scene technician, crime scene analyst, senior crime scene analyst, or reconstructionist.

Crime scene kit: Various portable kits used at a crime scene to collect evidence.

Crime scene search: The actual process of searching a crime scene for evidence.

Crime scene sketch: A rough drawing that is not proportional or to scale. A police officer or the initial crime scene investigator usually creates it.

Crime scene survey: The informal "looking over" or scanning of the crime scene.

Crime scene worksheet: A document listing the major tasks at crime scenes used to avoid forgetting any specific task.

Crystal violet: A dye stain commonly used for latent fingerprint examination on the sticky side of tape.

Cutaway: A crime scene drawing that has a portion partially cut away (such as a portion of a wall) to allow the viewer to see inside.

Cyanoacrylate (superglue) fuming: The process of using the fumes from cyanoacrylate ester (superglue) to locate latent fingerprints.

Cylinder rotation: The direction the cylinder of a firearm rotates during the firing process. It differs between various firearms. For example, Colt and Smith & Wesson revolvers rotate in opposite directions.

Cylinder: The housing for the multiple chambers for cartridges in a revolver.

DC flash: The older bulb-type camera flash as opposed to the electronic strobe of today.

Decubitus ulcer: *See* bedsore.

Defense wound: Wounds (typically on the hands and forearms) that are usually stabbing and incised-type wounds from warding off blows.

Definitive markings: Markings on evidence that are exclusive of all others.

Delegation: The referral of authority.

Demonstrative evidence: Evidence that demonstrates something such as a crime scene drawing for trial purposes.

Dental impressions: Impressions made by teeth in partially eaten food or in flesh.

Dentition: Teeth.

Depression: A mental state often associated with reduced functioning, feelings of sadness, despair, and so on.

Depth of field: In photography, referring to what portion of an image is and is not in focus.

DFO: A dye stain used to visualize latent fingerprints.

Diffusion filter: A filter used to soften or reduce the amount of light reaching the film when taking a photograph.

Digital photography: Photography using a digital camera that saves images on electronic media such as a memory card or disc.

Direction of flight: The trajectory of a blood drop, which can be established by its angle of impact and directionality angle.

Directionality angle: The angles between the long axis of a bloodstain and a predetermined line on the plane of the target surface that represents zero degrees.

Directionality: Established by the bloodstain pattern's assumed geometric shape after coming into contact with a surface.

Disclaimer: An indication on a crime scene drawing that indicates it is not to scale.

Distortion: In photography, refers to images typically taken with a wide-angle lens (wider than 28 mm).

Documentation process: The process of recording a crime scene, usually thought of in terms of photography, drawing, and narrative report.

Double gloving: The practice of wearing two sets of gloves simultaneously when working with hazardous evidence.

Draw-back effect: Blood that has been drawn backward into the muzzle of a firearm.

Drip pattern: Bloodstain patterns resulting from blood dripping into blood.

Druggist's bindle: A folded piece of paper that is used to contain small amounts of powdered substances; commonly used by pharmacists, especially in foreign countries.

Dusting: The process of using a latent fingerprint brush to spread powder, thus enabling one to visualize the latent print.

Dye number: The identifying number assigned to a specific color of fabric dye. This can be a form of class evidence.

Ejector: A device found on the bolt of a firearm that kicks the spent cartridge casing from the firearm, as extraction and recycling.

Electric trigger: In explosives, where the detonator is electric in nature as opposed to a burning fuse–type detonator.

Electrocution contact points: The point(s) at which an electric current entered and left the body during an electrocution.

Electronic shutter release: A remote shutter trigger for a camera that functions by radio signal or mechanical cable.

Electrostatic detection apparatus (ESDA): An instrument that subjects documents to a combination of static electric charge, vacuum, and vibration to visualize indented writing.

Elevation drawing: A drawing showing the details of a vertical surface, such as a wall.

Entry wound: The point at which a projectile, such as a bullet, entered the body.

Evidence report: A document that records items of physical evidence along with identifiers, such as engravings and serial numbers.

Exit wound: An injury caused by the exiting of a projectile, such as a bullet.

Expectorated blood: Blood blown out of the nose, mouth, or a wound as the result of air pressure and/or air flow acting as the propelling force.

Exploded view: A drawing where the walls are dropped down to the same plane as the floor; it displays both the overhead and elevation views in the same drawing.

Explosive charge: An amount of explosive used to make a bomb.

Exposure meter: An electronic meter or gauge that records the amount of light at a specific location for the purpose of photography.

Extension cable: In photography, a cable attached at one end to the camera and at the opposite end to the flash unit thereby allowing the flash to be used at a distance and angle from the camera.

Extortion: The obtaining of money or things of value by the use of force or threat of force.

Extractor: A device on the bolt of a firearm that facilitates the removal of the spent cartridge casing from the firearm.

Fabric pattern analysis: The process that compares torn fabric and weave patterns with other samples.

False positive: A test that gives a positive result that is not the result of the substance for which tested.

Fetish: In forensics and psychology, the sexual attraction to an object, such as women's clothing, and especially shoes and underwear.

Fiber: A strand of a natural or synthetic material usually associated with textiles.

Field-work forms: Formatted documents that assist the analyst with investigative procedures so as to do them properly, correctly, and in a timely manner.

Film speed: In photography, the speed of the film referred to as ISO (ASA and DIN), that indicates how sensitive the film is to light.

Filter: In photography, a piece of glass that fits over the lens and is color tinted or opaque. It allows, removes, or alters various light frequencies.

***Final Exit The*:** A book that explains how to commit suicide successfully.

Fingerprint: Impressions in the form of patterns resulting from contact of one of the palmar surfaces of the body with another object; usually associated with oils, perspiration, or other contaminants on the friction-ridge surface.

Fingerprint camera: Usually a fixed-focus 4 × 5 formatted camera to allow for the photography of fingerprints at a 1:1 ratio.

Fingerprint photography: The recording of fingerprints on film or digital media.

Firearm: A device designed to launch a projectile by the expansion of gases resulting from the rapid burning of a propellant.

Firing pin: A pin or nipple on the face of the bolt, or coming out of the center of the bolt, whose purpose it is to detonate the primer, which in turn initiates the propellant in the cartridge.

Fixed-focus camera: A camera that has a set focus (ie, no adjustments are possible). Typically found in fingerprint cameras.

Fixed lividity: The settling of the blood within a deceased person that is purplish in color and after a period of time sets. This means that when you press on the pattern, it does not blanch white from the pressure. *See also* Livor mortis.

Flight path: Path of the blood drop from the point of origin to the point of impact.

Floor plan drawing: An overhead line drawing of a room, house, or structure.

Flow pattern: Paths taken by blood as result of gravity or movement.

Fluorescein: A reagent used to visualize trace amounts of blood. It is used for pattern interpretation in bloodstain pattern analysis.

Fluoresce: Emission of electromagnetic radiation, such as visible light, after having been excited by exposure to other radiation, such as ultraviolet light. It remains only so long as the exciting radiation is present.

Forensic anthropology: The study of the humans in all places and all times from the legal viewpoint.

Forensic archaeology: The study of ancient humans and their surroundings.

Forensic entomology: The study of arthropods as they relate to forensics, such as postmortem interval (PMI), or time since death.

Forensic odontology: The study of detention as it relates to forensics.

Forensic photography: The use of image recovery or pictures to aid in the investigation of crime.

Forward spatter: Result of blood traveling in same direction as the source of energy causing the spatter.

French curves: A drafting implement that is a system of varying curves to aid in the connecting of lines in drawings.

Gentian violet: A dye stain used in latent fingerprint recovery, commonly used on cellophane.

Graffiti: Clandestine "tagging" or putting one's marks on objects.

Grid method: A method of drawing a crime scene in which squares are used to represent 1 ft^2, typically as $\frac{1}{4}$ -in. equals 1 ft.

Grid search: A search pattern consisting of a series of parallel search lines with a second series perpendicular to the first, so as to create a series of squares (evident when diagrammed).

Grooves: In firearms, a series of depressed spiral lines in the walls of the barrel of a firearm whose purpose is to put a spin on the bullet for stability in flight.

Gunshot residue (GSR): The trace evidence left from the discharge of a firearm; includes barium, lead, and antimony. *See also* Primer residue.

Hackle marks: Stress marks on the broken surface of glass that determine from what side the force was applied.

Haze filter: A 1A camera filter used to block out ultraviolet light from the sun.

Head stamps: The flat back surface of a cartridge casing that bears such information as the maker, caliber, and other information, varying from brand to brand and country to country.

Heat fracture: A fracture of glass that meanders instead of having the more or less uniform lines of a mechanical fracture. The broken edges are smooth and glassy in appearance.

Hematrace: A blood reagent that is specific to humans.

Henry Fingerprint Classification System: A ten-print fingerprint classification system used to file fingerprints.

Hesitation mark: Scarring, healing, or fresh incised wounds, typically to the wrists, indicative of a person having attempted suicide.

High-order explosives: Very powerful but stable explosives, such as dynamite and TNT.

High-velocity impact spatter (HVIS): Fine bloodstain pattern resulting from the impact of a rapidly traveling object, such as a bullet.

Homicide: The killing of another human. *See also* Manslaughter.

Hot shoe: A device on a camera to which an external flash unit is attached. The hot shoe provides the electric impulse to fire the flash.

Hot spot: A blank spot on a photograph resulting from a flash reflecting directly back into the lens of the camera.

Identification: Identifying an object or characteristic into one or more "class characteristics."

Impact site: Point where force encounters a source of blood.

Impact spatter: Bloodstain "patter" resulting from an object or force impacting a blood-bearing surface.

Impression evidence: The signature (pattern) of an object that is left in another object when the two have come in contact with one another.

Incised defense wounds: Wounds that are wider on the surface than they are deep, typically with clean sharp edges from a sharp instrument, such as a knife. Usually found on the hands and forearms as a result of blocking the knife or grasping the knife blade. Sometimes associated with the predominate hand.

Incised wound: A wound that is longer on the surface than it is deep.

Indented writing: Writing that is three-dimensional as the result of pressure from the writing implement. Sometimes found two or three pages under the original document.

Individual characteristics: Points of identification found on evidence that are unique to that item.

Individualization: The identification of an object to the exclusion of all others. Also referred to as a *positive identification*.

Industrial fatality: The death of a person while working (eg, falling from a scaffold).

Infrared (IR) light: A light frequency that is slightly above the visible frequencies and is designated long-wave and short-wave ultraviolet light. Commonly used to look for body fluids and trace metal.

Infrared filter: A filter used in photography to visualize the infrared light frequencies that are below the visual spectrum.

Infrared photography: Photography using the infrared spectrum to visualize bruises and scars, as well as faded or eradicated inks.

Initiator: In explosives, the substance used to cause combustion of the explosive (eg, a match).

Ink analysis: The study of inks for components, often using light frequency or thin-layer chromatography.

Inked print: An inked impression pattern of the palmar surfaces of the body as well as tires, shoes, and so forth. *See also* Known prints.

Instrument analysis: The analysis of a substance using instrumentation such as the gas chromatograph–mass spectrometers, Fourier Transfer Infrared Spectrophotometer.

Iodine fuming: Heating of iodine crystals to visualize latent fingerprints.

Keying: The practice of scraping a key along a car to damage the paint.

Known prints: An inked impression pattern of the palmar surfaces of the body, tires, shoes, etc. *See also* Inked prints.

Known sample: Material for which the origin is known; used to compare with unknown samples for identification purposes.

L-shaped ruler: A larger photo scale that is L-shaped and resembles the ABFO#2 scale.

Lacerated wound: Wounds with torn edges or edges separated by crushing or tearing.

Laceration: A wound that is typically longer on the surface than it is deep; result of tearing, as opposed to the cutting of incised wounds.

Lands: The elevated surfaces inside the bore of a gun barrel that helps impart spin to the bullet to stabilize it in flight.

Laser: Usually referring to a laser light used in forensics for a multitude of tasks.

Latent print adapter: A tube-type clear adapter placed on the lens of a camera to take a 1:1 ratio photograph of fingerprints.

Latent print camera: A camera that is typically 4- × 5-in. format film and a fixed-focus lens.

Latent print card: A 4- × 5-in. card on which latent fingerprints are affixed with tape.

Latent print envelope: The custody envelope used to store latent fingerprints.

Latent print: A print that is left by one of the palmar surfaces of the body and is not readily visible.

Leg wires: The electric wires coming from the end of a blasting cap (squib).

Lens hood: A hood-type fixture on the end of the camera lens barrel used to keep out light glare.

Leucomalachite Green: A presumptive blood reagent that is nonspecific.

Lifting: The removal of a latent fingerprint from a surface by using tape.

Ligature: A rope, belt, or anything else used as a noose or binding.

Ligature mark: A pattern mark on the skin surface associated with binding or hanging.

Line search: A search pattern in which everyone is lined up shoulder to shoulder.

Livor mortis: A pattern or stain left when gravity forces the blood to settle in the portion of decedent closest to the ground. *See also* Postmortem lividity.

Locard's Exchange Principle: Whenever two objects come into contact with one another, there will be a mutual exchange of matter; also known as Locard's Theory of Transfer.

Long-wave ultraviolet light: Light in the ultraviolet light frequency.

Low-order explosives: Less powerful explosives, often associated with less stability as well (eg, black gunpowder).

Low-velocity impact spatter (LVIS): A bloodstain pattern that is the result of no force being applied to the blood-bearing surface; blood that exceeds its surface tension and falls, thereby leaving a pattern.

Luminescence: The emission of light through phosphorescence, bioluminescence, or chemiluminescence; found among some insects and marine life; used in forensics with reagents such as luminol.

Luminol: A blood reagent that gives off a bluish glow and can be photographed and used in bloodstain pattern analysis.

Macro lens: A camera lens used to document very small items or details.

Macro photography: The photography of very small items or patterns.

Macro twin-flash unit: A camera flash unit consisting of two flash heads for macro or close-up photography.

Macro view: The overall crime scene.

Magazine: A box type container for firearm cartridges found in rifles and semi-automatic pistols.

Maggot masses: A mass of fly maggots that are concentrated in an area of a body opening, either natural or one caused by injury.

Magnetic powder: A latent fingerprint powder that has fine metal flakes inside to allow a magnetic wand to be used to spread the powder.

Magnetic wand: The device or brush used to spread magnetic latent fingerprint powder.

Major case cards: Inked or known fingerprint cards that also include the sides of the palms of the hands as well as the fingertips.

Manner of death: The type of death: natural, accidental, murder, or suicide.

Manslaughter: The killing of another human without "malice aforethought" but without consideration for the danger of their actions. *See also* Homicide.

Manual of Operations (MOO): A manual spelling out the operational policies of an organization, such as a crime lab.

Manual of Procedures (MOP): A manual spelling out the protocols of an organization, such as a crime lab.

Manual operation: In photography, the human determination of aperture, shutter speed, and focus of the camera as opposed to the computer control of the automatic camera.

Manufacturer's Safety Data Sheet (MSDS): Documents spelling out the makeup of a product along with the dangers and precautions required.

Master operation: The camera flash system that allows the flash to control other flash units referred to as *slaves.*

Mechanical fracture: A spiderweb pattern occurring when a force breaks glass, bone, or substances of similar makeup.

Medical misadventure: Indicates the mistake of a doctor or medical practitioner with regard to treatment of a patient.

Medication worksheet: A document in which medications are listed, with relevant information such as dosage, strength, and other related information.

Medium-velocity impact spatter (MVIS): A bloodstain pattern resulting from an object impacting blood at 5 to 25 ft/sec.

Mental illness: A disease of the mind or personality, evidenced by behavior, and any psychiatric illness listed in the *Diagnostic and Statistical Manual* (DSM) of the American Psychiatric Association.

Method of Operation (MO): The pattern behavior of a criminal. *See also* Modus operandi.

Micro view: A view of the scene or evidence from the standpoint of one item at a time.

Minimum qualifications (MQ): The fundamental requirements for a position.

Misting: Blood that has been reduced to a fine spray as a result of the energy or force applied to it.

Modus Operandi (MO) report: A report documenting the method of operation of a particular criminal.

Molybdenum disulfide: A small particle reagent (SPR) used in the recovery of latent fingerprints on wet surfaces.

Mongolian spots: Bluish or purple spots commonly found on the small of the back and the buttocks of Asian and American Indian infants and small children; sometimes confused with bruises.

Motor vehicle accident (MVA): The collision of two or more motor vehicles or a single motor vehicle with a fixed object or pedestrian.

Multifunction lens: A camera lens that has multiple functions, such as wide angle, standard, telephoto, and macro.

Muzzle: The opening in the end of a gun barrel.

Mylar sheet: A plastic-like material on which latent fingerprint lifts are commonly placed.

Narrative report: The portion of the investigative report that is in story format and logical sequence.

Natural death: A death resulting from causes that are not intentional or accidental.

Nebulyzer: A device used to administer medication to persons with breathing difficulties, such as asthma.

Negative control: In scientific testing, that sample without the unknown. It should not react, indicating the material is not contaminated.

Negative print film: A photographic medium, usually of celluloid, on which an image is recorded and in negative (ie, opposite from the actual view), as opposed to a positive, photograph, or slide.

Neutron Activation Analysis (NAA): A method used to analyze gunshot residue.

Ninhydrin: A chemical that reacts to amino acids. When used in fingerprint detection, it produces a purple latent print.

Noise: In digital photography, equivalent to grain on film. When the image is greatly enlarged, a snow-like image on the photograph, usually in black or gray.

Oblique lighting: In photography, a light less than perpendicular or at right angles. It is used to cause shadowing to show contour.

OBTI: A human-specific blood reagent.

ORI number: The originating facilities identification number on the FBI fingerprint card.

Overlay: In infant deaths, the occurrence of an adult completely or partially rolling over an infant who is sleeping in the adult bed, resulting in suffocation of the infant.

Overhead line drawing: The overhead line drawing, aerial, or "bird's-eye" view of a structure.

Painting with light: In photography, the process by which several flash units are flashed over a long distance to light the area up during night-time photo operations. Used with lighting unlit roads.

Palmer Method: A method of handwriting popular in the 1930s but still found in use today.

Panning: A method of pivoting with a camera in the direction of a moving object to keep it in sharp focus.

Passive pattern: Pattern created when blood exceeds its surface tension and falls freely from its source to impact.

Patent print: A latent print that is three-dimensional and easy to see with oblique lighting.

Pattern evidence: Any kind of evidence with a specific pattern or design (eg, shoe prints, tire prints, fingerprints).

Perimeter stains: Bloodstains that consist only of an outer periphery because the central area has been removed by wiping or flaking after the liquid blood has partially or completely dried.

Personal Digital Assistant (PDA): A device used as a minicomputer that allows notetaking and even report writing and drawing. Some have photographic and voice recording abilities as well.

Petechiae: Small red dots caused by bursting blood vessels, usually as a result of pressure. They are associated with suffocation and are usually found in the eyes, eyelids, and inside the lips.

Petechial hemorrhage: The process by which a small blood vessel ruptures.

Phenolphthalein: A presumptive blood reagent that is nonspecific.

Photo macrograph: A photograph taken through a lens designed for extreme detail of small objects.

Photo microscopy: The process of taking photographs through the microscope.

Photographic log: A document that lists all photographs taken along with pertinent information, such as *f*-stop, shutter speed, and camera type.

Photographic report: A report of photographs taken and their description.

Photographic transparencies: Commonly referred to as *slides*. They are photographic positives.

Photomicrograph: A photograph taken through a microscope lens.

Physical developer: A reagent used in the development of latent fingerprints.

Physical evidence: Evidence that can be seen or held.

Pistol grip: The handle of a firearm, typically a handgun.

Plan of operation: A detailed plan or schedule for some task.

Plastic prints: In latent fingerprints, a three-dimensional print pattern in blood, paint, clay, etc.

Point (area) of convergence: The common point (area) on a two-dimensional surface over which the directionality of several blood drops can be traced.

Point (area) of origin: The point at right angles to the point of convergence and projecting into three-dimensional space; it indicates the original position of the blood source when it was acted on by a force.

Point of impact: The point at which one object or substance contacts another.

Polarizing lens filter: A double glass camera lens filter that removes glare from the sun or other light.

Positional asphyxia: The process by which a person dies of suffocation because of being in a position that did not allow for sufficient movement of the diaphragm (eg, "hog-tied" person).

Positive control: In scientific testing, a surface that has a known control sample on it. Its reaction to a reagent indicates the reagent is working properly.

Positive print film: Also known as *color slide* or *transparency film*.

Postmortem interval (PMI): The time since death, often determined by the study of entomologic activity.

Postmortem lividity: The settling of the blood in a decedent resulting from the draw of gravity.

Pour patterns: In arson cases, patterns indicative of an accelerant being used to start the fire.

Presumptive test: A test that implies something is what it is thought to be (eg, positive presumptive blood test implies that the substance being tested is blood).

Primary crime scene: Usually the scene at which the crime was initially committed.

Primer residue: Residue commonly found on the back and web portion of the hands, consisting of barium, lead, and antimony. *See also* Gunshot residue (GSR).

Primer: An initiator usually associated with firearms ammunition.

Projected blood: Blood that impacts a surface as the result of an applied force.

Projected pattern: A blood pattern that was sent out under force or pressure.

Prone: Lying in a face-down position.

Property crime: A crime in which the object of attack was property.

Proportion: In crime scene drawings, objects are drawn to relative representative size, although not to scale.

Pupae: The larval stage of insects.

Pupate: The process by which the insect larvae progress to the adult stage.

Quarrying explosives: Very powerful but stable explosives that are used to move large quantities of rock (eg, ANFO, or ammonia nitrate fuel oil mixture).

Radial fracture: That part of a mechanical fracture that radiates out in a relatively straight line from the point of impact.

Reconstruction: To put something, such as a crime scene, back together.

Reconstructive agent: A chemical reagent such as luminol that allows one to visualize bloodstains for the purpose of determining what occurred.

Recycle time: In photography, the time required for a flash unit to fire and fully recover in order to fire again.

Reversed print: A print that is a negative image. The furrows are recorded instead of the ridges of a fingerprint.

Rhodamine 6G: A chemical dye stain used for visualizing latent fingerprints.

Ricochet: Deflection of blood after impact with a target surface; results in staining of another, different target surface.

Rigor mortis: A part of the decomposition process in which bacteria cause the stiffening of the muscles.

Ring lights: A camera flash unit used for extremely detailed photographs, such as insects and teeth.

Rope burn: An abrasion friction burn resulting from the rapid or pressurized movement under pressure of a ligature or binding.

Satellite spatter: Small droplets of blood that break off from the parent drop because of force or surface texture.

Scale: A specific ratio of measurement in a drawing or photograph as compared to the same object in real life.

Scanning electron microscopy (SEM): A method used to analyze gunshot residue.

Scene survey: The overview or scanning of the scene to note where points of interest are located.

Secondary crime scene: Typically, a crime scene other than where the initial crime occurred (eg, dump site in a killing).

Secondary device: In bombing, a second explosive device in the same general location, often booby-trapped.

Secondary crime scene: A scene different from the location of the initial or primary scene.

Secretor: The process by which about 75% to 80% of humans can have their blood type detected from body fluids, such as semen.

Semen: Male ejaculate, possibly containing spermatozoa.

Serial number: A numeric registration number on any given object, such as a camera.

Shelf life: The period of time in which a reagent can be stored before it is useless.

Shored wound: A wound resulting from the projectile striking the plane of the target at an almost parallel angle.

Short-wave ultraviolet light (UVS): Part of the light spectrum (220- to 320-nm) that is above the visual light spectrum and is used to visualize semen and other body fluids as well as trace metal.

Shutter speed: The speed at which the diaphragm of a camera lens is opened and then closed.

Signature: In pattern evidence, the pattern that is indicative of a specific object or type of object.

Single-lens reflex (SLR) camera: A camera in which you look at your object of interest through the lens by a system of prisms and mirrors instead of a viewfinder as in other camera.

Single print system: The Automated Fingerprint Identification System (AFIS), which is a filing and search system capable of searching with a single fingerprint or portion thereof.

Slave operation: In photography, a camera flash unit that is controlled by another flash referred to as the *master*.

Small particle reagent (SPR): Molybdenum disulfide solution that is used to recover latent fingerprints on wet surfaces.

Spatter: Bloodstains that are the result of force having been applied to the blood.

Spines: Scalloped edges and small points around the circumference of a blood drop.

Spiral search: A method of crime scene search used by people who go around in circles.

Squib: A blasting cap; an initiator for explosives.

Stab defense wounds: Wounds caused by fending off an attack and sometimes associated with the nonpredominant hand.

Stab wound: A wound that is deeper than the opening on the surface.

Standard lens: In photography, a 50mm lens.

Standard operating procedure (SOP): The protocols used for most procedures.

Static dust lifter: A device producing static electricity to attract patterns on a surface, such as a floor.

Statute of limitations: Legal term for the outer limit of time for which you can still prosecute someone for a crime.

Stellate wound: A wound caused by debris from the initial wound.

Sticky-side powder: A latent fingerprint powder or slurry mixture used to recover latent prints from the sticky side of tape.

Stippling: The tattoo-like pattern on the skin of the victim resulting from burning and unburned powder beneath the skin. *See also* Tattooing.

Striations: Impression patterns resulting from movement of one or both objects, such as the striations left on a bullet as it travels through the bore of a barrel (firearm).

Strobe flash: An electronic camera flash.

Subarachnoid hemorrhage: A bleeding within the skull that can be associated with impact.

Subdural hemorrhage: A bleeding in the skull between the dural and arachnoidal membranes as a result of trauma.

Sudan Black: A chemical fingerprint stain.

Suicide: The taking of one's own life.

Suicide note: A note or letter left explaining why someone took their own life.

Superimposition: A method of placing an x-ray or other transparency over a photograph to make a possible identification.

Supine: To be lying face up, as opposed to prone, which is face down.

Swipe pattern: A bloodstain resulting from a stained surface passing parallel to a surface and coming into slight contact with it, thereby leaving a stain.

Sworn staff: Staff who are "officers," or who carry a badge and firearm, as opposed to civilian staff.

Sync speed: The speed at which a camera shutter and flash work together, usually 1/60th of a second.

Tardieu spots: Petechial hemorrhages caused by the force of gravity, such as in an arm hanging down.

Tattooing: The pattern of gunshot residue that has embedded itself in the skin as the result of a gunshot. *See also* Stippling.

Technical photography: Photography of a scientific or technical nature.

Telephoto lens: A camera lens that brings distant objects closer by magnification.

Telephoto photography: The photography of distant objects, such as is used in surveillance work.

Tempered glass: Hardened glass, such as that used in the side and back windows of cars, that is fracture resistant and breaks into small non-sharp pieces.

Ten-Print System: A fingerprint filing system in which all ten fingerprints are required. *See also* Henry Fingerprint System.

Theory of transfer: The principal by which Locard states that as we move about, we not only leave minute evidence, we take away minute evidence as well, *See also* Locard's Exchange Principle.

Thermal fracture: A fracture of glass resulting from heat in which the pattern meanders and has smooth edges.

Thread count: The number of threads in a fabric in a given amount of material surface.

Time fuse: A fuse that burns at a specific time.

Time of death: The time at which a person was declared dead or without life.

Tool marks: The impression, or "signature," of a tool after it contacts another, softer surface.

Topographic map: A map that has contour lines indicating elevation.

Trace evidence: Physical evidence that is very small, often microscopic, in size; also a term used for hair and fiber evidence.

Trace metal detection test (TMDT): A test using the chemical reagent 8-hydroxiquineline with short-wave ultraviolet light to detect minute traces of metal.

Trajectory: The flight (pattern) of a projectile, such as a bullet. It drops as a function of both gravity and loss of energy.

Transfer evidence: Small trace evidence that we leave and take away from a scene; the basis for Locard's Principal.

Transfer pattern: Bloodstain patterns created when a wet, bloody surface comes into contact with a second surface. A recognizable image of all or part of the original surface may be evident in the pattern.

Triangulation: A method of documentating the location of an object by taking measurements from the object to two known points.

Ultraviolet (UV) light: May be of long- or short-wave frequency; often used to locate body fluids and trace metal.

Undetermined death: A death in which no determination was made as to the manner and/or cause of death.

Un-du: A chemical that allows for the removal of tape without destroying fingerprints on the sticky side.

Unknown prints: Prints of interest usually believed to belong to the suspect.

UV filter: A filter that allows the passage of ultraviolet light.

Vandalism: The intentional destruction or defacing of the property of another.

Vehicle Identification Number (VIN): The serial number of a motor vehicle.

Videography: Documentation or recording of moving photography using magnetic media.

Viewfinder: The aiming window on cameras that are not single-lens or twin-lens reflex camera.

Visible print: A fingerprint that can be seen without the aid of any treatment.

Void: The absence of stains in an otherwise continuous bloodstain pattern.

Walkthrough: The process by which investigators are taken on a "tour" of the crime scene so as to inform them of the case.

Wave castoff: Small blood drop that originates from a parent drop because of the wavelike action of the liquid in conjunction with striking a surface.

Weave pattern: The pattern created when threads are interwoven to make fabric.

Wide-angle lens: A lens that allows the camera to record a wider area. Commonly referred to as a *35mm lens*.

Wipe pattern: The pattern left when an object is moved laterally through an existing bloodstain.

Writer's palms: In fingerprint examination, the side of the palms of the hands.

Writing style: The way or manner with which one writes or prints.

Index